THE JEWS IN AUSTRALIA

Jews form only a tiny slice of the Australian population, yet their influence on Australian society has been immense. A dozen Jewish convicts arrived with the First Fleet in 1788. They were forerunners of a comfortable Anglo-Jewish community – which was dramatically challenged and enriched by a wave of European immigrants fleeing from Nazi persecution. In recent decades, new groups from places as diverse as the Soviet Union, Israel and South Africa have brought their own measure of cultural challenge and influence.

Among many remarkable individuals, Sir Isaac Isaacs was the first Australian-born Governor-General, and Sir Zelman Cowen a distinguished successor. The legacy of Sir John Monash, Australian commander-in-chief during World War I, continues at Monash University in Melbourne. A few names – Peter Singer, Arnold Zable, Frank Lowy, Henry Szeps, Professor Ron Penny, Richard Pratt, Slavor Gregorian – give a sense of the range of Jewish contribution today.

The Jews in Australia traces the community's history, explores what makes it different from others around the world, and draws fascinating comparisons between the Melbourne and Sydney components, each with its distinctive institutions and particular character. Though the very success of Jewish integration into Australia's diverse society has sharpened community debate about such key issues as intermarriage and the shifting roles of women, the dominant picture is of a thriving and vibrant community.

Suzanne D. Rutland is Chair of the Department of Hebrew, Biblical and Jewish Studies at the University of Sydney. Her many books include *Edge of the Diaspora: Two Centuries of Jewish Settlement in Australia* (2001). She has been president of the Australian Jewish Historical Society, Sydney, and of the Australian Association for Jewish Studies.

THE JEWS IN AUSTRALIA

SUZANNE D. RUTLAND

CAMBRIDGE
UNIVERSITY PRESS

477 Williamstown Road, Port Melbourne, VIC 3207, Australia

Cambridge University Press is part of the University of Cambridge.

It furthers the University's mission by disseminating knowledge in the pursuit of education, learning and research at the highest international levels of excellence.

www.cambridge.org
Information on this title: www.cambridge.org/9780521612852

© Suzanne Dorothy Rutland 2005

This publication is in copyright. Subject to statutory exception and to the provisions of relevant collective licensing agreements, no reproduction of any part may take place without the written permission of Cambridge University Press.

First published 2005

A catalogue record for this publication is available from the British Library

National Library of Australia Cataloguing in Publication data

Rutland, Suzanne D. (Suzanne Dorothy), 1946–.
The Jews in Australia.
Bibliography.
Includes index.
ISBN 0 521 61285 3.
ISBN 9 78052161 2852.
1. Jews – Australia – History.   2. Australia – Ethnic relations.   I. Title.
994.004924

ISBN 978-0-521-61285-2 Paperback

Cambridge University Press has no responsibility for the persistence or accuracy of URLs for external or third-party internet websites referred to in this publication, and does not guarantee that any content on such websites is, or will remain, accurate or appropriate.

CONTENTS

List of Illustrations — vii

Acknowledgements — ix

Introduction — 1

1 Convicts and Early Settlement — 11

2 Waves of Migration — 22

3 A Place in Australian Society — 36

4 The Watershed Years — 51

5 Diverse Voices — 66

6 Israel and Zionism — 79

7 Transformation or Disappearance? — 93

8 Jewish Women — 106

9 The Broader Community — 120

10 Recent Immigrants — 135

Conclusion	148
Appendix 1: Synagogues	163
Appendix 2: Parliamentarians	167
Appendix 3: Hostels, 1945–1960	171
Notes	174
Bibliography	186
Index	194

ILLUSTRATIONS

Sir Moses Montefiore	4
Rosetta Nathan and Moses Joseph	16, 17
Bridge Street, Sydney	18
Synagogue of the East Melbourne Hebrew Congregation	24
Margaret Street Synagogue, Brisbane	26
Karnofsky family shop, Kangaroo Valley, New South Wales	27
George Judah Cohen	39
Isaac Isaacs	44
John Monash	48
An antisemitic cartoon	55
Sydney David Einfeld	64
Dr Nahum Goldmann and Maurice Ashkanasy	71
Isi Leibler and Ari Volvovsky	75
An anti-Zionist cartoon, 1946	84
Israeli President Moshe Katzav, Ambassador Nati Tamir, Mark Leibler and Dr Ron Weiser	89
Mount Scopus College, Melbourne	98
Sydney Jewish Museum	103
Dr Fanny Reading	108

Josie Lacey, Margaret Gutman, Nina Bassat, Diane Shteinman, Ezer Weizmann and Dr Philip Bliss	110
Professor Zelman Cowen	126
'Mo' in his renowned make-up	133
Roy Steinman at Moriah College, Sydney	139
Graph showing antisemitic episodes since 1990	156
Peter Wertheim and Jeremy Jones	160

ACKNOWLEDGEMENTS

I have worked in the field of Australian Jewish history since 1968, and this book is the product of my research over that whole period. There are so many people who have assisted me over the years and to whom I owe a debt of gratitude. With this present publication, there are two people whose names stand out and, indeed, they have been a constant source of help, encouragement and advice over many years. Professor Konrad Kwiet, Roth Lecturer in Holocaust Studies in the Department of Hebrew, Biblical and Jewish Studies at the University of Sydney, read the manuscript not once but twice and his suggestions and comments have been most helpful. Helen Bersten, honorary archivist of the Australian Jewish Historical Society, Inc, (AJHS) also read the entire manuscript and contributed to its accuracy. In addition, other people kindly read and commented on sections of the text, including Professor Colin Tatz, Professor Gideon Shimoni, Dr Ron Weiser and Jeremy Jones. I would like to also thank the team of volunteers at the Australian Jewish Historical Society, particularly Mr Joe Ben Mayor, who scanned in most of the photographs, which come from the archives of the AJHS. In addition, I would also like to thank the Jewish Agency Research and Strategic Planning Unit and Department for Jewish Zionist Education for permission to use material from a survey commissioned by them on the recent Jewish waves of migration to Australia. My editor, Kim Armitage, and the publication team at Cambridge University Press, have also provided me with much support and assistance.

Suzanne D. Rutland
Sydney, 2005

INTRODUCTION

The history of the Jewish people spans four millennia, from the time of the biblical patriarch, Abraham, to the present day. Judaism is one of the oldest religions and the first monotheistic one. Throughout its history, the Jewish religion has not remained static and its ability to adapt and evolve helps to explain its survival into the modern era. The belief in one God, in moral ethics based upon the Ten Commandments, and in the covenant between God, the Children of Israel and the Land of Israel, set out in Genesis, the first book of the Torah (Hebrew Bible), have remained central features. The covenant is symbolised by the circumcision of all males at the age of eight days, a practice that has distinguished Jews throughout the ages. The belief in the common origins of the Jewish people with the Abrahamic covenant explains the ethnic identity of Jews today, so that Jewish identity is best understood as ethnic and religious.

The first two millennia of Jewish history centred in and around the Land of Israel, but already in 586 BCE, after the destruction of the First Temple in Jerusalem, the first dispersion took place. Known by the Greek word '*diaspora*', meaning dispersion, the first major Jewish settlement outside Israel was established in Babylon at that time, although Jews were permitted to return to what was then called Judah after 550 BCE, the start of the Second Jewish Commonwealth. This lasted until 70 CE, when the Second Temple was destroyed during the first major Jewish rebellion against the Romans, who captured many of the rebels and took them as slaves to Rome. The second phase of dispersion, from 70 CE, led to Jewish communities eventually being established throughout the world. In each case the Jewish community existed as a minority, struggling for survival against the forces of anti-semitism, which often aimed at the physical destruction of Jewry. Jews were also threatened by the pressures of assimilation, which undermined distinctive Jewish religious practice and belief through the assumption of the host society's culture.

During the medieval period, Jews lived either under the crescent, with Islam, or the cross, with Christianity, and two different strands of Jewish tradition emerged. The main centre of Jewish life in the Muslim world was Spain, so that Jews deriving from Mesopotamia, Spain, Portugal and North Africa became known as Sephardi (literally Spanish), whilst the main area of Jewish life under Christianity centred around the Rhineland, so that Jews deriving from northern, central and eastern Europe are called Ashkenazi (literally German).

These themes of diaspora existence are central to the story of the Jews in Australia — which emerged initially from English Jewry. Australian Jewry is one of the youngest diaspora communities established on the 'edge of the Diaspora', with only New Zealand Jewry being further away from the Jewish centre of Israel.

Jewish life in England

The emergence of Jewish life in England is a fairly recent phenomenon in the span of Jewish history. The first organised Jewish communities developed after the Norman invasion of 1066 when Jews were encouraged to settle in England because of their financial skills. This period was fairly short-lived, as Jews were expelled in 1290 after a century of increasing anti-Jewish persecution and massacres, such as the one that occurred in York in 1190 at the time of the Third Crusade. For the next three and a half centuries, Jews were not permitted to live in England. When William Shakespeare wrote his well-known work, *The Merchant of Venice*, there were no Jews living openly as Jews, and his famous Jewish character, the avaricious Shylock, was based on an earlier Italian work — although a community of secret Jews had already moved to England from Portugal.

The origins of present-day British Jewry were thus embedded in the Sephardi tradition of secret Judaism. After the expulsion of the Jews from Spain in 1492, many sought refuge in Portugal, but they were all then informed of the 1497 expulsion edict, which was followed immediately by the forced conversion of most of Portuguese Jewry to Catholicism. Many of these converted Jews, known as Conversos, or by the derogatory term *'marranos'*, meaning 'swine', practised their Judaism in secret for over a century, particularly in Portugal. At the end of the sixteenth century, it became easier for these New Christians to escape, and a number settled in the Netherlands, where they were able to practise their Judaism openly from the beginning of the seventeenth century, and in England. While a *converso* community, whose Jewish connections were recognised, was established by the 1590s during the reign of Elizabeth I, the first open Jewish service was not held until 1655 when the Dutch rabbi of Portuguese origins, Menasseh ben Israel, arrived to seek the official readmission of Jews. In a petition of 13 November 1655, Menasseh requested of Oliver Cromwell:

> 1. The first thing which I ask of your Highness is that our Hebrew nation be received and admitted into this mighty republic under the protection and care of your Highness like the citizens themselves, and for greater security in the future I entreat your Highness, if it is agreeable to you, to order all your commanders and generals to defend us on all occasions.[1]

This petition was considered at a special Whitehall Conference held in December 1655, which failed to come to a definitive conclusion, despite Cromwell's desire to promote Jewish settlement in England because of their financial skills and mercantile connections. Menasseh ben Israel died during his return journey to Amsterdam, a broken man, but his visit resulted in the open practice of Judaism in London even though the expulsion order of 1290 was never officially revoked. Summing up the significance of these events, historian of British Jewry, David Katz, has written: 'Although Jews in England would not become fully emancipated until the middle of the nineteenth century, their residence here rested on a secure foundation with the admission at the Whitehall Conference that "there is no Law that forbids the Jews return into *England*" '.[2]

Sephardi Jews flourished during the second half of the seventeenth century under the tolerant regime of English society. On 23 June 1700, Solomon de Medina was the first Jew to be knighted. They had their own religious structure headed by a *haham* (rabbinical leader, Hebrew for 'wise man').

Sir Moses Montefiore, scion of a leading Sephardi family, a number of whom were founding members of Jewish communities in Australia

This community was reinforced during the eighteenth century with the arrival of Ashkenazi Jews fleeing European persecution and discriminatory measures, and seeking a better life in England. They established separate religious organs, out of which emerged the chief rabbinate, later led by Dr Nathan Marcus Adler (1803–1890), one of the most influential figures of Anglo-Jewry. Adler, who was German born, filled the position of chief rabbi of British Jewry for almost half a century (1845–1890) and his ideas were continued by his son, Dr Hermann Adler (1891–1911). Nathan Adler recognised that the Ashkenazi Jews had become sufficiently acculturated to consider themselves English, and had lost their skills in Hebrew and Yiddish,[3] and he began to modernise, reorganise and anglicise the Ashkenazi community. He introduced a shorter form of the service and English sermons. Synagogue worship came to possess an air of organised formality and decorum, which was foreign to the Eastern European Jewish tradition. It became typical of English orthodoxy to build a single cathedral-like synagogue, unlike the small, intimate synagogues of Eastern Europe.[4]

As a result of Adler's policies, Anglo-Jewry developed a distinctive religious outlook, which combined 'orthodoxy and efficiency, piety and dignity, and modernity of method with strict adherence to tradition'.[5] Its communal life was well organised and religious practices were modified to meet the challenges of emancipation. These developments reflected both Jewish tradition and English culture; they emerged from a process of evolution rather than revolution, just as British democracy emerged gradually through parliamentary reform over the course of the nineteenth century. The anglicising of Judaism was to be of great importance in the development of the early Australian Jewish community, which was reliant on the British chief rabbinate until the 1930s.

The European experience

The Jewish experience on continental Europe was very different from that of Anglo-Jewry, as the well-established Jewish communities in western and eastern Europe were affected by enlightenment and revolution. In the West, emancipation occurred suddenly at the end of the eighteenth century, largely as a result of the French Revolution of 1789 and the Napoleonic conquests, when the discriminatory ordinances against Jews, forcing them to live in ghettos and restricting their movement and activities, were lifted and they were granted equality. In the East, the process took much longer, and was much less complete, so that Jews living in Tsarist Russia continued to suffer from discrimination until the revolution of 1917.

As the ghetto walls were gradually broken down and Jews were accepted into the general community, Jewish life and religious practice faced great challenges. In response, various initiatives were introduced to reconcile traditional Judaism with the modern lifestyle. These included the development of modern Orthodox, Reform and Conservative Judaism, and the more secular responses of Zionism and Bundism, a movement that sought to combine Yiddish culture with Judaism's ideals of social justice.[6] As a result of these developments, being a Jew could no longer be equated with the rigid practice of Judaism. The Jewish way of life was no longer a uniform one, since it manifested in many forms, and Jews came to see Jewish identity as a range of options: religious, cultural or national, or various combinations of these.

Initiatives to reconcile traditional Judaism with modern lifestyles were first introduced by the reformers in Germany in the early nineteenth century. Many Westernised German Jews found the traditional synagogue service, with its nasal singsong, occasional bargaining for the recital of prayers and lack of decorum, completely distasteful. Their desire to create a more dignified and aesthetic service resulted in the establishment in 1818 of a liberal temple in Hamburg, the Israelitischer Tempelverein, where the playing of organ music, a desecration of the Jewish Sabbath according to orthodox Judaism, was also introduced. This marked the beginning of the Reform movement, which at first did not have a sufficient philosophy to justify its ritual changes. Abraham Geiger (1810–1870) provided this philosophical basis by emphasising that Jewish spiritual and ethical values were more important than outward manifestations of Jewish practice and worship. During the 1840s, three Reform conferences held in Germany further consolidated Reform theology.

Two leading Jewish thinkers responded to Reform Judaism which they saw as going too far, and created two other branches of Modern Judaism. Rabbi Samson Raphael Hirsch (1808–1888), who coincidentally attended the same university as Geiger, developed the neo-orthodox approach, which demonstrated that secular knowledge and aesthetic forms of worship were not inconsistent with Jewish tradition. Rabbi Zacharias Frankel (1801–1875) developed Conservative Judaism as a middle-of-the-road compromise between the rigidity of orthodoxy and the extremism of Reform. This movement accepted the need to adapt Judaism to modern challenges, but stressed that the principles of change must be found in the historical dynamics of the Jewish people. The Conservatives maintained that Judaism could not dismiss important traditions embedded in the community.

In addition to religious change, the challenges of nineteenth-century developments in Europe produced secular responses, Of these, the growth of political Zionism was most important. The father of modern political Zionism was Theodore Herzl (1860–1904), a secular Jew who was born in Budapest and became a journalist and writer after studying law in Vienna. As the Paris correspondent of a leading Viennese newspaper, he covered the Dreyfus Affair of 1894, when a French army captain, who was also Jewish, was unjustly accused of selling secret documents to Germany. Herzl was aroused when he heard French protestors at the trial chanting 'Death to the Jews'. He elaborated the theory that the only answer to antisemitism was Jewish self-determination through the 'return to Zion'. In 1897, he founded the World Zionist movement at the first Zionist Congress, which was held at Basle in Switzerland.

In the same year, another secular organisation, the Bundist movement, also held its founding meeting as the General Jewish Workers' Association in Lithuania. Its response to antisemitism was opposed to Herzl's, with its leaders arguing that the only way to solve the problem was to change the local society. They wished to achieve such change through a synthesis of non-revolutionary Marxism, Yiddish culture and Judaism's ideals of social justice. The movement was anti-religious and anti-Zionist.[7] Many Bundist refugees took these ideals with them to Western Europe and the United States.

The New World

Both Reform and Conservative Judaism established themselves in the United States in the late nineteenth and early twentieth centuries. Between 1840 and 1880, about 300 000 German Jews settled, and they established the reform movement there. It became more radical than in Europe, partly because of 'liberal' Christian influences. Under the leadership of Rabbi Israel Wise, who built the Reform movement in Cincinnati, the guiding principles of United States Reform were developed, being formalised in the Pittsburgh Platform in 1885. This changed the traditional belief in a personal Messiah to belief in a universal Messiah. As the United States was seen as 'the new Zion', so the positive aspects of Jewish dispersion were emphasised, and Reform Judaism argued that this dispersal enabled Jews to carry Jewish ethics and morality to the world and so hasten the coming of the Messianic Age. The idea that the Bible was literally inspired was rejected, and only its moral laws were seen as binding. All laws that did not adapt to the habits of modern civilisation, including kosher dietary laws and strict Sabbath observance, were abrogated. Reform Judaism wished to retain the ethical values of traditional Judaism, whilst rejecting the strict observance and ritualism of orthodoxy.[8]

From 1880 to 1920, over two million Eastern European Jews fled the pogroms in Tsarist Russia and sought a new life in the United States. Many of these newcomers were more attracted to Conservative Judaism – for which Solomon Schechter had developed an organised structure – than Reform, so that by 1915 it had emerged as a third force in US Judaism.

Australian Jewish responses

In Australia, in the nineteenth and early twentieth centuries, the situation was very different. Australian Jewry was more conservative, and the limited reaction to these overseas developments underlined the weaknesses of the Jewish communities. These weaknesses were to prevail until the major immigration influxes before and after World War II.

Daniel Elazar and Peter Medding have described the Jewish communities that developed in the nineteenth century as having emerged within a frontier society. Louis Hartz, in his seminal work, *The Founding of New Societies*, described such societies:

> [they were] fragments that were broken off, as it were, from
> European civilisation, and had to implant themselves in new soil,
> pursuing lines of development that reflected their European heritage
> but were, nevertheless, substantially different because of the
> transplantation. These fragments began their separate development
> from the point at which they were separated from European
> civilisation as a whole, maintaining patterns common to the
> civilisation they left behind in forms that remained more or less frozen
> or took radically different directions from those of their original
> civilisations, which continue to undergo adaptations of their own.[9]

This pattern of development was evident in the case of Australian Jewry.

The various Jewish settlements in the Australian colonies began as fragments of Anglo-Jewry. As a result of their small numbers and lack of Jewish learning, the early Australian Jews were fearful of any change and their pattern of religious life remained frozen in the Anglo-Jewish mould. The waves of European Jewish immigrants who arrived between the 1850s and the 1930s were too few in number and too dispersed geographically to radically change this fossilisation of Jewish life. The communities that spread throughout Australia continued to follow the Anglo-Jewish pattern, even when Anglo-Jews were no longer numerically dominant. The newcomers who arrived before the 1930s did attempt to introduce changes, but only in a few instances were these to be lasting. Significant changes began only in the 1930s, with the refugees from Nazi persecution.

The general Australian community was predominantly British in origins until after World War II. This British fragment maintained English culture in the Antipodes, and a distinctive Australian lifestyle was slow to emerge. The Jewish community sought to conform to middle-class English standards and, as a result, became 'more British than the British'.[10] This was reflected in the early 'cathedral' synagogues established in Sydney and Melbourne, which maintained a 'high church atmosphere'.[11]

The transplantation of Jewish life from the insular ghetto societies of Europe to the free and open Australian society led to a high level of assimilation of Australian Jewry. Every effort was made until the 1930s to minimise outward differences, with the majority gentile population creating an ideology of non-distinctiveness.[12] Most Jews considered themselves Australians of the Jewish religion, and their response to the nineteenth-century challenges of modernisation was limited and conservative. The various communities developed one uniform reaction – the Anglo-Jewish form of modern orthodoxy developed by chief rabbis Nathan and Hermann Adler – and this remained rigid and standardised. All the other forms of modern Judaism and Jewish identification were either not considered or were rejected. Australian Jewry remained isolated from the mainstreams of Jewish thought,[13] with its leadership concentrated in the hands of a few prominent Anglo-Jewish families who seemed more concerned with civic recognition than with Jewish consciousness, and this situation changed only with the arrival of the pre- and post-World War II refugees and Holocaust survivors.

Peter Medding argued, in his study of Melbourne Jewry in the early 1960s, that after 1933 they moved 'from assimilation to group survival'. His thesis was supported by contemporary observers of the period. In 1955, Sydney David Einfeld, a leading figure in Australian Jewry, delivered a major address on post-war Jewish immigration to the National Council of Jewish Women in Sydney, part of which was reported in the *Council Bulletin*:

> The absorption of Jews from overseas had a tremendous social and cultural impact on the relatively isolated Australian Jewish community, which was predominantly of a conservative British outlook ... The newcomers have served the synagogues, the Jewish Day Schools and Young People's camps and have participated in all communal organisations and appeals, especially for Israel.
>
> Without the coming of these migrants, the Australian Jewish community would have stagnated and perhaps have faded completely. Migration means new life, new vigour and new enthusiasm. When the history of the Australian Jewish community was written, Mr Einfeld said, he felt that the period of 1934 to 1954 would be aptly and properly described as the time when Jewish life was preserved, enriched and even revitalised by the enormous influence extended by the Jewish migrant from Europe.[14]

The period from 1934 until 1954 was indeed a watershed in Australian Jewish history. The immigrants brought with them a new and stronger identification with Judaism and Jewish consciousness, transforming every aspect of Jewish life in Australia. The pre-war refugees laid the basis for key changes, and these were built on and extended by the post-war immigrants, who were much more numerous. Their experiences during the Holocaust added a new dimension to Australian Jewry, influencing and changing the attitudes of the established community. The Australian Jews, in turn, assisted in the rapid integration of the Jewish refugees into Australian life, so that the transformation was a two-way process. Jewish life was diversified, with various strands of religious, cultural and social life emerging as Australian Jewry finally incorporated the nineteenth-century changes that had resulted from emancipation and secularisation in Europe. With this, the community came of age.[15]

1
CONVICTS AND EARLY SETTLEMENT

Australian Jewry commenced with the arrival of a dozen Jewish convicts in 1788 on the First Fleet – the beginnings of European settlement. Australia was the first modern state where Jews were present from its very beginning. There are many fascinating Jewish convict stories, some representing success, others further tragedy. Jewish convicts were not able to establish an organised Jewish community, which had to await the arrival of the first free British immigrants after the late 1820s.

The Jewish convicts

Transportation of the unwanted criminal elements from Great Britain, which started in 1788, ended in New South Wales in 1840 and in Tasmania in 1853. Of the 151 000 convicts transported to the eastern coast of Australia, it is estimated that about 800 Jewish convicts had arrived by 1845. Most of them came from London, were of working-class background and were male. Only 7 per cent of Jewish convicts were female, compared with 15 per cent of Christian convicts. This is because Jewish females were more sheltered within the stronger Jewish family structure. The average age of the Jewish convicts was twenty-five, but ranged from as young as eight to some elderly people.

The majority came from a European Ashkenazi background and were largely second and third generation. When the first generation arrived in England from Europe, they were impoverished but usually observant of Jewish law, kept the Sabbath and so did not work on Saturdays. This meant that they were excluded from the main forms of lower-class employment – in the newly emerging factories or as servants. The only occupations that enabled them to continue Sabbath observance were those of storekeepers in the East End markets of London, or hawkers and peddlers. Their children and grandchildren at times drifted away from the strict practice of their religion, and some became involved in petty crime. Most Jews were transported for thieving, pick-pocketing, receiving stolen goods and the circulation of false coins, and very few for violent crimes. The majority managed to reform and to establish themselves successfully in the new colonies.

There are many fascinating stories, such as those of First Fleeter, John Harris, known as Australia's first policeman, and James Larra, the Parramatta publican who opened the Freemason's Arms there in 1794. Rabbi John Levi and Dr George Bergman told these and other stories in their pioneering study, *Australian Genesis*. Perhaps the best known is that of Esther Abrahams, who was arrested at the age of sixteen for stealing two yards of black lace. Expecting her first child, Esther was to be transported to the United States, but following the revolution and declaration of independence, she was amongst those on the First Fleet to Botany Bay. Despite her pleading with the authorities, she was sent on the boat *Lady Penrhyn*, where a young marine, Lieutenant George Johnston, befriended her. She became his mistress, and after twenty-five years of living together, with six children born to the union, the Reverend Samuel Marsden finally married them in 1814. Esther's fame is largely due to her partner, who played a key role in the rebellion against Governor Bligh in 1807, and was nominally in charge of the colony until the next governor arrived. George Johnston was recalled to England to face trial for mutiny, found guilty and cashiered from the army. However, he was permitted to return to the colony, and continued farming his Sydney estate at Annandale, named after his birthplace. Esther largely severed her ties with Judaism. All her children were baptised in the Church of England, and she was married by Marsden and received an Anglican burial. However, she drew closer to the Jews of the colony in 1829 as she faced a heart-breaking trial due to family conflict, when her second son, Robert, accused her of being insane because he feared losing his inheritance. Her lawyer, David Poole, was Jewish, as was her neighbour, Jacob Isaacs, her only character witness. With her dark hair and oriental looks, Esther's Jewish ancestry was clear. She founded a dynasty, with her great, great grandson, Sir David Martin, becoming Governor of New South Wales in 1989.

A number of convicts became successful businessmen and auctioneers. At times, this success proved to be mercurial, and many in the small community were severely affected by the depression of the early 1840s. One such success story was that of Solomon Levey, who arrived in 1815, accused of stealing a bag of tea from his mother. Levey was 'co-partner in the creation of one of the great mercantile houses of New South Wales . . . [his] prison had become his promised land'.[1] The business partnership of Solomon Levey and Daniel Cooper created one of the largest trading companies in the colony, plying between the Pacific Islands, South America and even South Africa. Daniel Cooper's home, Juniper Hall, which is still standing in the Sydney suburb of Paddington, is evidence of the wealth he acquired. Solomon's brother, Barnett Levey, was attracted to the new colony in 1821. He was the first Jewish male free settler and became known as the father of Australian theatre. Other members of Levey's family arrived later, including another brother, Isaac, who became a founding figure of the Sydney Jewish congregation. Solomon Levey returned to London in 1826 to sponsor the establishment of a colony on the west coast of Australia – the Swan River settlement – but this venture proved to be a disaster. Solomon died in London at the early age of thirty-nine. Samuel Lyons, who arrived on the same transport as Levey in 1815, built up a spectacular business, building Lyons's auction mart in George Street, Sydney. A third success story was that of Moses Joseph. He was convicted for stealing and arrived in Sydney on the *Albion* in 1827, when he was assigned to the firm of Solomon and Levey. Within five years he was granted a ticket of leave, opened a tobacco shop, and later generated much of his wealth from trading in gold. Unlike the earlier convicts, he was to play a central role in the development of Jewish life in Sydney. His success led to most members of his own and his wife's family emigrating to Australia; they were to play a central role in the development of Judaism across the Tasman in New Zealand.[2]

Establishing Jewish life

It took over a generation for an organised Jewish community to emerge. The Church of England operated as the established religion, and during the early years of transportation all convicts were compelled to attend Anglican services on Sundays, preceded by the humiliating church parade. Many of the convicts were Irish Catholics, who deeply resented being forced to attend Protestant services. This enforced religious observance led to Sydney's first church being burnt to the ground shortly after it was built. As Governor John Hunter wrote in 1799:

> About a month past, some wicked and disaffected person, or persons, in consequence of a Strict Order which I saw it absolutely necessary to issue, for Compelling a decent attention upon divine Service, and a more soberly and orderly manner of Spending the Sabbath Day, took an opportunity of a Windy and dark Evening and Set fire to the Church . . . and it was completely consumed.[3]

Not only was religious worship enforced Anglicanism but, as the education system also emanated from the church, the teaching of reading, writing and arithmetic was all done through the Protestant Bible. Despite efforts to change this situation, the Anglican Church controlled the early education systems until the introduction of the Denomination Education Boards in the 1840s. The strong personalities of some of the early ministers, such as the Reverend Samuel Marsden, combined with the evangelical approach of Governor Lachlan Macquarie, ensured that it was difficult for other denominations to function.

The profile of the Jewish convicts was another limiting factor. Almost all were poorly educated members of the working class with little or no knowledge of their Jewish traditions or literacy in the Hebrew language, so essential to Jewish worship. They arrived without the necessary ritual objects for worship, such as prayer books, prayer shawls, phylacteries, *mezzuzah* (small portion from the Torah placed on doorposts) or the actual Torah scrolls. In the early years, they had to focus on their physical survival and on building up new lives in an unfamiliar land. They simply did not have time for their ancient faith. In addition, the extreme shortage of Jewish women meant that men had to choose Christian partners. This was problematic for Judaism as the religion stems from the mother, who needed to go through a rabbinic conversion to be considered Jewish. Throughout the nineteenth century, the issue of conversion to Judaism was an extremely volatile one, resulting in significant splits within congregations.

Following a pattern of Jewish tradition, the first moves for establishing an organised form of the religion took place in 1817 when a Chevra Kadisha (literally Holy Society), a Jewish burial society, was formed in Sydney. In 1820, Abraham Levy applied for a section of the Devonshire Street cemetery, later to become Central Railway, to be allocated as a Jewish burial ground, but this request was not acceded

1 CONVICTS AND EARLY SETTLEMENT

to until 1832, when the area was consecrated.[4] Judaism throughout the colonies usually began with the consecration of a burial ground, and Jewish cemeteries scattered throughout country areas of Australia are evidence of the early patterns of settlement. There are a number of reasons for the importance placed on Jewish burial. In Judaism, the concept of standing before God in judgement after death is very strong. As convicts aged, and became more aware of death and of returning to their maker, they tended to become more concerned with their lack of Jewish observance and wanted at least to have a Jewish burial. Another factor was the strong belief in resurrection of all Jews during the Messianic Age. This belief necessitated a Jewish burial, without which one would not be resurrected.[5]

The first services in the colony of New South Wales were conducted from 1820 by emancipist Joseph Marcus, one of the few convicts with Jewish knowledge. Marcus was already elderly and infirm when he started to take services in private homes, and he died in 1828. The last four lines of the well-known hymn, 'Adon Olam' (Lord of the universe), are inscribed in Hebrew letters on his tombstone, which now stands in the Pioneers' Cemetery at Botany Bay.

Walter Jacob Levi, a free settler, called a meeting in June 1828 to express sympathy for the persecuted Jews of Tsarist Russia. He then organised a second meeting, to be held at the tavern of emancipist Abraham Polack, but he died tragically in the intervening period. Polack chaired this meeting, and then wrote on behalf of the fledgling community to Governor Ralph Darling, requesting use of a recently vacated government building for the Jewish High Holydays. Darling, who displayed the traditional antisemitic prejudice, wrote: 'It is hard if they cannot procure some other representative'. As Levi and Bergman described it, 'the brutal words "Put away" tell of its fate and bear silent witness to Darling's prejudice'.[6] The formation of a Jewish congregation had to wait another few years.

The Sydney Synagogue

Judaism became an organised religion after the arrival of free British settlers in the late 1820s. After the Napoleonic wars, England experienced an extended period of economic recession. Financial difficulty, and a sense of adventure, attracted the sons of some of the leading Anglo-Jewish families, including the Montefiores, the Furtados and the Mocattas, to Australian shores, where they were to make their mark on the development of an organised religious life. Phillip Joseph Cohen

Rosetta Nathan and Moses Joseph (opposite), the first couple to be married according to Jewish rites in Sydney in 1832

arrived in the colony of New South Wales in 1828, with authority from the chief rabbi to perform Jewish marriages. He was to conduct the first Jewish marriage between Rosetta Nathan and Moses Joseph in 1832.

A key event was the arrival of Rabbi Aaron Levy, a judge on the London Beth Din (ecclesiastical court), who came to Sydney in 1831 to facilitate the divorce between a convict and his wife, who did not wish to go to the colonies. Rabbi Levy brought with him the colony's first Torah scroll, prayer books and other ritual objects, and while in Sydney healed a schism between emancipists led by Joseph Simmons and Phillip Cohen, who had started services at his property on the corner of George Street and Martin Place. A properly

1 CONVICTS AND EARLY SETTLEMENT

constituted congregation was formed in 1831, with Joseph Barrow Montefiore as its first president, and in 1833, Reverend Michael Rose, the first qualified minister, arrived – although he remained in Sydney for only three years. After that, Solomon Phillips served the congregation in a part-time capacity. Another community employee was Polish-born Mordecai Moses, a scripture reader and dealer in London. His son, George Moss, had arrived as a free settler in 1830, but Mordecai was convicted of forgery and arrived in chains in 1836. He was assigned to take care of the cemetery, and in 1839 was appointed collector and caretaker (shammas) of the Sydney Synagogue, a position he filled until his retirement and death a quarter of a century later.[7] In

An etching of the rented property at 4 Bridge Street, Sydney, that was the first premises in Australia to be fully fitted out as a synagogue

1837, premises were rented and fitted out as a synagogue at 4 Bridge Street, and this was to serve the community for five years, until the congregation was in the position to purchase land and build its own synagogue in York Street.[8]

Australia's first purpose-built synagogue was opened with ceremony in 1844. It was built at the cost of £4000 on land bought by Moses Joseph in 1841, with subscriptions from the Jewish community and donations from one hundred Christians sympathetic to the Jewish cause. The synagogue was designed in the Egyptian style and was considered a handsome structure, but the community was faced with a debt of £1000. They decided to apply to the colonial government for financial assistance, and the Legislative Council granted their request and also allocated £150 annually for the minister's stipend. This was a most unusual decision, given that Jews in the Old World were still fighting for full emancipation. When approaches were made, the governor, Sir George Gipps, felt that such funds could only be given to Christian denominations, and the Colonial Office in Britain supported this position. In the end, funds were found from the general supplementary estimates, and Gipps's successor, Sir Charles Fitzroy, wrote home to his superiors, explaining that 'I considered it advisable to accede . . . the members of the Jewish religion being a numerous, respectable and influential class in the community, contributing largely to the public revenue'.[9]

During this period, Sydney's Jews established the other elements of Jewish community structure, with the creation of philanthropic bodies and educational establishments. Thus, by the end of the 1840s the Jewish community was a small but well-regarded group within the colony, which was soon to gain its independence from the Colonial Office.

Judaism spreads

The second penal colony to be established was in Van Diemen's Land, renamed Tasmania in 1855, and a number of Jewish convicts were sent out there, with some deciding to remain after gaining their ticket of leave. One of the most famous of the convict stories is that of 'Ikey' Solomon, who is considered to be the prototype for Charles Dickens's Fagin, in *Oliver Twist*. The brothers Judah and Joseph Solomon arrived in Hobart in 1819 and successfully established themselves once they were emancipated. Judah built himself a mansion in Argyle Street, in the heart of Hobart Town. Abraham Reuben arrived in Tasmania in 1827, convicted for stealing one sovereign and half a crown. He served his term with only one punishment recorded in the 'Black Book', and married a free settler, Rosetta Marks. They had ten children, became synagogue members when it opened, and Reuben was to become the first Jewish alderman in Hobart Town. He is one of the few Jewish convicts with a significant number of Jewish descendants in Australia today – Sydney-based Mordecai Moses being another one.

As in Sydney, the first step towards organised congregational life was the consecration of a cemetery. Three months before he died in 1828, emancipist Bernard Walford successfully obtained a section of land in the Hobart cemetery, which was consecrated for Jewish burials. A similar request in 1832 for a land grant for a Jewish cemetery in Launceston was rebuffed, much to the chagrin of the Jews living there.

The Jewish population in Van Diemen's Land grew slowly, with most free settlers choosing Sydney over Hobart Town. The 1842 Census showed 259 Jews out of a total of 42 000. Most were listed as shopkeepers: of the 802 shopkeepers recorded in that Census, about a quarter were Jewish. An organised congregation was formed in 1842, and in 1843 the foundation stone for the Hobart Synagogue was laid in what had been the garden of Judah Solomon's mansion in Argyle Street. The synagogue, designed in the Egyptian architectural style, was opened in July 1845. Once the synagogue was opened, Jewish convicts, who had been forced to attend Sunday Anglican services, were permitted to attend the Sabbath services, and the convict benches in the synagogue are still there.

The Jews of Launceston also wanted to build a synagogue and applied for a land grant, but the governor, Sir Benjamin Franklin, rejected this request. They then appealed to the Colonial Secretary, as well as to Sir Moses Montefiore, also without success. The *Launceston Examiner* supported the Jewish cause and the synagogue, built with the assistance of many Christian donations, was finally opened in 1846. Tasmanian Jewry had passed its heyday by the late 1840s, but its two synagogues in Hobart and Launceston are the oldest standing today.

At a site that was to become the city of Melbourne, the Port Phillip Bay Association purchased land from the Aborigines in 1835. Judah and Joseph Solomon of Van Diemen's Land were two of the seventeen-member association, and the only ones with purely commercial interests. As all the others were pastoralists, they probably provided much of the capital. They were soon joined by members of their family as well as other emancipists and free settlers. Melbourne's Jewish population increased slowly from 57 in 1841 to around 200 in 1850.

Jews were concentrated in Melbourne's commercial life, particularly in the clothing business, owning 25 of the 47 drapery stores. Already in 1839, four years after the Port Phillip Bay settlement began, the first Jewish services were held and a charitable society formed. Two years later, a Jewish Congregational Society was formed at the home of Asher Hymen Hart, with Michael Cashmore its first president.

The small community applied in 1843 for land for a cemetery, granted by Sir George Gipps, and in 1844 also received a land grant for a synagogue in Bourke Street. In 1847, the foundation stone was laid, and the synagogue, with seating for 150 worshippers, was consecrated in 1848. Membership was divided between privileged and unprivileged, and a person had to be an ordinary member for six months before they could be promoted to the privileged level, a decision that created ill will amongst members. In addition, Jews who married out could not become privileged members or be called to the Torah. Circumcision of sons of mixed marriages also proved a vexed problem. After employing for a short period Walter Lindenthal as teacher, the congregation appointed Reverend Moses Rintel from Sydney as their teacher in 1849, and he served the Melbourne community for thirty-one years in this capacity, which demonstrated their understanding of the importance of Jewish education.[10]

South Australian Jewry began to develop during the same period. An 1834 Act of Parliament established South Australia as a free colony, with eleven Royal Commissioners, one of whom was Jacob Montefiore, cousin of Sir Moses and brother of Joseph Barrow Montefiore. By the 1840s, a number of members of leading Anglo-Jewish families had settled in Adelaide, including the Montefiore family and the family of Jonas Moses Phillipson, whose young brother-in-law, Philip Levi, became an extremely successful trader and businessman. They were joined by emancipist Emanuel Solomon who, together with his brother Vaiben in Sydney, developed an inter-colony trading business, and was later to become a successful auctioneer and property developer.

Jewish services started in a private home in 1846, and in 1848 the congregation was officially formed, purchasing land in the city centre in what became known as Synagogue Place and consecrating its synagogue in 1850. It was a small stone building which could seat 150 worshippers, had a women's gallery, and was also built in the Egyptian style. A larger synagogue was built next door in 1872. Unlike Tasmania, the Jews of South Australia enjoyed full religious equality. Already in 1846, when services were just beginning, they were granted some state aid, although they did not use this grant.

Thus, during the 1840s Australian Jewry established itself, with purpose-built synagogues opened in Sydney, Hobart, Launceston, Melbourne and Adelaide within a six-year period. However, they were a tiny if well-established minority. Over the next half century, they were to be reinforced by further waves of emigration from the European continent as well as from Britain.

2
WAVES OF MIGRATION

Australian Jewry experienced three waves of immigration between 1850 and 1930 – German Jews and others arriving during the gold rushes, refugees from Tsarist Russia from 1880 to 1914, and Polish Jews after 1918. However, the numbers arriving with each of these waves were comparatively small, and Australian Jewry remained a tiny, isolated outpost of the Jewish world until the 1930s.

The gold-rush era

Gold was discovered in New South Wales in 1848, and shortly afterwards larger goldfields were found in Victoria. Amongst those adventurers who came were some young Jewish men, often from Germany. German Jews had been very active in the 1848 democratic revolutions and, when they failed, many sought a democratic life in the New World, mostly in the United States.

Travel to Australia by sailing ship was a lengthy journey, and after arriving they faced a difficult journey to the goldfields. Abraham Abrahamsohn, who initially worked at the Californian goldfields and then travelled to Australia, described these hardships:

> During the march it rained without letup, so that a compass was our guide. The paths were bottomless and our hardships incredible. We often had to swim horse and wagon across water, and strip, and carry our goods to the other shore on our heads. When, after a trip of one hundred and sixty miles, we had reached Mount Alexander, our horse, which until then had been fed on grass, was so weak that it

could not continue. We had no other choice than to burn our implements during the preparation of a meal, and rest for a day.

After a journey of eight days with the thus, less burdened horse, we reached the Bendigo River, along which the canvas tents of thousands of workers extended for miles.[1]

Abrahamsohn started work as a prospector, but after a series of mishaps he returned to his trade as a baker. Having amassed quite a fortune, he became homesick and decided to rejoin his family in Germany. His experiences were typical of most Jews on the goldfields, who tended to be traders and hawkers, the middlemen who supplied goods for the miners, rather than diggers themselves.

The capital cities

The discovery of gold had a radical impact. Within a decade, Victorian Jewry experienced a ten-fold increase, making it the largest Jewish community in Australia. In 1848, the Jewish population numbered only 200; by 1861, it had increased to 3000. The tiny synagogue built in 1848 by the Melbourne Hebrew Congregation, known as She'arith Yisroel (Remnant of Israel) proved too small, and larger premises were constructed in Bourke Street, consecrated in 1855. They served the congregation for seventy-five years. A dispute over actions of its minister, Reverend M. Rintel, led to his leaving the congregation in 1857. With the support of his brother-in-law, Henri J. Hart, he founded the Mikveh Israel Melbourne Synagogue, later better known as the East Melbourne Hebrew Congregation. It received a government land grant for its first city premises in 1859. However, this proved unsuitable, and in 1870 the congregation received government permission to sell the property. They moved to a new site in Albert Street, where the new synagogue was consecrated in 1877. Rintel served the congregation until his death.

As the German Jews rose up the social ladder, many moved south of the Yarra River to the newly developing area of St Kilda. By the 1860s, they were sufficiently well established to build a third synagogue in Melbourne, the St Kilda Hebrew Congregation, consecrated in September 1872. Its membership was largely successful German Jewish immigrants, with Moritz Michaelis being considered its founding father. Its first minister was German-born Rabbi Elias Blaubaum, who served until his death in 1903. He also founded and edited the *Jewish Herald*, which started as a fortnightly in 1879. The *Herald* was

The synagogue of the East Melbourne Hebrew Congregation is the oldest synagogue still standing in Melbourne

the first long-running Jewish paper in Melbourne – after the failed second attempt of the *Australian Israelite*, which was published by Solomon Joseph from 1871 to 1875.

Efforts were made in the 1870s and 1880s to establish Reform Judaism in Melbourne. Reverend Dr Dattner Jacobson, a native of

Vienna and a maverick character, established the Temple of Israel in 1881, but when he left for the United States in 1885, the congregation disintegrated.[2] Melbourne then had three synagogues, Anglo, German and Eastern European, which reflected the ethnic diversity of the community; but all three remained under the orthodox rubric.

In Sydney, a schism occurred in 1859 over the circumcision of the son of a gentile woman whose husband was a member of Samuel Cohen's family and a director of David Cohen & Co. As a result, the breakaway Macquarie Street Congregation was formed. In 1862, the Reverend Alexander Bernard Davis was appointed minister of the York Street Synagogue. He proved to be a unifying leader, serving the community for over forty years. Davis managed to engineer a conciliation with the Macquarie Street Synagogue and the two congregations united to build the Great Synagogue, which was opened in 1878 near the corner of Park and Elizabeth streets. Modelled on the tradition of the London Great Synagogue, it has remained an impressive historic landmark of Sydney and has often been described as a Cathedral Synagogue. Built to accommodate over one thousand worshippers, the Great Synagogue remained the only Jewish place of worship in Sydney until 1914 and dominated communal life until the 1930s.

A number of Jewish families settled in Brisbane after the colony of Queensland separated from New South Wales in 1859. The Brisbane Hebrew Congregation was formed in 1865, under the leadership of Jonas M. Myers, who proved to be the backbone of the community for forty-three years. It took time, however, before a synagogue was built, and it was not until 1886 that the present synagogue in Margaret Street was built and consecrated.[3]

Country areas

By the 1860s, 60 per cent of Jews lived in Sydney and Melbourne, whilst 40 per cent lived in rural areas of New South Wales and Victoria. The story of Jews in rural Australia was one of rapid growth, followed by decline. They moved out of the cities, attracted by commercial or mining opportunities, but it proved too difficult to maintain Jewish life. By the early twentieth century, most country Jews had either assimilated or moved back to urban centres.

Jews were associated with the growth of rural towns outside Sydney, where they made significant contributions to economic and civic development. They also established the framework of a Jewish community, with the consecration of burial grounds according to

The Margaret Street Synagogue, built by the Brisbane Hebrew Congregation in 1886, is still the main synagogue in Brisbane

Jewish tradition and the building of small synagogues. By the second half of the nineteenth century, Jewish communities existed in Goulburn, Forbes and Maitland, where the synagogue was opened in 1879 and functioned for about two decades. The towns of Lismore, Grafton and Tamworth also attracted a number of pioneers who

The Karnofsky family shop in Kangaroo Valley, New South Wales, was typical of rural Jewish commerce

contributed to civic life and tried to establish the basis of Jewish communal life, without success.[4]

In Victoria, Jewish life developed mainly in the gold-rush towns. The foundation of the Ballarat Jewish community was typical. Ballarat historian, Nathan F. Spielvogel, described the first High Holyday service held at the Clarendon Hotel:

> 'Cohen. Six tomorrow night at the Clarendon Hotel'. The big black-bearded man nods his head to little Charlie Dyte and resumes his shouting.
>
> Away goes Dyte, squeezing himself through the noisy, taunting crowd, till he comes to another shop over the doorway of which is a crudely painted sign 'The Little Wonder'. Here on a box stands a thin, red-headed man, yelling 'All vool and a yard vide. Shirts! Shirts! Shirts! Dirt Cheap! Come in and see!'
>
> 'Bernstein', whispers Dyte. 'Six tomorrow night at the Clarendon Hotel.' *'Yosher Ko-ach* [May you have strength]' murmurs the red-headed one, and goes on with his yelling.
>
> Next evening about twenty men assemble in the large dining room of the Clarendon Hotel . . . young exiles from the ghettoes of Russia, Poland, Roumania, Germany and England . . . who had left their far off homes to seek their fortunes in the Golden South.[5]

From these beginnings in 1853, the congregation grew rapidly, and in November 1855 it consecrated its first synagogue. This land was reclaimed, the community received a new land grant, and the *Ballarat Times* described its second synagogue, opened in 1861, as 'sufficiently tasteful without being ostentatious'.[6] It is still standing today.

The congregation experienced problems with religious leadership, but it was able to attract the first fully ordained rabbi, Rabbi Samuel Herman, who served the congregation from 1864 to 1868 and headed the first Beth Din in Australia. Reverend Israel M. Goldreich followed, serving from 1868 to 1905, apart from a brief period in Sydney in 1874–1875. He was assisted by Newman Friede Spielvogel, a native of Galicia (the part of Poland under Austrian rule) who was 'ready to fight for what he regarded as the ancient landmarks of pure, simple, traditional Judaism'.[7] Spielvogel, a Hebrew scholar of international repute, contributed to Ballarat's reputation as a centre for Jewish orthodoxy and learning.

A gold rush started in Bendigo in 1852, and the first Jewish service was held in 1854. Two years later, a weatherboard synagogue was constructed following a government land grant and £100 subsidy. This synagogue was replaced in 1872 with a more permanent stone building, seating 500 congregants, and it functioned until the turn of the century.[8] Parallel developments occurred in Geelong, where a land grant for a cemetery was made in 1849, a synagogue was built in 1854, and replaced by a stone building in about 1860.[9] This community also experienced a decline in membership.

Jews also moved into rural Queensland, as far as Cooktown. A synagogue was opened in 1876 at Toowoomba, but the community experienced a decline, and by 1901 there were only twelve families remaining, with services held only during festivals. By 1917, most Jews had moved away and the unused building was in danger of collapse. An appeal enabled repairs to be made, but the synagogue remained empty. In 1928, the building was sold to the Lutheran synod.

Jewish education

Early efforts to establish Jewish schools were rewarded with the creation of the Denominational Education Boards, which provided government funding in the 1840s. In Sydney, the community received a land grant at Church Hill in 1850, but it was not until the early 1860s that the Sydney Hebrew School was established. A Public Schools Act was passed in 1866, but it was argued that the new Act applied only to Christian schools. Jewish parliamentarian, Jacob Levi Montefiore, raised the issue again in 1868, and this time the request for certification was granted.[10] The Sydney Hebrew Denominational School continued to function until 1882, when the Great Synagogue decided to close it down. Subsequently, Jewish education was provided in government schools through the Right of Entry programme established by the 1880 Public Instruction Act, which ended government funds for denominational schools in New South Wales.

In Melbourne, a Jewish denominational school was established in 1855, called the West Melbourne Grammar School. Unlike Sydney, the Melbourne Jewish community decided to maintain its separate school after the passage of the Victorian Public Instruction Act of 1872, which ended state aid to religious schools. This decision was based on the desire to maintain Jewish traditions through education, the belief that this should be supported by private rather than state funds, and the belief that a Jewish school was needed because state schools used textbooks promoting Christianity. It reflected the differences between the two communities. Even in the nineteenth century, Melbourne Jewry was more 'Jewish conscious', so that 'although both communities were concerned with minority equality', the Sydney community 'stressed minority non-distinctiveness whereas the Melbourne community stressed minority identity'.[11] The school finally closed in 1898 after experiencing difficulties due to the 1890s depression. In 1895, the United Jewish Education Board was established to provide Jewish education in government schools, paralleling the establishment of the Sydney Board of Jewish Education in 1882.

Eastern European immigrants

Tsar Alexander II was assassinated in 1881 by a group of five radical students, one of whom was Jewish. His successor, Alexander III, exploited anti-Jewish sentiment to provide an outlet for Russian unrest. He introduced anti-Jewish legislation through the May Laws of 1882, with forced expulsions in the Jewish Pale of Settlement, and he encouraged pogroms, or violent attacks on the Jews. One victim, John Sackville, who was to become a leading retailer in Melbourne, described to his son the brutality he had experienced: 'they breathed down my neck. I was just a boy you know, but to them I was a little Jew and they let me have it. They kicked me and thrashed me with leather thongs fixed to a heavy piece of lead'.[12]

Many Jews sought to escape from Tsarist rule but only a tiny number came to Australia and, as most arrived via England, they were already exposed to the English language and culture. Between 1881 and 1921, Australia's Jewish population increased by around 11 000 from 9125 to 21 615, with only about 3000 Eastern European refugees contributing to this increase. The main reason for the much smaller number of Eastern Europeans choosing Australia was the problem of distance. The long sea voyage was a strong deterrent – and many had not heard of Australia. Most chose the United States, which was seen as the '*goldene medina*' (golden country) and attracted over 2 000 000 Jewish immigrants between 1880 and 1924. Britain's Jewish population increased seven-fold from 35 000 to 250 000, until the Aliens Immigration Act of 1905 reduced immigration. Canada accepted 120 000 Jewish refugees in the period 1900 to 1931 and South Africa took in 40 000, mainly due to chain migration from Lithuania.

Despite the small numbers of Russian refugees, there was a strong antisemitic outcry against their arrival in Australia, particularly when it was mooted that Baron de Hirsch wished to promote Jewish settlements there. Anti-Jewish immigration sentiment was expressed by trade unions, some politicians and in the general press. The *Bulletin* and *Truth* both highlighted the economic peculiarities of Jews, and during the Russian immigration scare the *Bulletin* commented:

> Even the Chinaman is cheaper in the end than the Hebrew ... the one with the tail is preferable to the one with the Talmud every time. We owe much to the Jew – in more sense than one – but until he works, until a fair percentage of him produces, he must always be against democracy.[13]

Disturbed by this rising antisemitism, established Australian Jews expressed concerns about the arrival of a flood of Eastern Europeans. This became the prevailing pattern of the wider Australian society towards any new wave of immigrants.

Religious life expands

More Eastern European Jews settled in New South Wales than in Victoria, which was severely affected by the depression of the 1890s. The New South Wales Jewish population increased steadily from 3266 in 1881 to 10 151 in 1921. In Victoria, a decline in numbers from 6459 in 1891 to 5907 in 1901 reflected its economic problems. However, the refugees were more dispersed in New South Wales.

With the growth of Sydney's Jewish population, a number of new congregations were formed, but not all managed to survive. Eastern European newcomers formed the Druitt Street congregation in 1881, with the Reverend A. D. Wolinski as its minister. When he accepted a position at the Great Synagogue, the congregation folded. The Baron de Hirsch Memorial Aid Society was formed in 1898 to service the needs of the newcomers, with Yiddish-speaking Rabbi Isador Bramson as its first minister. It faced a financial struggle, and its appeal for assistance to the Great Synagogue fell on stony ground, resulting in its closure. The Newtown Hebrew Congregation was formed in 1883, but for almost two decades operated as a small minyan (prayer group of ten men), holding services in private homes and rented halls. It was not until 1912 that it purchased land for its synagogue, which was finally built and consecrated in 1919. The first suburban synagogue opened in Bankstown in 1914, more than thirty years after the consecration of the Great Synagogue in 1878. The Central Synagogue was formed in 1912 with the aim of introducing the Polish *minhag* (custom) into Sydney, and in 1916 it rented a property in Napier Street, Surry Hills. With the shift of population to the eastern suburbs, the congregation decided to amalgamate with the Bondi-Waverley congregation (established in 1918), and in 1921 it purchased land, thus laying the foundation for its synagogue in Bondi Junction.[14]

Many of the Eastern European refugees moved to country areas, with new communities formed at Newcastle in 1905 and Broken Hill in 1911. The Newcastle congregation was founded by the Cohen family, which moved its family trading company from Maitland with the opening of the railway line. It was strengthened with the arrival of Eastern European newcomers who were also attracted to the mining town of Broken Hill, where the small congregation consecrated its synagogue and employed Reverend Zallel Mandelbaum as its first minister.

Despite the formation of new congregations, New South Wales Jewry continued to be dominated by Sydney's Great Synagogue. Rabbi Francis Lyon Cohen became the city's first ordained rabbi in 1905, and he remained its leading religious figure until his death in 1934.

Most of the European newcomers to Melbourne settled in the inner-city suburb of Carlton. This became the first area of settlement for successive waves of immigrants and, for over half a century, the heart of Jewish life. By the turn of the century, a number of more orthodox Jews formed their own minyan in Carlton, which came to be known as the Stone minyan, after one of its founders. It was to form the basis of the Carlton United Hebrew Congregation, established in 1912. In the 1920s, Carlton continued to attract Polish Jews who had escaped the 'cold pogrom' caused by the economic discrimination and hardships in the newly created independent Poland.

The newcomers also laid the basis for activities that drew on Yiddish, a language that combined medieval German, Hebrew and Slavic languages to express the unique Eastern European Jewish culture. Yiddish theatre started in the early 1900s, as a result of the efforts of Samuel Weissberg. A Yiddish library and meeting centre, the Kadimah (meaning 'forward'), was founded in Carlton in 1911. The Kadimah played a central role for the Yiddish-speaking newcomers over the next half century. Whilst most arrived poverty-stricken, they suffered even more from the cultural desert that they experienced in Australia, and the Kadimah had, by 1913, become 'an oasis at which they could renew their contact with an intellectual life without which they would have been like lost souls'.[15] Many Kadimah members were affiliated with the Bund, a movement founded in Tsarist Russia in 1897. Bundist philosophy advocated that the answer to the 'Jewish problem' lay in secular Jewish socialism and the development of Yiddish culture, rather than the creation of a Jewish state as advocated by Zionism. In October 1915 they moved from Bourke Street, where the premises were too small, to 313 Drummond Street, Carlton.

Another development in Victoria was the formation of Jewish agricultural colonies. In response to the fear of poor Russian Jews flooding Australia, a Jewish Land Settlement Committee was formed in Melbourne. Two Russian Hassidic Jews, Moshe and Bere Feiglin, arrived in Melbourne in 1912. Escaping the pogroms, their family had settled in Palestine, where they became successful farmers. However, in 1911 their father had a vision that there would be a major catastrophe, and he decided to send four of his sons to different parts of the world. When Moshe Feiglin arrived in Melbourne, he was employed at a Melbourne factory where he had to start work while it was still dark, making it difficult for him to observe morning prayers. One of his compatriots said to him: 'Moshe, you live in the dark; you may as well pray in the dark'.[16] Unwilling to accept this situation, Moshe Feiglin went to the Land Settlement Committee and offered to start a Jewish agricultural colony. The settlement at Shepparton proved successful, and in the 1920s another one, this time short-lived, was founded at Berwick.

Victorian Jewry had, by the 1920s, developed a different, more pluralistic, profile than New South Wales Jewry. Yiddish culture did not become entrenched in Sydney for a number of reasons. Many of the Eastern Europeans became hawkers, and their itinerant lives and need to acculturate quickly led them to learning English, which disconnected them from their Yiddish cultural roots. The more dispersed nature of their settlement meant that there was no comparative development to Carlton, and no prominent personalities emerged to establish new movements such as Melbourne's Kadimah. Additionally, the dominant role played by the Great Synagogue, which maintained Anglo-Jewish conformity, contrasted with the three different congregations of Melbourne.

Two smaller capital cities also developed because of Eastern European migration. Some Russian Jews had escaped from the pogroms via Siberia to Manchuria, where they established communities such as Harbin. Some decided to move to Australia, which did not require a visa before 1914. Since Brisbane was the first port of call, they disembarked there. Officials who did not understand Russian met every boat and asked to be shown a passport. One Jewish refugee, an ex-soldier of the Imperial Army, showed a coloured theatre programme and got away with it![17]

The new arrivals found the Anglo-Judaism of the Brisbane Hebrew Congregation strange and formal, and they built their own synagogue, known as the Deshon Street Shule, in South Brisbane in 1910. This area became known as 'little Jerusalem', as one could hear Yiddish and Russian spoken everywhere as well as smell the 'titillating [sic] aroma of Jewish cooking'.[18] For a short period, Yiddish culture flourished in Brisbane. Most of the Russian Jews were manual labourers. They formed a Jewish Workers' Association based on Bundist principles, and established a Yiddish library. Efforts to set up a Yiddish theatre failed, and the association petered out after 1918.

Fremantle was the first port of call in Western Australia for immigrants coming from Europe and Palestine, and in the 1890s the Jewish community in the West developed rapidly. A synagogue opened in Fremantle in 1887, but the Perth Hebrew Congregation quickly overtook this community. In 1897, it employed Reverend (later Rabbi) David Freedman, who served the congregation for over forty years until his death in 1939. A Hungarian-born but British-trained graduate from Jews' College, London, Freedman was able to communicate with both the Australian-born and the foreign Jews.[19] However, a small group of newcomers opposed the anglicised customs of the Perth Hebrew Congregation. They broke away to form a more orthodox community known as the Palmerston Shule.

Gold was discovered in Western Australia in the 1890s, attracting Jews from many areas. They settled in the gold-rush towns of Coolgardie and Kalgoorlie, and within a short time congregations were formed and synagogues built. The Coolgardie congregation lasted only a decade, from 1896 to 1905. The community in Kalgoorlie was more permanent, operating from 1901 until 1969.

Characteristics of Australian Jewry

Rabbi Jacob Saphir, a rabbinical emissary from Jerusalem, visited Australia in the 1860s. He recorded in his diary[20] the high level of acceptance of Jews: 'there is no discrimination between nation and nation. The Jews live in safety, and take their share in all the good things of the country.'[21] He noted that they were orthodox in name but not in practice, giving the example of one religious Jew who was concerned that the *shochet* (ritual slaughter) did not follow Jewish law correctly. As Saphir put it, 'this was his excuse to buy meat from the Gentile, while adhering to the Jewish ritual to salt the meat. Many others followed his example.'[22] He criticised Dr Adler, Chief Rabbi of the British Empire, for not providing better rabbinical leadership. He also highlighted the problem of assimilation through intermarriage because of the shortage of Jewish women, noting that many Jewish men took non-Jewish women into their households to assist them as servants and ended up marrying them. In addition, there was inadequate religious leadership, so that 'each man goes his own way and does what is pleasing in his own eye'.[23]

Despite the growth of the Jewish population, with the new waves of immigrants from Germany, Tsarist Russia and Poland in the 1920s, the dominant characteristics of Australian Jewry continued. Efforts were made in the 1920s to overcome the problem of assimilation, because intermarriage was increasing despite a more equal balance between the sexes. These efforts included projects to increase synagogue membership, and the creation of communal centres and Jewish sporting organisations. In Sydney, the Maccabean Hall was opened in 1923 in Darlinghurst, to serve as a Jewish War Memorial and community centre. Two years later, the first interstate sporting competition was held in Melbourne, leading to the staging of the annual Jewish Sports Carnivals. Jewish cultural life expanded with new publications, such as the *Australian Jewish Chronicle* in 1922 in Sydney and the first Yiddish paper, *Oistralier Leben* (Australian life), in Melbourne in 1931.[24] In addition, overseas leaders, such as Chief Rabbi Dr Herz, began to visit Australia.

These efforts failed because of the oligarchic and conservative nature of the leadership, the weakness of Jewish education, the dispersion of the community in the suburbs and the decline of the country communities. Many Jews married out and lost their Jewish identity. Sydney Jewish leader Victor Cornfield wrote in a letter to the *Hebrew Standard* in 1929:

> Our community has a dread of making a 'faux pas', which might endanger its social standing in the general scheme of things. Our leaders are at the tremble lest they be singled out as Jewish and prefer to keep in the background when prominent Jewish men and women come to our shores either as a visitor or with a message.[25]

Although this observation is an exaggeration, it is an apt summation of the fear of any action that would make the community distinctive. Jews were more concerned with being Australian, and thus fully accepted within the general society, than with being Jewish.

3
A PLACE IN AUSTRALIAN SOCIETY

By the end of the nineteenth century, Jews had become a well-established minority with identifiable settlement and occupational patterns, making them more visible than their 0.5 per cent of the total population may have predicated. Although there was some anti-Jewish prejudice, most enjoyed success in economic, political and social life. Observers, both Jewish and non-Jewish, remarked on the high proportion of Jews active in public life. An article published in 1922, entitled 'One Hundred Years of Judaism in Australia', claimed:

> 'Every country has the sort of Jews it deserves.' Berthold Auerbach made this epigram about his own race and if there is any truth in it, New South Wales has deserved exceedingly well. In every branch of our activities since the earliest times, members of the Jewish community have taken a large and distinguished part.[1]

They were a very acculturated group, who spoke English and were so well integrated that 'their outward manner was hardly distinguishable from them [non-Jewish Australians]'.[2]

Patterns of settlement

Australian-born Jews made up 58.4 per cent of all Jews by the end of the nineteenth century and, combined with a further 17.8 per cent born in Britain, made a total of 76.2 per cent. Of the remainder, 5.7 per cent were born in Germany and Austria, 12.2 per cent in Eastern Europe, with others coming mainly from southern and western Europe.[3]

By 1900, most Jews lived in urban centres, largely in Melbourne and Sydney. As already noted, the peak of 40 per cent living in rural areas in 1861 declined to 19 per cent in 1901 and further to 13.1 per cent in 1921, whilst the Jewish population of Hobart decreased from 282 in 1881 to only 121 in 1921, and Adelaide Jewry declined from 840 in 1891 to 743 in 1921. In the two large cities there were specific settlement patterns: in Melbourne, moving from Carlton, the first area of settlement, to the southeastern suburbs of St Kilda, Caulfield, Prahran and Malvern, and in Sydney, moving from the city centre of Haymarket, Surry Hills and Darlinghurst to Bondi and Bellevue Hill. However, well-known Australian demographer, Charles Price, has argued that these settlement patterns were too dispersed to be described as a 'ghetto', and cannot be equated with the type of Jewish concentrations that developed in the Lower East Side of New York or the East End of London at the turn of the century.

The shift to the suburban areas reflected a move up the economic ladder into the merchant and professional classes during the early twentieth century. In Sydney in the 1870s, 89 per cent of the Jewish population were concentrated in the Town Hall area. By 1901, 77.6 per cent had moved to Surry Hills, Darlinghurst, Paddington, Glebe and Newtown, 5.4 per cent to the working-class and lower-middle-class suburbs of the southwest, 11 per cent to the residential suburbs of Woollahra, Waverley and Randwick, and 6 per cent were scattered in other areas. By 1921, 33.9 per cent of Sydney Jewry were living in the eastern suburbs, and this trend continued in the 1930s. Melbourne experienced a similar move up the socio-economic ladder, with only 12.5 per cent living in the southeastern suburbs in 1871, increasing to 40.7 per cent by 1921. Many of the Jews living in St Kilda were well off and opted to send their children to private schools such as Scotch College and Wesley, where they imbibed 'the English middle class values to which many Jews aspired'.[4]

Perth Jewry is one of the most geographically isolated Jewish communities. The distance to its nearest Jewish neighbouring community, Adelaide, is 2832 kilometres. The community grew rapidly as a result of the 1890s gold rushes, and by 1911 Perth was the only Jewish centre outside Sydney and Melbourne that numbered over 1000. The community also moved away from the city centre, first to Mount Lawley[5] and then to the northern suburbs of Coolbinia, Menora, Yokine and Dianella. Perth developed a stronger Jewish community than the other smaller capital cities for a number of reasons. Its Jewish population was less dispersed, being concentrated around Mount Lawley. It has enjoyed a stability of religious leadership, with Rabbi David Freedman (1897–1939), Rabbi Louis Rubin-Zacks (1939–1961) and Rabbi Shalom Coleman (1966–1985), who was replaced by the present incumbent, Rabbi David Freilich. Most immigrants came from Tsarist Russia and Palestine, especially the northern town of Safed, so moulding the community's unique character. From 1881 to 1921, 9 per cent of Perth Jews came from Palestine, and from 1921 to 1930 this increased to 39 per cent. Most arrived almost penniless, disembarking at Fremantle, the first port of call. Later this pattern was reinforced by chain migration.

The immigrants to Australia continued the urban, middle-class traditions of their forebears so that, as in Europe, they were 'a minority in more than a religious sense as the concentration in commerce and the concomitant lack of Jewish labourers and farmers illustrates'.[6] Almost none became farmers; in 1901 only 2.2 per cent were engaged in agriculture, compared with 40 per cent of the general population, and only 10 per cent were unskilled workers. There was a relatively high concentration in finance and property (7 per cent, compared with 2 per cent of the general population), the sale and manufacture of textiles (24 per cent, compared with 4 per cent), and general dealing (48 per cent, compared with 9 per cent).[7] The number of professional men increased gradually, a fact commented on in the *Jewish Herald*:

> It is, indeed, gratifying to note how gradually the petty occupations for which our people have so often been twitted are passing away to make room for the learned professions – the skilful doctor, the astute lawyer, the clever architect or to the contracting manufacturer and the enterprising merchant. A transformation in our wonted occupations has already set in, and it is gaining larger proportions from year to year.[8]

Jews tended to prefer self-employment and occupations that were not subject to discrimination, even though there is no evidence of discrimination against those who sought employment in big commercial firms, as there was against Catholics.

Commercial life

Amongst the early businessmen, there were a number of rags to riches stories. Some of these businesses are still well known, even though the founding families no longer run them. Names such as Myer Stores and Wynvale Wines pay tribute to the entrepreneurial skills of early immigrants.

George Judah Cohen, businessman and community leader

In New South Wales, prominent nineteenth-century Jewish firms included David Cohen & Co., Feldheims, Gotthelf & Co. and Hoffnung & Co. The Cohen family's firm was established in 1836 in West Maitland, where Samuel Cohen opened a general store. From these humble beginnings, the firm David Cohen & Co., named after Samuel's younger brother, David, developed into one of the most influential commercial houses in the state. After the death of his father, Samuel Cohen, in 1861, George Judah Cohen took control of the company at the age of nineteen, and in 1879 he moved to Sydney. George Judah further developed the company, as well as later becoming director of the United Insurance Co., the Commercial Banking Co., the Australian Gaslight Co., and Tooth & Co., serving on these boards for over forty years. Following in his father's footsteps, Sir Samuel Cohen also contributed to the New South Wales Kindergarten Union, serving as its president. Sir Samuel's son, Major-General Paul Cullen, has also had an outstanding career both in business and civic life, as president of Austcare, amongst other organisations.

The Melbourne counterparts of the Cohen family were the Michaelis/Hallenstein families, who were German immigrants closely associated with the St Kilda Synagogue. Moritz Michaelis arrived in Victoria in 1853, developed a tannery business with his nephew, Isaac Hallenstein and, by the time he died in 1902, was one of the hundred wealthiest men in Victoria. Other successful businessmen included Phillip Blashki, a native of Poland and designer of cricket's Sheffield Shield; Aaron Waxman, described as the 'doyen of Melbourne's Jewish moneylenders'; and German immigrants Joseph Kronheimer, a tobacco importer, and Hugo Wertheim, a sewing machine and piano importer. Barnett Snider, an English immigrant, developed an enormous clothing warehouse in Flinders Lane, which gained the nickname Schnorrers Lane (Beggars Lane) because of its large number of Jewish clothing businesses. Snider later became president of the Victorian Chamber of Manufactures.

By far the most outstanding of the Eastern European Jewish immigrants was Sidney Baevski Myer. He was born Simcha Baevski in 1878 (adding the name Myer later) and arrived in Australia in 1897. After working as a hawker and then running a store in Bendigo, he moved to Melbourne in 1911 and bought the block of land that became the site of the renowned Myer Emporium. Myer acquired other retail stores, expanding his shopping empire throughout Victoria. His first marriage, to a Jewish girl from Ballarat, ended in divorce, and in 1920 he married into the prominent Baillieu family, gradually severing his links with Judaism. His retail company, Myer Stores, went public and is still trading with branches across Australia.

Another refugee from Russian Poland, John Sackville (née Zak), also settled in Melbourne and contributed to the clothing manufacturing industry, as well as founding a remarkable family dynasty that is still contributing to Jewish and civic life. Writing about his grandfather, Justice Ronald Sackville stressed John's 'humility – for all his business success he has lived modestly . . . Most of all, his faith in the Almighty has remained unshakeable'.[9]

Samuel Wynn, renowned for Wynvale Wines, also fled the Russian pogroms, arriving in Australia in 1913. He believed in the value of manual labour and initially worked on the land, but his wife was not suited to country living and so they settled in Melbourne, where he went from cellar-hand to the owner of a wine shop in Bourke Street in 1918. This marked the beginning of an outstanding career, which saw Wynn develop from wine shopkeeper to restaurateur and, subsequently, winemaker. From 1925 he became involved with wine production, and in 1951 he rescued the Coonawarra Estate in South Australia, making the area famous for its claret production. He was also active in the Jewish community, assisting other immigrants, developing Yiddish culture through Kadimah, and as a leading Zionist. Indeed his son claimed that Wynn's life was 'not a rags to riches story for, although his material achievements were certainly great, they were hardly memorable. His real achievements were spiritual'.[10]

Those successful businessmen also contributed both financially and in leadership to public charity. Sir Adolph Basser, a native of Cracow in Poland, who made his money selling spectacles and later jewellery, donated £40 000 to found Basser College at the University of New South Wales and £100 000 to the University of Sydney to develop nuclear research and establish an electronic computer. Abram Coppleson, another Eastern European immigrant, contributed to medical research by founding the Coppleson Institute at the University of Sydney. Jews were active in the United Ancient Order of Druids, which provided medical, friendly, sick, unemployment and funeral benefits to 23 000 members, as well as being prominent in the Freemasons. John Goulston, who was highly regarded for his 'frequent active interest in the cause of charity',[11] became Deputy Grand Master in 1918 and Grand Master from 1924 to 1928. He was the only Jew in the British Empire to achieve that rank.[12]

Politics

Before 1933, the number of Jews involved in politics was disproportionate to their small population. In Europe, Jews were often excluded from political processes on religious grounds. Before emancipation at the end of the eighteenth century, communities had court Jews, known as *shtadtlanim*, who negotiated with the outside authorities. Even after emancipation, Jews had to struggle for full equality.[13] In Britain, the first Jewish parliamentarian, Lionel de Rothschild, did not take his seat in parliament until 1858 despite being re-elected consistently over a ten-year period, because he refused to swear the oath on a Christian Bible. Even in the comparatively open Australian society Jews, as a minority, still felt the need to have individual representatives in the political process. Membership of colonial parliaments was seen as a mark of distinction, and since Jews were concerned with achieving full equality, their active involvement in political life was typical of their aspirations to attain English middle class values and respectability.

Once given the opportunity to stand for parliamentary elections, a comparatively large number of Jews took advantage of their newly found rights. The first Jew to be elected was Lionel Samson of Western Australia in 1849. Ten years later, Saul Samuel (1820–1901) was elected to the New South Wales Legislative Assembly. This was the start of an illustrious political career spanning almost forty-five years during which he became the first Jew to achieve ministerial status in the British Empire, and from 1880 to 1897 was Agent-General for New South Wales in London. Sir Saul was the first Australian Jew to be knighted, in 1882.

Sir Julian Salomons, another prominent politician, served for various periods from 1870 to 1889 in the Legislative Council, and was Solicitor-General and vice-president of the Legislative Council. He was appointed Chief Justice of New South Wales in 1886, but he resigned after a few days because Sir William Windeyer, a leading figure in Sydney, accused him of 'always breaking down mentally'.[14] Analysing this event, Morris Forbes argues that antisemitism played a part. Salomons was appointed Agent-General to London in 1899, retiring from that position in 1900.[15] Other leading politicians in New South Wales included Henry Emanuel Cohen, John J. Cohen and Sir Daniel Levy. In 1917, the New South Wales Legislative Assembly did not sit on Yom Kippur (the Day of Atonement) because the speaker, Cohen, and the deputy speaker, Levy, were both observant Jews.

There were twenty-one Jewish parliamentarians in New South Wales and fifteen in Victoria before 1914. It has been claimed that 'a Victorian Jew played a major part in each fundamental public question as it arose in the nineteenth century'.[16] These figures included Nathaniel Levi (Rabbi John Levi, who served as chief senior rabbi of Temple Beth Israel in Melbourne, is a direct descendant), Jonas Felix Levien, Isaac Alfred Isaacs, Ephraim Zox, Max Hirsch, Edward Cohen and Charles Dyte. In the 1895 Victorian parliament there were seven Jewish members of the lower house and two of the upper house, comprising 7 and 4 per cent respectively in the two legislatures. Ephraim Zox commented that if 'the Jews were represented in proportion of their number to the general population, there would be only half a Jew in parliament'.[17] Jews were also active in local government, with Sir Benjamin Benjamin being the first Victorian Jew and the first Melbourne mayor to receive a knighthood in 1889.

Of the prominent Jewish figures of this period, the two outstanding names by far are Sir Isaac Isaacs and Sir John Monash. Indeed, the story is told that when the Australian prime minister, James Scullin, went to advise the King, who subsequently appointed the first Australian-born governor-general, he had two names in his pocket – Isaacs and Monash.

Sir Isaac Alfred Isaacs was born in Melbourne in 1855, son of a poor immigrant family from Poland.[18] He began his career as a teacher at Yackandandah and Beechworth state schools, and then entered the civil service while studying law at night. He graduated with first class honours in 1880, and later gained his Master of Arts degree. In 1882 he was admitted to the Bar, and took silk in 1899. While developing his successful legal career he became involved in politics, and from 1892 to 1901 represented Bogong in Victoria. He served as solicitor-general from 1892 and attorney-general from 1894 to 1899.

Isaacs played a prominent role in the movement for federation and in 1897 was chosen as the Victorian representative to the Federal Convention. His position reflected the general approach of Victoria, where the desire for federation was strong, whereas in New South Wales, the only colony that supported free trade, opinion was divided because of the fear that federation would interfere with its economic interests. Isaacs was supported by co-religionist Vaiben L. Solomon of South Australia, in contrast to Sir Julian Salomons, who opposed federation as disadvantageous to the interests of New South Wales.[19]

After Federation, Isaacs entered federal parliament, representing Indi from 1901 to 1906, and was appointed attorney-general in the

Isaac Isaacs, Australia's first native-born governor-general

second Deakin ministry. In 1906 he was appointed to the High Court, where he served with distinction for twenty-four years, eventually being promoted to chief justice in 1930. Six months later, he was appointed Australia's first native-born governor-general, serving in this position for six years. Isaacs died in 1948, aged ninety-two years.

Isaacs was a considerable scholar, known for his verbose and rhetorical speaking style and his strong conviction of his own infallibility. He was also noted for his persistence, linked with an outstanding ability for hard work. In the late 1890s, Alfred Deakin described him:

> A clear, cogent, fiery speaker, he set himself at once to work to conquer the methods of platform and parliamentary debate and in

both succeeded. He was not trusted or liked in the House. His will was indomitable, his courage inexhaustible and his ambition immeasurable. But his egotism was too marked and his ambition too ruthless to render him popular. Dogmatic by disposition, full of legal subtlety and the precise literalness and littleness of the rabbinic mind, he was at the same time kept well abreast by his reading of modern developments and modern ideas.[20]

These comments sum up Isaacs's strengths and weaknesses. His intellectual brilliance and reformist policies won him support, but not personal liking. His unpopularity cannot be traced merely to jealousy or antisemitism, but was a result of his dogmatism, which at times led to controversy within the Jewish community as well. The greatest division was over Deakin's proposal for a referendum to introduce general scripture lessons based on the Christian faith. Both Isaacs and Theodore Fink, another Jewish parliamentarian, voted in support of the proposal, much to the chagrin of the Jewish community. In the last years of his life, he again conflicted with the community over political Zionism.

Isaacs maintained a strong connection to Judaism, but could not always be described as a 'Jewish politician' — rather than a politician who happened to be Jewish.[21] When R. Bowman, a member of the Victorian Legislative Assembly, made a derogatory interjection in relation to the Jewish people, Isaacs reproached him but did not make any effort to defend his religion. This was in contrast to Ephraim Zox, who protested strongly when faced with criticism of Jews and who was active in community leadership, serving as president of the Melbourne Hebrew Congregation, and to Sir Julian Salomons, whose speech 'I would be a fool and a poltroon . . .' was a strong statement of pride in his Jewish heritage.[22]

Social and cultural life

The father of the Australian theatre, Barnett Levey, and of Australian music, Isaac Nathan, were both Jewish. Levey was the first Jewish male free settler to arrive in New South Wales, and his exploits in creating the first theatre, the Theatre Royal, have already been described. The son of a cantor in England, Nathan left his traditional background, his second wife being a Christian, and became part of the royal court. He is most famous for putting Byron's 'Hebrew Melodies' to music. He fell out of favour at court, and decided to emigrate to New South Wales. He composed the first Australian opera, *Don John of Austria*, the libretto being written by the economist, merchant and parliamentarian, Jacob Levi Montefiore. As a member of a minority group, he felt a sense of empathy with the indigenous Australians, and in 1849 he published 'The Southern Euphrosyne', a work that was partly literary and partly musical, combining Talmudic and Aboriginal legends.

In art, names such as Joseph Wolinski, Emanuel Phillips Fox and Miles Evergood (of the Blashki family) were well known, while Maurice Brodsky's weekly journal, *Table Talk*, contributed to Australian journalism. Two important Australian academics, philosopher Professor Samuel Alexander, and historian and folklorist Joseph Jacobs, both left their native land at the age of eighteen and made their mark in England. Jews on the whole were not sportsmen, but Ernest S. Marks was active in a number of amateur sporting bodies, as well as serving as Sydney's first Jewish mayor in the 1930s.

The armed forces

Given their strong sense of loyalty to the British Empire, which had provided them with a safe, democratic environment, Australian Jewry's strong support for the war effort during the 1914–1918 war was not surprising. Indeed, a number had volunteered to fight in South Africa during the Boer War. There was a high level of enlistment for World War I: 13 per cent of Jewish males compared with 9.2 per cent of the overall population. Three hundred soldiers were killed, and a number were mentioned in despatches, with Leonard Keysor awarded a Victoria Cross. Apart from a sense of loyalty, this high level of engagement was also due to a desire to counteract the antisemitic view that Jews made poor soldiers.

Rabbinical leadership strongly supported the war effort, with Rabbi Francis Lyon Cohen of the Great Synagogue, Sydney, and Rabbi Jacob Danglow of the St Kilda Hebrew Congregation, Melbourne, advocating that all members contribute through enlisting or working on the home front. All the leading rabbis wished to serve as chaplains at the front, but the Great Synagogue decided that it could not dispense with Cohen's services. Rabbi David Freedman of Perth served as chaplain until 1918, when Danglow replaced him.

It is thus understandable that the Jewish community supported the two conscription referenda called by Prime Minister Billy Hughes. In Sydney, John J. Cohen and Daniel Levy were founding members of the Universal Service League. Before the referendum of October 1916, Cohen used the example of Moses before he entered the Land of Canaan to stress that no Jew could morally object to conscription:

> No responsible leader could permit any section of the people to escape its equal burden in the perils and the sufferings and the anxieties of the nation's welfare. Nay, further, that the shirker who avoided his personal share was a sinner against God as well as against his neighbour.[23]

This stance, which reflected the community's patriotism as well as its largely middle-class composition, contrasted with opposition to conscription from the Irish Catholics, who were anti-British and largely working class. On the whole, the workers were opposed to conscription, and both referenda failed to attract sufficient votes.

The most successful Jewish soldier during this period was Sir John Monash who, as a civilian soldier and a Jew, rose to become commander-in-chief of the Australian Imperial Force. Apart from Leon Trotsky, who led the Red Army from 1917 to 1921, Monash has been the only Jew outside Israel to lead an army in modern times. He was very aware of his situation and, after the war, he said that he told himself: 'Remember that you are a Jew and if you muck it up, our people will be blamed for it'.

Monash came from a humble background, born to immigrant parents from Prussian Poland. His father, Louis, arrived in Melbourne in 1853, aged twenty-five, seeking to assist his foundering family fortunes. A few years later he returned to Germany, where he met and married Bertha Manasse and in 1864 they travelled to Melbourne. One year later, John Monash was born. When he was nine, his family moved to Jerilderie, where his father opened a store, but John's teacher, William Elliot, recognised his abilities and advised the family to send him to Scotch College in Melbourne. He matriculated with first class honours in German and French in 1881, and enrolled in an Arts degree, but had to suspend his studies for two years for financial reasons before graduating in Arts and Civil Engineering. The Melbourne Harbour Trust employed him from 1892 to 1894, but he was retrenched because of the depression, and started his own business as a patent attorney and consulting engineer, specialising in reinforced concrete.

He joined the University regiment, and continued as a civilian soldier with the Fourth Battalion Victorian Rifles and then the Military Garrison Artillery, where he served for twenty-one years. In 1913 he joined the Thirteenth Infantry Brigade. With the outbreak of war, Monash enlisted as a brigade commander with the Fourth Infantry

John Monash was commander-in-chief of the AIF during World War I

Brigade, and in January 1915 he embarked for Egypt. He served throughout the Gallipoli campaign and was responsible for the Allied withdrawal, which he executed with minimal loss of life. After a period training troops in Alexandria, he was appointed commander-in-chief of the Third Division (one of five), promoted to major-general and sent to France.

With his engineering background, Monash proved to be a brilliant tactician with tanks, which were being used for the first time. He held off the German offensive on the Somme in March 1918 and, following further battle successes, was appointed commander-in-chief in June, replacing Sir William Birdwood. The combined Australian, British and Canadian troops won a major victory under Monash's leadership on 8 August. The German commander, General Ludendorff, described this as a 'black day of the German army' and, in recognition of his outstanding contribution, King George V knighted Monash in the field four days later, the first time a British monarch had taken such action for three hundred years.

After the war, Monash served as director of repatriation until 1920, and then was appointed chairman of the Victorian Electricity Commission. He was awarded an honorary Doctorate of Law in 1920, and later completed his doctoral thesis in engineering, dealing with the Australian victories in France in 1918. He was appointed vice-chancellor of the University of Melbourne in 1923. While not an observant Jew, Monash always acknowledged his Jewish roots, and in 1927 he agreed to be the first president of the Zionist Federation of Australia. He died in 1931 after a number of years of illness. Monash University in Melbourne is named in his honour.

Economic depression

Australia faced two major economic depressions with high unemployment, in the 1890s and following the New York stockmarket crash of 1929. In each depression, the Jewish community was affected in a similar manner to the rest of Australia. Victoria was more affected than the rest of Australia during the 1890s, and Melbourne Jews experienced many financial collapses, with notables such as former lord mayor, Sir Benjamin Benjamin, becoming bankrupt. A number moved to other states, some even going as far as South Africa. During the Great Depression of the 1930s, Jewish welfare organisations assisted those in need. In New South Wales the Jewish Employment Bureau, established in 1927, was particularly active. Rabbis and ministers agreed to salary reductions because of the financial problems their congregations faced.

Economic depression tended to result in increased antisemitism, and this was the case during both depressions. In the 1890s, anti-Jewish feelings were fostered in the 'yellow press' such as *Truth*, owned and edited by demagogue John Norton. Extreme right-wing political movements emerged for the first time in Australia after 1929. Antisemitism was part of their platform, and they often expressed admiration for Nazi ideology. These movements included the New Guard in New South Wales led by Eric Campbell, the Social Credit movement, and the Australia First movement. The strongest opposition during both depressions was directed at Jewish refugees – from Tsarist Russia in the 1890s and, after 1933, from the ever-escalating tragedy of European Jewry due to Nazism and Fascism.

4
THE WATERSHED YEARS

The watershed years for Australian Jewish history occurred with the refugee flight from Nazism in the late 1930s and the survivor emigration in the aftermath of World War II. There had been some Jewish immigration from Poland during the 1920s, but the population from 1921 to 1933 remained static. In 1933, there were only 23 000 Jews in Australia. Between 1938 and 1961, the community almost trebled to 61 000, with around 9000 refugees arriving between 1938 and 1940, 17 000 survivors arriving between 1946 and 1954 from Europe and Shanghai, and a further 10 000 until 1961, including those who escaped at the time of the 1956 Hungarian revolution. These three waves completely changed the nature of the Australian Jewish community, but Jews continued to constitute only 0.5 per cent of the overall population because of the hostility that was expressed towards Jewish immigration.

Anti-refugee hysteria

Proposals to admit Jewish refugees met with a hostile reception. Known as 'anti-refo' feeling, this manifested itself in the late 1930s and continued after 1945 in general newspapers, in statements by some members of parliament and in resolutions passed by pressure groups such as the forerunner of the Returned Services League (RSL) and the Australian Natives' Association.[1] Extreme feelings were also expressed in daubing and damage to property, particularly in areas of Jewish concentrations in Melbourne and Sydney.

These negative reactions were due to Australian isolationism. Most Australians favoured immigration from Britain and opposed admission of large numbers of aliens for fear that they would undermine Australian living standards. Until the 1930s, Australian immigration policy was grounded on the principle of being 98 per cent Anglo-Celtic, and was dependent on British consular officials in Europe. Immigration's keystone was the 'White Australia' policy, which virtually excluded all Asians after Federation in 1901. Australian xenophobia reflected 'a dislike of something different, a primitive fear and distrust of the new and the unknown'.[2] Immigrants were resented because of the fear of economic competition and 'their challenge to previously well-settled, easy going concerns'.[3] In the case of Jewish immigration, there was the added element of antisemitism, which became 'a handy peg on which to hang any personal hatred or antipathy'.[4]

Before World War II, anti-refugee feelings were both anti-foreign and anti-German. Australians had, in the recent past, fought a war against Germany, while another appeared imminent. German and Austrian Jews were also accused of being arrogant and overbearing. At a time when antagonism towards Germany was gaining momentum, Australians were not very welcoming to ex-German citizens, and during the war many of the refugees were interned as 'enemy aliens'.

Newspaper reports and leaders of organisations such as the RSL claimed that shiploads of Jews would arrive to the detriment of Australian workers and, after the war, ex-servicemen, their wives and British immigrants. The fear was expressed that Jewish immigrants would be involved in smuggling opium and other contraband, and would introduce criminal elements into Australia. Other concerns included the accusations of illegal Jewish immigration, and that unemployed refugees would become a charge on the state.

The problem of sweatshops was highlighted. In May 1939, Sir Frank Clarke, president of the Victorian Legislative Council, attacked the refugees:

> Hundreds of weedy East Europeans . . . slinking, ratfaced men under five feet in height and with a chest development of about twenty inches . . . worked in backyard factories in Carlton and other localities in the North of Melbourne for two or three shillings a week pocket money and their keep . . . One group here tendered the supply of 100,000 articles of women's silk underclothing at seven and a half penny each. No Australian factory could compete with such prices and pay awards.[5]

4 THE WATERSHED YEARS 53

Allegations were also made that owners of small businesses were prepared to cut prices in order to attract a clientele, and similar charges were made after the war. Although Jews were not always specifically mentioned, the term 'refugee' tended to be synonymous with 'Jews', as the majority of the pre-war refugees were Jewish.

Another concern was that Jewish immigrants would form unassimilable colonies in Sydney, especially in Kings Cross and Bondi, and in Melbourne, especially in Carlton, and these would become foci of racial tension. In 1939, a leader in the *Sunday Sun* claimed:

> The situation that so many people said would occur has come to pass in Potts Point. Refugees from foreign persecution have taken it over like Grant took Richmond ... Small, hardworking groups of men and women have established factories for turning out shirts and other articles at cut rate prices ... The very isolation that everyone wished to avoid has happened under our noses.[6]

After the war, the fear was expressed, as in this letter in the *Sydney Morning Herald*, that they would take over accommodation at a time of an acute housing shortage, disadvantaging Australian ex-servicemen:

> First, refugees are intensely competing for and getting houses Australians would normally occupy. Many of our people have been evicted and are in great distress but no known refugee lives at Herne Bay or under canvas. Men who enlisted, leaving homes and shops, returned to find them occupied by refugees ...[7]

The letter also claimed that refugees were prepared to pay huge key-money bribes, and that those who had built or bought blocks of flats demanded exorbitant rents. Poor health was cited as another reason for keeping refugees out.

Professionals, such as doctors, expressed strong opposition to refugee immigration. In 1938, a restrictive quota of only eight foreign doctors to be registered annually in New South Wales was introduced. Thirteen European Jewish doctors completed the final three years of their medical studies at the University of Sydney in 1950, only to find that not all of them could be registered.

The fear was expressed that the refugees would create political tensions. After the war, the conflict between Jewish settlers in Palestine and the British mandatory authorities provided further fuel for those who opposed Jewish immigration, especially after the bombing of the King David Hotel in June 1947. These events aroused the ire of many

Australians who believed that Australia should not import anti-British Jewish terrorists. In addition, Zionism and Communism were often linked and, with the growing Cold War hysteria in the late 1940s, this added to their undesirability as immigrants. There was also a concern about dual loyalty.

One of the most vocal opponents of Jewish refugees was Henry Baynton Gullett, Liberal member for Henty, Victoria. In December 1946, he stated in parliament that although 'men of the Jewish faith have played a very distinguished part in Australia's affairs':

> we are not compelled to accept the unwanted of the world at the dictate of the United Nations or any one else. Neither should Australia be a dumping ground for people whom Europe itself, in the course of 2,000 years, has not been able to absorb.[8]

Gullett alleged that Jewish immigrants were 'setting up sweat shops, cornering housing and evading income tax'.[9]

Jack Lang, former premier of New South Wales and in federal parliament in 1946, constantly criticised Labor's immigration policies in his paper, the *Century*, and attacked Arthur Calwell, the minister for immigration, in parliament. For example, Lang claimed that Jewish refugees stranded in the Middle East had boarded the *Strathmore* at Port Said, taking berths withheld from prospective British immigrants.[10] In reply, Calwell described Lang as 'this Australian Julius Streicher' (a notorious German antisemite convicted at the Nuremburg trials), and the *Sydney Jewish News* commented that Lang's attack was 'the most venomous of all references to Jews and aliens during the recent session of Parliament, including Gullett's attack'.[11]

One of the strongest pressure groups opposing alien immigration in general and Jewish immigration in particular was the RSL. The president of the New South Wales branch, Ken Bolton, became a leading advocate for the cessation of alien and Jewish immigration. He believed that these newcomers deprived Australian ex-servicemen of accommodation and employment. Bolton began his campaign in 1946 with the statement 'let us not beat about the bush . . . they are German Jews of the same ilk as those who have come before'.[12] Leaders of the Australian Natives' Association were also critical of Jewish immigration. The association's president, P. J. Lynch, stated in 1947 that Australia must not become a 'dumping ground for European refuse now causing trouble in Palestine . . . as Jews in Palestine were murdering and flogging British subjects'.[13]

An antisemitic cartoon typical of the populist press, Bulletin, 4 December 1946. *The original caption read: 'The Pied Harper – The Commonwealth Statistician's review supports the impression that permanent-migration figures are unfavorable. In August, a year after the end of the war with Japan, Australia received 1941 immigrants, but permanent departures totalled 2606'.*

Cartoons in the populist press, such as the *Bulletin* and *Smith's Weekly*, highlighted the anti-Jewish stereotype. Jews were portrayed as incapable of assimilating. They created sweatshops and worked long hours for low wages, thereby undermining Australian living standards. They were also moneylenders, who controlled the banks and the media and, since they were not primary workers, they were undesirable immigrants. In addition, Jews were often portrayed as godless people out to destroy Christianity and lacking morality. They were wealthy, indicating that they were greedy and obsessed with money. The Jewish concept of the Chosen People led to the well-known accusations of international control and world conspiracy theories. Above all, Jews were physically undesirable – ugly, with hooked noses and foreign accents. The word 'Jew' did not always appear on these cartoons, but the visual representation made it clear that the negative message was referring to Jews who, if they were given the chance, would take over the country.[14] While some scholars, such as Professor W. D. Rubinstein, have denied the impact of this anti-refo hysteria,[15] most have illustrated how it led to the government introducing quotas to restrict Jewish immigration to Australia both before and after the war.[16]

Discriminatory policies before the war

Hitler's assumption of power and the persecution of Jews in Germany after 1933 created a refugee problem, which by 1938 reached crisis point. As each new Nazi policy was implemented, the Australian government was pressured to change its immigration policies concerning 'aliens'. Australia was seen as a suitable place of refuge because of its small population, low birth rate and democratic traditions. In both London and Australia, Jewish representatives requested the Australian government to permit more Jewish refugees to settle, but until 1936 such requests met with a negative response. Only aliens with £500 in their possession, or dependent relatives of residents, were allowed to enter, so that few Jewish refugees arrived before 1936.

Due to the intensification of Nazi antisemitism and the slow improvement of economic conditions, there was a gradual relaxation of immigration policies concerning aliens. The government reduced the landing money to £50 in 1936, and agreed that a responsible Jewish organisation could act as guarantor. Aliens without a guarantor needed £200, and there was a quota system for the issue of landing permits. At the government's instigation, the Australian Jewish Welfare Society was formed in 1937, under the presidency of Sir Samuel Cohen, to co-ordinate efforts for Jewish refugees. It replaced the German Jewish Relief Fund, created in 1936 to assist German Jews escaping from Nazism.[17]

Following the Nazi Anschluss with Austria in April 1938, the Jewish refugee problem worsened as a further 180 000 Jews came under Nazi rule. President Franklin Delano Roosevelt convened an international conference to discuss the refugee crisis. Held in Evian, France, in June 1938, thirty-eight countries were represented. The negative position of the Australian government, which announced that it would not liberalise its alien immigration policy from an annual quota of 5000, or 15 000 over three years, was representative of all participating nations. Australia's delegate, Thomas W. White, declared that 'as we have no real racial problem, we are not desirous of importing one by encouraging any scheme of large-scale foreign migration'. As Australian historian, Paul Bartrop, stated, 'Australia typified the world's approach as it stood in mid-1938'.[18]

After the devastation of the Kristallnacht pogroms in Germany and Austria in November 1938, the Australian High Commissioner in London, Stanley Bruce, who had been a conservative prime minister in the 1920s, recommended that the quota should be doubled to 30 000 over three years. However, the government decided against this proposal. In a major ministerial statement on 1 December 1938, the Minister for the Interior, John McEwen, reconfirmed that Australia would admit 15 000 refugees over a three-year period.[19] The government took no action on a proposal by the Jewish Freeland League to create a Jewish colony in the Kimberley area of Western Australia and, despite the efforts of Dr Isaac N. Steinberg who arrived in 1939, this proposal was rejected in 1944. The outbreak of war in September 1939 ended the flow of refugees; by this stage some 7200 had arrived, 5080 of them in 1939.

The war years

During the war, Australian Jewry became aware of the Holocaust. Following the announcement by Anthony Eden on 17 December 1942 of the Allies' recognition of the massacre of Jews in Poland, the United Jewish Emergency Committee was formed in Sydney by Dr Jona M. Machover (a leading Zionist, originally an émigré of the Russian revolution who settled in London and was stranded in Australia during the war), while in Melbourne the United Jewish Overseas Relief Fund was formed under the presidency of Polish-born Leo Fink to raise funds and collect goods to assist their suffering brethren in Europe. The Palestine Jewish community cabled the Australian government, informing it of the slaughter of Polish Jews and seeking 'to open the gates of free countries to those who seek refuge from that inferno on earth'.[20] By 1943, communal documents recorded the destruction of three to four million European Jews, and in November 1943 a resolution endorsed by all Australian Jewish communities, referring to 'the parlous state of European Jewry', was presented to Prime Minister John Curtin. It urged him to support Jewish immigration to both Australia and Palestine, and to participate in 'any international scheme for the provision of relief to the survivors of Nazi atrocities'.[21] Even so, most people were not aware of the full extent of the Holocaust or the exact details of the extermination programme until after the war, and the Australian government made no positive response to these appeals.

Lack of understanding of the plight of European Jews was evidenced in the fact that refugees from Germany, Austria and later Hungary were labelled as 'enemy aliens' and were required to report to the local police, to receive a police pass if they wished to travel outside their police area, and to surrender their radios. Some 'enemy aliens' were interned initially at Hay in New South Wales and later at Tatura, Victoria.[22] Here they joined 2400 refugee internees who were sent by Britain on the *Dunera*, and some internees from Singapore and other parts of Asia.

The story of the *Dunera* became notorious in the wake of British hysteria about Nazi agents among refugees. The *Dunera* was dispatched with 2542 men on board. Included in the transport were 200 former Italian Fascists and 251 German prisoners of war, mostly seamen. The majority of the passengers were 'C' class aliens, those who had been classified as potentially least dangerous. As the *Dunera* was built to accommodate only 1600 passengers, the overcrowding led to insufferable conditions during the voyage. The food was described as inedible, and the crew often behaved with barbaric cruelty. Many refugees were beaten and all had their belongings ransacked. Trying to make the best of their situation, they gave lectures, formed Torah study groups, and even wrote a constitution on board. After their arrival on 6 September 1940, they continued these activities at the Hay and Tatura camps. The constitution was refined and a sort of college was set up, where camp inmates could study anything from mathematics to metaphysics and a great variety of languages. A makeshift theatre company, a rabbinic academy (*yeshiva*) and Zionist study groups were also established. Many of the *Dunera* internees returned to Britain towards the end of the war. Around 1000 remained, most of whom volunteered for service in Australian Military Forces employment companies, which engaged them in essential non-military wartime work.[23]

The total number of Jewish refugees reaching Australia between 1933 and 1945 was 8200. Their status was eventually redefined as 'friendly aliens'. Of the 3500 men between the ages of eighteen and forty-five, nearly every one volunteered as soon as refugees were permitted, and 1200 were accepted for service. Of the rest, most were engaged in industries classified as essential to the Australian war effort, while some also contributed to the scientific war effort.

Post-war immigration

The Pacific war radically changed attitudes within Australia. Many policy-makers believed that Australia must populate or perish. Ben Chifley was appointed Minister for Post-war Reconstruction in December 1942, and in late 1943 an inter-departmental committee was established to report specifically on immigration.[24] A subcommittee, set up to investigate white alien immigration, stressed that in order to foster immigration to Australia, white aliens must be 'regarded as an asset and not a person admitted on sufferance'. It recommended that to 'ensure future safety and fullest economic development' the Commonwealth 'should be prepared to accept any white aliens who can be assimilated and contribute satisfactorily to economic development and against whom there are no objections on the grounds of health, character or (while the ban is still in force) enemy alien nationality'.[25]

These criteria became central to post-war immigration policy. The main concern with non-British Europeans was that they were healthy and could add to the work force, especially for activities such as road building, hydroelectric schemes and other work in remote areas. The subcommittee proposed continuation of the landing permit system, but that landing money requirements should be reduced, as artisan types were more suitable than businessmen. In order to avoid delay, it was suggested that an immigration section be established in Australia House, London, with the authority to issue permits.

In regard to Jewish immigration, the subcommittee recommended an end to the pre-war plan of admitting up to 15 000 refugees. It was felt that on the whole the 7000–8000 refugees already admitted were not desirable, as 'most of them, probably 80 per cent, settled in Sydney and Melbourne and soon became conspicuous by their tendency to acquire property and settle in particular districts, such as King's Cross, Sydney'.[26] The subcommittee claimed that professional and university-educated Jewish refugees had greater difficulty adjusting than the artisan class. In addition, it felt that the Polish Jews, who arrived before 1938 and mainly worked in textile industries in Melbourne, 'could not be regarded as desirable types of migrants'.[27] Overall, Jewish immigrants were depicted as less desirable than any other European immigrants.

Arthur A. Calwell was appointed Australia's first Minister for Immigration in July 1945. Under his leadership, Australia evolved an immigration policy that, for the first time in Australian history, regarded non-British immigrants as a viable immigrant source.[28] In his first ministerial statement, Calwell stressed Australia's need to build up its population, and stated that it would not be possible to maintain and develop present population figures without some immigration.[29] With this first statement, Calwell began his role as the architect of Australia's post-war mass immigration programme.

Calwell appointed Tasman H. E. Heyes as his new head of department. Heyes was a typical upper-class Anglo-Saxon, who reflected the 'gentleman's antisemitism' of the Melbourne Club of which he was a member and which traditionally excluded Jews through the blackballing method. Under Heyes's direction the department expanded rapidly. Among the early appointments was Noel W. Lamidey, an English immigrant who had arrived in Australia in the 1920s and was sent to Australia House in 1946 as Chief Migration Officer. During the war, Lamidey had acted as secretary to the Aliens Classification and Advisory Committee, which dealt with matters relating to internment and restrictions on aliens. At Australia House, he played a key role in both British and Continental emigration to Australia.

Even before the end of the war, Australian Jewry began to consider post-war Jewish immigration. Many recent newcomers were deeply moved by the enormity of the destruction of European Jewry and were determined to do everything possible to assist in the rehabilitation of survivors through sponsoring their emigration to Australia. After Calwell's appointment, he met with Jewish community leaders, Alec Masel and Paul Morawetz, to discuss a memorandum on this issue. Calwell agreed to the introduction of a 'humanitarian' immigration programme whereby 2000 survivors of the concentration camps with family sponsors in Australia would be admitted in the twelve months from August 1945.

The announcement of this agreement led to an outcry, even though this quota was significantly lower than the annual number of 5000 before the war. These negative attitudes of the general Australian public had important repercussions for post-war Jewish immigration. In the face of prejudice, antisemitism and his somewhat insecure position within his party and Cabinet, all of which caused concern to Calwell, he introduced measures to limit the number of Jewish refugees. Charles Glassgold, the representative from the American Joint Distribution Committee in Shanghai in 1949, summed up their essence:

> I have to transmit to you some information which should by now not be shocking to any Jew, but which nevertheless still horrifies one. From a most unimpeachable source there comes to me a statement made by the new Australian Consul in Shanghai that casts the pall of futility over the prospect of Australian migration. The Consul said to my informant substantially the following:
> 'We have never wanted these people in Australia and we still don't want them. We will issue a few visas to those who have relations there as a gesture'.[30]

These restrictions included a new 25 per cent limitation of Jewish passengers on all ships, and in 1948 the extension of this quota to planes. Only a few hundred Jews were permitted to immigrate from Shanghai after July 1947, following a top-secret report of the consul-general, Major-General O. C. W. Fuhrman, painted Jews as the criminal element of Shanghai. A 'gentleman's agreement' in January 1949 set the quota for Jewish immigrants to 3000 per annum, and then eased the 25 per cent quota on ships and planes. The 'Iron Curtain embargo' in December 1949 effectively excluded Jews who originated from countries under Soviet rule, and there were special discriminatory policies towards Jews of Middle Eastern origins, including India.

Calwell's fear of the negative effect of Jewish immigration on his overall policies was most clearly evidenced in regard to the International Refugee Organisation. Under the IRO agreement, after July 1947, Calwell agreed to admit workers from the displaced persons camps in Europe on a two-year work contract, and 170 000 displaced persons arrived in the next four years, with a further 29 000 under personal sponsorship. Jews were virtually excluded from the programme, as only young, single Jews were permitted and they had to sign an extra clause agreeing to work in 'remote areas of Australia'. The definition for being a Jew was based on racial not religious grounds and, as a

Jewish member of the selection team commented at the time, 'Hitler could not have done better'.³¹

In carrying out these policies Calwell was supported fully by his departmental officers. These measures were continued under the Liberals with Harold Holt as Minister for Immigration from 1950 to 1955. But the policy was disguised, and when the Jewish leadership questioned the government, it claimed that 'there is no discrimination . . . between Jewish and non-Jewish displaced persons'.³²

Jewish responses

With the pressures of the arrival of the Jewish refugees, the Australian Jewish Welfare Society in Sydney grew rapidly by 1938 from a small group run largely by volunteers into a large organisation with fourteen full-time employees at the Maccabean Hall in Darlinghurst. With financial assistance from the Refugee Economic Corporation, founded by US philanthropist Charles J. Liebman, Mutual Enterprises was created to assist refugees to establish themselves in business, and Mutual Farms to settle refugees on the land. A training farm was opened at Chelsea Park, Baulkham Hills. In Victoria, Jewish Welfare developed under the leadership of Isaac Herbert Boas. It provided 'sustenance grants' to newcomers,³³ purchased land for farms in Shepparton and assisted the refugee children at Larino.

While the established Australian Jews did try to provide material assistance, they were concerned that the refugees should adjust immediately, discard any foreign behaviour and become 'one hundred per cent Australian'.³⁴ An official of Jewish Welfare met every boat and, where possible in Sydney, they were taken immediately to the Maccabean Hall and issued with instructions that stressed:

> Above all, do not speak German in the streets and in the trams. Modulate your voices. Do not make yourself conspicuous anywhere by walking with a group of persons all of whom are loudly speaking in a foreign language . . . Remember that the welfare of the old-established Jewish community in Australia as well as of every migrant depends on your personal behaviour. Jews collectively are judged as individuals. You personally have a grave responsibility.³⁵

The editor of the *Hebrew Standard*, Alfred Harris, reinforced this message and criticised refugees for 'congregating in and about King's Cross and Bondi; perhaps not realising that in so doing they are looked upon as forming colonies which is positively undesirable'.[36] The refugees were strongly encouraged to settle on the land.

Employees and leaders of Jewish Welfare in both Sydney and Melbourne epitomised this patronising attitude, causing tensions between the established community and the newcomers. Walter Brand, who assumed the office of 'general secretary' of Jewish Welfare in Sydney in 1940, could speak only English and treated the refugees with a lack of consideration.[37] President, Saul Symonds, defended Brand's approach, and there were similar issues in Melbourne with president Boas.

After the war, Australian governments, both Labor and Liberal, insisted that the reception and integration of the refugees was the Jewish community's responsibility. No government funds were to be expended on Jews because of the fear of political repercussions. The sponsors of the refugees and the Jewish Welfare Societies assumed the task of finding accommodation, including hostels (see Appendix 3), and helping those in need. Boats were met, immigrants were helped with finding employment or setting up in business through interest-free loans and there were two schemes, Save the Children and the Jewish Welfare Guardian Scheme, to assist orphan survivors of the Holocaust.[38] Refugee integration was an immense undertaking for Australian Jewry to finance alone, and they appealed to overseas Jewish communities, particularly in the United States. The absorption of post-war Jewish immigrants thus became a joint enterprise between local and overseas Jewries. This financial assistance first came from the American Joint Distribution Committee, the Hebrew Immigrant Aid Society and the Refugee Economic Corporation. After 1952, it was taken over by the Conference on Jewish Material Claims Against Germany, which provided substantial funding from 1952 to 1965.

Melbourne Jewry, with its stronger Eastern European origins, was more pro-active in assisting survivors. Assistance came through the United Jewish Overseas Relief Fund (UJORF) under the presidency of Leo Fink, who believed that emigration was necessary for full rehabilitation. UJORF members also believed that the Australian Jewish Welfare Society lacked drive and carried out its activities merely as a philanthropic concern, while because their organisation represented Polish Jews, most of whom had lost immediate family in Europe, it saw the immigration question as 'a matter of life and death'.[39] UJORF amalgamated with Jewish Welfare and sponsored as many survivors as possible. Fink persuaded Calwell to waive the 25 per cent quota in the case of the *Johan de Witt*, which arrived in March 1947 with

Sydney David Einfeld, champion of the Jewish survivors

600 Jewish survivors among its 700 passengers, its reception co-ordinated by Sydney David Einfeld. In this, he conflicted with his more conservative Sydney colleague, Saul Symonds.[40]

As a result of Melbourne's more aggressive approach, 60 per cent of survivors, mainly from Poland, settled in Melbourne, with 40 per cent in Sydney and very few elsewhere. The leadership of Perth Jewry encouraged survivors to travel on to either Melbourne or Sydney. After Symonds's sudden death in 1952, Einfeld assumed the presidency of Jewish Welfare in Sydney and the tensions between the two major centres dissipated. Einfeld dedicated himself to the needs of the newcomers, constantly visiting Canberra with Walter Brand in efforts to persuade the government to liberalise its policies.

5
DIVERSE VOICES

Immigration before and after World War II had an enormous impact on Australian Jewry. Until the 1930s, the Jewish community was governed in an authoritarian fashion from the leadership of the synagogues. The struggle for democratic leadership, spearheaded by the pre-war Jewish refugees, is a fascinating chapter in Australian Jewish history. The diversity of communal organisations indicates the many forms of Jewish identification in Australia – whether religious, Zionist, cultural or ethnic.

A representative structure

Until World War II, there was no federal body representing Australian Jewry. When the Australian colonies federated in 1901, an attempt was made to create a federal structure, but failed due to intense Melbourne/Sydney rivalry.[1] The organisational structure changed radically following Hitler's rise to power and the refugee crisis, which challenged the comfort and complacency of the established Australian Jewish leadership. In New South Wales, the Advisory Board formed in 1932 to represent the synagogues was forced to broaden its structure, with other community organisations gaining representation in 1936. Formed in 1921, the Victorian Jewish Advisory Board was restructured in 1938. However, it was not until the devastation of European Jewry became known that a representative federal body for lay leadership was created, in August 1944.[2] Named the Executive Council of Australian Jewry (ECAJ), its formation marked a watershed in Australian Jewish history.

The catalyst for the creation of the ECAJ was the formation of the Australian Council of UNRRA (United Nations Relief and Rehabilitation Administration) to assist in solving the problem of the 'displaced persons'. The Department of External Affairs convened a meeting of this new organisation in February 1944, and representatives of three Jewish organisations, the Australian Jewish Welfare Society, the Jewish Advisory Boards and the United Emergency Committee for European Jewry, attended. Subsequently, two further organisations sought to affiliate, but the Department was reluctant to accept too many Jewish organisations. The departmental secretary stressed that 'You will appreciate that it is necessary to restrict membership to the most representative organisations, otherwise the membership of the Council would increase to a number which would make its effective working most difficult'.[3] Two Jewish representatives were finally chosen, Dr Leon Jona of Melbourne and Gerald de Vahl Davis of Sydney. These experiences, combined with the community's concern for the tragedy of European Jewry, led to the decision to form an all-Australian Jewish Council.[4]

The first official interstate meeting took place in Melbourne on the weekend of 5–6 August 1944, hosted by Alec Masel, president of the Victorian Jewish Advisory Board. Its aims were to affirm the creation of an Australian roof body, finalise the constitution, and discuss the major issues facing the community. As the *Sydney Jewish News* later commented, the delegates were 'seized by a realization of their heavy responsibilities' and 'quickly settled to their business'.[5] The meeting unanimously approved the formation of a body to represent Australian Jewry called the Executive Council of Australian Jewry. Its aims were set out as follows:

> To represent and speak officially on behalf of Australian Jewry
> To take such action as it considers necessary on behalf of Australian Jewry in matters that concern Australian Jewry or Jewry in other parts of the world.

At its second conference in Melbourne in January 1945, the constitution was ratified and the first committee of management was elected, to be based in Melbourne, and with Alec Masel as president.

The formation of the ECAJ was a vital development for Australian Jewry. The editor of the *Jewish Herald* wrote that a united national body was needed to deal with key issues such as antisemitism, immigration and relief, and the absence of such a body 'has entailed a very severe handicap':

Such consultation as did exist between the states was at best a vague and shadowy thing. There was not only the absence of common counsel with all that meant in the way of hesitancy and confusion, but there was also the disservice rendered at Canberra and in other official quarters, by the spectacle of the Jews speaking with a dozen voices.[6]

Immediately after the war, the immigration of Jewish Holocaust survivors to Australia was a major concern for the ECAJ, as was the creation of the State of Israel.

The constitution established the structure for the ECAJ, and it has remained basically the same. Its work has been based on the principle of rotation between the two major Jewish centres of Melbourne and Sydney. The constituents are the various roof bodies of Victoria, New South Wales, Western Australia, Queensland and South Australia, together with the Hobart Hebrew Congregation, and later the Australian Capital Territory.

The structure of the ECAJ is built on the state representative councils. The formation of Boards of Deputies in New South Wales, Victoria, South Australia, Queensland and Western Australia changed the organisational structure of Australian Jewry. This process mainly took place after the formation of the ECAJ in 1944 and, in the case of the smaller Jewish communities, was a consequence of the need for equivalent structures. These roof bodies are the central lay authority and official mouthpieces of the respective Jewish communities. Amongst their many activities, they deal with policy matters relating to Jewish immigration, support of Israel, co-ordination of appeals in the community, ex-servicemen, public relations – involving defence work against the growth of antisemitism, and the promotion of goodwill between Jews and non-Jews. In recent years, community security has become a major concern. In addition, they are concerned with developments in overseas Jewry.

The New South Wales Jewish Advisory Board was reconstituted on a broader basis in 1945, as the New South Wales Jewish Board of Deputies. In the first elections held in 1945, twenty-five Jewish organisations were represented and the contest was portrayed as the synagogues opposing the Zionists.[7] By 2003, the Board had sixty-two constituent organisations representing almost every aspect of organised Jewish communal life.

Initially, the New South Wales Board represented Sydney Jewry's organisational structure only, and there was no direct franchise for the deputies. Demands for further democratisation, spearheaded by former Viennese lawyer Dr Hans Kimmel, resulted in a constitutional committee being established in 1948. One quarter of the deputies would be elected by direct general franchise, and in 1954 this was extended to 50 per cent. New South Wales is the only state to have this form of franchise. Sydney Jewry created a local community appeal structure, known as the Jewish Communal Appeal, in 1967. Over the years, its fundraising capacity has expanded, and its significant financial support enables the Board to function effectively.

The struggle for constitutional change of the Victorian Jewish Advisory Board occurred earlier than in New South Wales. Major reforms were introduced in 1938 and again in 1942, when the base of the Board was widened to include all representative Jewish organisations. Following the New South Wales example, the Board changed its name to the Victorian Jewish Board of Deputies in 1947 – and in 1988 it would become the Jewish Community Council of Victoria. Standing committees were created for finance, public relations, education, immigration and other such matters as were established by a two-thirds majority of the Board.[8] From 1947, the Board met on a monthly rather than a quarterly basis.

Further demands for democratisation were met in 1955, when a number of changes were proposed, including direct representation for each 150 voters.[9] The first ballot under this new system was held that October.[10] However, direct general franchise was not maintained in Melbourne, and the lack of a central fundraising structure has contributed to funding problems in recent years.

The ECAJ also established closer links with overseas world Jewish organisations such as the World Jewish Congress, founded in 1936 in Geneva to represent diaspora Jewry. An Australian section was established in 1941 but, at its annual conference in 1947, the ECAJ leadership decided to affiliate directly with the World Jewish Congress and the section was closed.

There were significant problems associated with this structure, but every attempt to change the constitution failed. As a result, the ECAJ faced constant problems. As Robert Goot, president of the New South Wales Jewish Board of Deputies, summed up in 1982:

> The ECAJ has never been, in my view, an ideal organ for the representation of Australian Jewry. It is very much a compromise body – compromising its headquarters between Sydney and Melbourne; compromising its programs by abysmal funding;

compromising its national representation by distance, cost of travel and inadequately funded administration and communal facilities but ultimately relying on compromise to ensure a consensus on political attitudes.[11]

This is harsh criticism, but the various crises in the ECAJ's history illustrate its validity.[12] Yet, as Robert Goot also pointed out, the structure of the ECAJ 'may be imperfect, but it is still the most representative organ of Australian Jewry'.[13] In all key issues, the ECAJ was recognised as the official representative body of Australian Jewry, and its leaders were outstanding people who presented the concerns of the community in an effective manner.

Claims Conferences

The West German government proposed in 1951 that both moral and material reparations should be made for the destruction of European Jewry by allocating funds to the various diaspora communities. Following a meeting that year in New York, an organisation called the Conference on Jewish Material Claims Against Germany was incorporated in the United States to lodge a claim on heirless property in West Germany in the name of the Jewish people. After lengthy negotiations between the government of Israel, the Conference and West Germany, an agreement was signed at Luxembourg in September 1952 whereby Germany paid compensation for heirless communal property as well as individual restitution until 1965.

Australian Jewry engaged in a great debate, mirroring reactions in other parts of the Jewish world, over the issue of German compensation. Some favoured accepting reparations, as it was only right that the former perpetrators should assist the victims of Nazism; others considered reparations as 'blood money' and believed that there should not be any relationship with Germany.[14] These differences of opinion were reflected in the opposing positions taken by New South Wales and Victoria. The New South Wales Jewish Board of Deputies voted in support of Israel's position, whereas in Victoria, under Maurice Ashkanasy's presidency, the ECAJ opposed negotiations with West Germany.[15] Further debate and discussion, with Sydney Einfeld strongly supporting reparations, led to a reversal of the Victorian position, and in July 1952 the Australian Jewish community decided to participate in German reparations through the ECAJ.[16]

5 DIVERSE VOICES

Dr Nahum Goldmann (left), president of the World Jewish Congress, at the home of Maurice Ashkanasy in December 1969

There was also an intense debate about who should represent the claimants. In Sydney, the Association of New Citizens, led by Dr Max Joseph, believed that it should be the representative body. Dr Joseph argued that the Association represented the victims of Nazism and as such was entitled to the funds.[17] This view was strongly opposed by Einfeld, who believed that only the ECAJ could represent the claimants.

The first Claims Conference to distribute funds from the West German government was held in 1954. This assistance proved invaluable for the absorption of Jewish immigrants, since the local community could raise only 25 per cent of the money required and Claims allocations replaced earlier funds from US Jewish welfare organisations. The community could not have managed without this outside financial assistance, because there was no government funding for Jewish immigrants. The ECAJ presidents (alternatively Ashkanasy and Einfeld)[18] travelled overseas to represent Australia's interests at the Claims Conference meetings. At times, conflicts arose over the allocations of funds. For example, in 1955 Ashkanasy obtained an allocation of £36 000 over three years for Mount Scopus College in Melbourne.[19] The Sydney community was very bitter at the size of this grant, especially as their

Jewish day school, Moriah College, had not received any financial assistance.[20] Einfeld managed to negotiate its first allocation in 1958.

The 1952 Claims Conference agreement also allowed for individual restitution for Nazi victims, and the United Restitution Office was created to help administer such claims. In 1953 Einfeld, then president of the ECAJ, was appointed to its governing board through the efforts of Dr Nehemiah Robinson of the World Jewish Congress. This appointment provided official recognition of the ECAJ's work on behalf of Jewish refugees from Europe.[21] A United Restitution Office was set up in Australia, with branches in Sydney, Melbourne, Brisbane, Adelaide and Perth, to assist individuals in their reparation claims.

Nazi war criminals

Immediately after the war, Nazi collaborators and war criminals entered Australia. Many came through the International Refugee Organisation, which brought in 200 000 European displaced persons between 1947 and 1950. Australia took in the fourth largest number of displaced persons, after the United States, Canada and Israel.

There are a number of reasons why Nazi war criminals entered Australia and the other Western countries at this time. The Australian selection procedures were inadequate, with no formal policy. The focus was on the exclusion of 'enemy aliens' (Germans and Italians) rather than on Eastern European fascists, many of whom had joined the Waffen SS. These Eastern Europeans used various tactics, such as lying about their war record, presenting forgeries, and removing their SS tattoos, in order to evade exclusion from the immigration programme. Australian security tended to rely on dubious overseas sources, including the International Refugee Organisation selection officers, who often were superficial in security investigations. Overall, there was a preoccupation with weeding out communists because of growing Cold War tensions, and by 1949 and 1950 the pressure was to process as many people as possible. The number of Jewish displaced persons on the transports to Australia was very small, and those who were selected often experienced antisemitism, and in some cases even recognised a camp guard.

The organisation that was most active in following up these claims was the Jewish Council to Combat Fascism and Anti-Semitism, which interviewed and collated many of the stories. In relation to Bonegilla near Albury–Wodonga, the largest immigrant reception centre, they reported:

The superintendent in charge of the camp is Major Kershaw, but in actual fact the camp is run by his aide who is a Balt by the name of Lipsius. Mr Lipsius is well known in the camp as a former Stormtrooper. He is very much disliked, not only by the Australian staff, but also by all non-Baltic migrants, who say that he appoints only Balts to all the best jobs in the camp. As far as can be verified by observation, there seems to be truth in this statement. It is a fact that the whole of the camp is in the hands of Mr Lipsius. Nothing can be done in any department without reference to him. The chief Education Officer refers to him as the 'Minister of Labour'.[22]

While it is difficult to verify this passage, one employee at Bonegilla was Konrad Kalejs, who worked there as a processing clerk for three years. Kalejs claimed that he had been a farmer during the war. He became an Australian citizen, and then left for the United States in 1959. When the Office of Special Investigations was established in the United States in 1979, it was revealed that Kalejs had in fact been a member of the Arajs Kommando (Latvian Security Auxiliary Police), a mobile killing squad that had travelled throughout Latvia carrying out mass shootings of Jews and other civilians.

When data of Nazi and antisemitic activities in the migrant camps was presented to the Department of Immigration, it was disregarded because of the communist links of the Council to Combat Fascism and Anti-Semitism. The government claimed that the charges were 'actuated by religious or national bias and that the charges made cannot be substantiated'[23] and continued, until the 1980s, to deny that Nazi criminals had entered Australia.

In early 1986, discussions between the World Jewish Congress and ECAJ president, Leslie Caplan, alerted the Jewish community that Kalejs might be deported from the United States, and the ECAJ made representations to the government. At the same time, Mark Aarons broadcast a series on 'Nazis in Australia' for *Background Briefing* on ABC radio. These two events acted as an important catalyst for Prime Minister Bob Hawke to establish the Menzies Review into whether Nazi criminals had entered Australia after the war. The Menzies Report stated that Nazis had indeed entered Australia, and recommended that action be taken. A Special Investigation Unit was created, under the leadership of Bob Greenwood QC, and later Graham Blewitt, and they investigated over 800 names. In the end, only three men were brought to trial, with only one trial, that of Ivan Polyukhovich, taking place in 1991. He was charged with the murder of twenty-four people in the forest surrounding Serniki, a little village in the Ukraine, but was not convicted. Closure by the Keating government of the Special Investigation Unit in 1992 meant that no further investigations have been initiated in Australia.

Asia/Pacific diaspora communities

The Australian Jewish community had long expressed concern for the survival of the small Jewish communities in Asia and the Pacific region. They were isolated, dispersed and small, with largely transient and non-native populations that lacked spiritual and educational leadership. In the early post-war years, Australian Jewry was itself struggling to absorb the mass immigration of Holocaust survivors, but by the 1960s was sufficiently well established to assist the small Jewish communities to its north. Isi Leibler, who in the 1960s founded Jetset Travel, which became the largest travel agency in South-East Asia, spearheaded this programme. Having a network of offices and a personal presence in the region placed Leibler in a unique position as communal leader and lobbyist for Israel. For over a quarter of a century the ECAJ, in partnership with the World Jewish Congress, worked to promote the religious and cultural survival of these Jewish communities. In 2003, the ECAJ was a founding member of the Euro-Asian Jewish Congress, which has led to regular meetings between the major Jewish communities in this region.

Oppressed diaspora communities

Jews in the Soviet Union had faced antisemitism, discrimination and the abuse of their basic human rights since the Stalinist era. The Soviet government denied this situation and sought to suppress any evidence of human rights abuses. For over thirty years, Australian Jewry took part in an international campaign for Soviet Jewry, which consumed much time, energy and resources. Whilst located on the periphery of the diaspora, Australian Jewry came to play an important, and at times innovative, role in this campaign. In 1962, Australia was the first country to raise the issue of abuse of human rights in the Soviet Union at the United Nations. Yet, this action resulted in a significant clash between New South Wales, represented by Sydney Einfeld, and Victoria, represented by Maurice Ashkanasy and supported by his young protégé, Isi Leibler, which almost destroyed the unity of Australian Jewry. Until the

5 DIVERSE VOICES

Isi Leibler (left) and Soviet refusenik Ari Volvovsky in 1989

collapse of the Soviet Union in 1989, political figures on both sides of the political spectrum, including Bob Hawke, Senator Joan Child and Malcolm Fraser, contributed to the campaign for the human rights of Soviet Jewry. At the same time, the broad Jewish community campaign of public rallies and other demonstrations, led by Marcus Einfeld, then Robert Goot and later Diane Shteinman and Sam Salcman, continued to highlight their plight.

Melbourne/Sydney schisms

The differences between the two major centres, Melbourne and Sydney, often led to major clashes, which threatened the unity of the community. One such clash, in the 1950s and 1960s, was over the role of the Left-leaning Jewish Council to Combat Fascism and Anti-Semitism (JCCF&A), formed in Melbourne in 1942. Initially, it worked closely with the Victorian Jewish Advisory Board (later Board of Deputies) and its members were the backbone of the Board's Public Relations Sub-Committee. A similar organisation, the Jewish Unity Committee, was formed in Sydney in 1945, and in August 1948 changed its name to the Sydney Council to Combat Fascism and Anti-Semitism. After a stormy period, it was finally accepted by the New South Wales Jewish Board of Deputies as a Board member in August 1949.

In the same period in Melbourne, an intense clash developed between the president of the Victorian Jewish Board of Deputies, Maurice Ashkanasy, and the JCCF&A, as a result of growing Cold War tensions. A number of the leading members of the latter, including its general secretary, Judah Waten, were communists or had Left-leaning sympathies, and this led to a climate of conflict within organised Melbourne Jewry. The organisations clashed over the anti-German immigration campaign, which opposed the mass immigration scheme for non-Jewish Germans signed by Immigration Minister Harold Holt in 1950. The Jewish community organised protest rallies in the capital cities, but the government was not swayed. Holt privately noted that it was chiefly 'Jewish interests' that had sought to arouse the public against German immigration, and that 'a small vocal minority should not seriously be regarded as expressing the will of the Australian people'.[24]

An open rift developed in the middle of this campaign when Ashkanasy's proposal in 1950 to exclude the JCCF&A from the Board of Deputies Public Relations Sub-Committee was defeated, and Ashkanasy resigned as president of the Board and the ECAJ. Melbourne's Jewish leadership gradually moved to the Right during 1951–1952, and Ashkanasy returned, largely as a result of the failure of leading JCCF&A members to acknowledge the revival of anti-semitism under Stalin, highlighted by the Prague Trials, a series of antisemitic show trials held in Czechoslovakia in the early 1950s. In these trials, eleven of the fourteen prosecuted for conspiracy against the state were Jews, eight of whom were executed. In the Doctors' Plot, nine doctors, six of whom were Jewish, were accused by Stalin of planning to assassinate Soviet leaders. A new Public Relations Committee was constituted in mid-1951, excluding members of the JCCF&A, and Ashkanasy returned to the Victorian Jewish Board of Deputies. The JCCF&A president, Sam Cohen, resigned from the Board, and in July 1952 the former was disaffiliated after it defied the latter by organising a protest demonstration against the first post-war German Ambassador, Dr Walter Hess.[25]

These divisions between the Left and Right wings of the Jewish community paralleled similar developments in the wider Victorian community. The Australian Labor Party excluded the JCCF&A in the early 1950s, and worked in close co-operation with a Bundist, Bono Wiener – but after the split with the Democratic Labor Party in 1955, the ALP resumed co-operation. Sam Cohen was endorsed on the ALP Senate ticket above Ashkanasy in the 1962 elections, resulting in Cohen's election and Ashkanasy's defeat.[26]

New South Wales Jewry did not experience such bitter conflict, and the Sydney Jewish Council gradually faded away. In Perth, the Western Australian Council for Jewish Affairs was disbanded in 1954. The differences between the Melbourne and Sydney councils reflected the intellectual climates of the two cities, since Victoria had a stronger history of Left-liberalism and was much more affected by confusion between communists and Left-liberals than was New South Wales. Differences between Sydney and Melbourne have continued, with crises over leadership in subsequent decades.

Conclusion

The structure of the Executive Council of Australian Jewry is very different from roof bodies in other parts of the English-speaking world. Australian Jewry drew many of its models from Anglo-Jewry but, because of its small size in the nineteenth century and the traditional Melbourne/Sydney rivalry, it did not imitate the structure of the British Board of Deputies, which is located in London and has a permanent secretariat. It is also different from the United States model, where a plethora of organisations operate on a federal level. While it is closest to Canada and South Africa, both these countries have their headquarters located permanently in one place, Toronto and Johannesburg, and both have a permanent, centralised secretariat and a much better funding structure.

The post-war democratisation process in Australia resulted from the broadening base of the various Jewish roof bodies. This is clearest in Victoria, where the Victorian Jewish Board of Deputies' representative organisation ranged from the ultra-orthodox to the progressives, from the Yiddish socialist Bundists to the Left-leaning and communist, from the Kadimah to the various Zionist organisations. The pluralistic co-ordination through the roof bodies was a direct result of the arrival of the Jewish refugees and survivors. The leadership of the roof bodies, at state and federal levels, moved from the old patrician leadership emanating from the synagogues to the key secular organisations, including the Zionist movement. Gradually, the newcomers came to play an active role in Jewish communal leadership. In Sydney, Dr Joachim Schneeweiss, who arrived in 1939 as a youth with his family from Germany, was the first newcomer to become a Board vice-president in New South Wales, and later ECAJ president. In Melbourne, Polish Jewish refugee and Zionist leader, Nathan Jacobson, also served as ECAJ president in the 1970s. The face of Australian Jewry had changed from purely religious to diverse and multi-faceted.

6
ISRAEL AND ZIONISM

While support for Zionism in Australian Jewry today is a *sine qua non*, this was not always the case. There was enormous resistance to the Zionist movement in its early years, and anti-Zionism remained a key platform until after World War II. Changing attitudes towards Zionism have contributed to the transformation of Australian Jewry. Events in Nazi-dominated Europe, combined with the arrival of refugees and survivors, resulted in a clearer understanding of the need for a Jewish homeland. Following the creation of Israel in 1948, anti-Zionist sentiment dissipated. Zionism shifted from being a fringe movement to a central focus of Jewish identification. By 1960, the Zionist movement of Australia had established itself 'in the vanguard of all communal efforts'.[1]

The beginnings of Zionism

Australian Jews became involved in assisting their less fortunate brethren in Palestine after 1850. Early support for Palestine was in the form of *haluka*, funds collected to support needy and pious Jews in the Holy Land. The first Australian campaign to raise funds for Palestine was in 1854, when Sir Moses Montefiore's appeal, supported by the British chief rabbi, raised £8000, compared with £20 000 in Britain.[2] Subsequently, a number of emissaries from Palestine travelled to Australia, the two best known being Rabbis Jacob Levi Saphir and Chaim Zvi Schneersohn, both of whom were in Australia between 1861 and 1863. Saphir's experiences were recorded in his travelogue, *Eben Saphir*, but his visit was a failure and the Melbourne Hebrew

Congregation had to assist him with his fare home. He later admitted that 'the toil and labour exceeded the reward'.[3] Schneersohn was more successful, as he raised funds to erect dwellings to house sixteen poor families in Jerusalem, a result mentioned in Moses Hess's classic work, *Rome and Jerusalem* (1860). In a footnote, Hess reported that the Dean of the University of Melbourne, who supported the appeal, stressed that 'it would not take long before the Jews regained possession of the land which belongs to them and which was promised to them'.[4]

Modern Zionism, meaning the desire to create a Jewish state by political means on the ancient soil of Israel, emerged in the second half of the nineteenth century. Following pogroms in Tsarist Russia in 1881, Leo Pinsker and others of the Hoveve Zion (Lovers of Zion) Movement reinforced the work of early Zionist philosophers, such as Hess. Little was known in Australia about this emerging Jewish nationalism in Europe, and efforts in the 1890s to establish a branch of the movement met with minimal success.[5]

Theodore Herzl, aroused by the savage antisemitism of the Dreyfus case in France, transformed the 'hitherto ethereal vision of a "return to Zion" into a practical political movement' in the 1890s.[6] However, the spokesmen for Australian Jewry did not accept Herzl's dream. It was described by the *Australasian Hebrew* as being on 'an impractical if dazzling scale'[7] and was opposed by the *Jewish Herald*. The anglicised elements of Australian Jewry objected to the calling of the first Zionist Congress in 1897. Since Australian Jewry was the only Jewish community that was neither represented at the Zionist Congresses nor an endorsee of the Jewish Colonial Trust, Herzl personally appealed for Australian support in a letter published in the *Hebrew Standard* in April 1901:

> The holding back of your share of help we noted with pain, but the day of your joining our common cause will come. So we call upon you not to forget in prosperity your unfortunate brother, also not to forget that on account of the name 'Jew', which he bears with pride, he suffers much. Are you willing to help those unfortunate brothers, do you wish to procure respect the whole world over for the name 'Jew'? Then join the Zionist cause, sign for shares in the Jewish Colonial Bank, and send delegates of Australian Jews, the coming summer to the Zionist Congress in London.[8]

There was no immediate response to Herzl's appeal. The Western Australian Zionist Association was established in 1900, through the efforts of Reverend David Freedman, but it was not until 1902 that the New South Wales and Victorian Zionist Leagues were established. Australia had two representatives at the sixth Zionist Congress in 1903, but the early Zionist bodies struggled to survive.

Percy Joseph Marks tried to resuscitate the Sydney Zionist movement with the formation of the Union of Sydney Zionists in 1908, and a Ladies Zionist Society was formed. In Melbourne, two rival societies emerged: Hatechiya (rebirth) in 1913, under the leadership of a new immigrant, Solomon Ashkanasy, and with a largely Russo-Polish committee, and Herzlia in 1915. Despite the fact that there were four Zionist organisations in Melbourne by 1917, the movement continued to stagnate.[9]

After World War I, the situation did not change radically, particularly in Sydney, despite the Balfour Declaration and British support for the concept of a Jewish homeland. Israel Cohen, the first Zionist emissary to Australia, undertook a fundraising tour for Keren Hayesod (the new Palestine Restoration Fund) in 1920. He sought to explain the meaning of Zionism, and so strengthen the movement in Australia. He commented on the community's devotion to the British Empire and noted that 'So fond were they of singing the National Anthem at gatherings that I was almost inclined to think that they regarded me not so much as an emissary of the Zionist executive, as an envoy of His Majesty'.[10] A total of £67 817 was pledged, with Perth Jewry alone subscribing £10 200, Melbourne £26 000, Sydney only £15 500, Newcastle a staggering £12 000, Brisbane £3100 and Adelaide £1017. Much of this money was pledged by relative newcomers from Europe, who later faced difficulties in redeeming their pledges.[11]

Zionist work continued to stagnate during the 1920s. In order to rectify this situation, Dr Alexander Goldstein, an executive member of the World Zionist Organisation, was sent to Australia in 1927. Under his impetus, the Australian Zionist Federation (later renamed the Zionist Federation of Australia and New Zealand, and then Zionist Federation of Australia) was formed at a combined Zionist meeting held in Melbourne. The Federation acted as an umbrella organisation for the various branches of the Zionist movement, and helped to coordinate activities and improve publicity.[12] Goldstein recommended the employment of a full-time professional and Mark Ettinger, a law graduate from London, was brought from Palestine to fill the position of general secretary in 1928. However, with the onset of the Depression, the Federation faced difficulties in maintaining this position, and in 1930 Ettinger left Australia and was not replaced.[13]

Australian Zionism continued to struggle in the 1930s without a professional infrastructure. It was marked by constant changes in leadership and a succession of short-lived organisations. Rabbi Israel Brodie of the Melbourne Hebrew Congregation, an outstanding person who later became chief rabbi of the British Empire, led the Zionist Federation, and faced many obstacles. The situation was not improved after Brodie's departure in 1936, when Rabbi Ephraim M. Levy of the Great Synagogue, Sydney, assumed the presidency.

Anti-Zionist sentiment

Major factors in the struggle of the Zionist movement included opposition from key rabbinical figures in Melbourne and Sydney; the position taken by the Jewish press, particularly the *Hebrew Standard*; and the anglicised nature of the community, including concerns about dual loyalty. The Zionist movement was also handicapped by the remoteness of Australia and the small size of the community.

Rabbinical leaders such as Reverend Alexander Bernard Davis (1860–1903), Reverend Joseph Landau (1890–1901), Rabbi Francis Lyon Cohen (1905–1934) in New South Wales, and Rabbi Dr Joseph Abrahams and later Rabbi Jacob Danglow (1904–1958) in Victoria, remained strongly opposed to Zionism. These rabbis believed that Jews were held together by religious and ethical ties, and were concerned lest Zionism be seen as compromising their allegiance to Australia. They were opposed to the secularisation of the Messianic idea, and rejected the concept that nationalism could solve the Jewish question. Only divine intervention, they argued, could determine the fate of the Jewish people. They followed the lead of Chief Rabbi Hermann Adler and other leading Anglo-Jews.

The Zionist message had less appeal in Australia because few Eastern European Jews, the mainstays of the Zionist movement, settled in Australia before 1920. The relative absence of antisemitism, together with active Jewish participation in all facets of public life, made many of the community suspect any movement which appeared to conflict with loyal British citizenship.

With the creation of the British mandate, opposition subsided, but when Zionism conflicted with British policy, many Australian Jews faced a crisis of conscience. Difficulties were experienced in 1928 with the Wailing Wall incident, when religious Jews placed a *mehitza* (divider) to separate men from women worshipping there during Yom Kippur, sparking Arab violence. Extensive Arab rioting in 1929 resulted in the Passfield White Paper, which sought to restrict Jewish immigration and land acquisition in Palestine. In both instances, the Australian Zionist movement protested against British policy, and their protests were criticised by the established leadership, which sought to defend British policy. Thus the Melbourne Jewish Advisory Board emphasised in 1928 that Australian Jews, as 'loyal British Jews', should make every effort to 'uphold the authority of the British Government ... and do nothing to embarrass it in its already difficult task'.[14]

One of the leading agitators against political Zionism was Alfred Harris, who served as founding editor of the *Hebrew Standard of Australasia* from 1895 until his marriage in 1908, and again from 1925. He supported Rabbi Cohen's position and opposed the pro-Zionist Rabbi Levy. The *Hebrew Standard* reprinted in 1937 an article entitled 'Zionism and Jewish Nationalism' by Claude G. Montefiore, who criticised Zionism. Rabbi Levy responded in the next edition, claiming that because of the ethnic character of Judaism, even in England, Montefiore would be considered as a Jew, not an Englishman, as 'even the friendly Englishman considered it absurd for a Jew to pretend he is an Englishman'. This argument resulted in a public rebuttal from two leading Australian Jews, Sir Isaac Isaacs and Sir Samuel Cohen. Levy's contract was not renewed. An untenable situation developed when Rabbi Falk, on instruction from the Melbourne Jewish Advisory Board, proceeded to act as senior minister, while Levy refused to stand down. It took time before this schism was resolved with Rabbi Levy's departure for England.

Harris continued as the mouthpiece for anti-Zionist feelings, attacking Zionism as 'unjust, dangerous to a degree, even cruel in its inevitable consequences and, after all, unattainable'.[15] The paper became the battleground between Sir Isaac Isaacs, a strong opponent of political Zionism, who considered the concept of a Jewish state to be undemocratic and opposed to the interests of the Arabs, and a much younger scholar, international lawyer Professor Julius Stone, whose booklet, *Stand Up and Be Counted* (1944), financed by the Zionist Federation, was a response to Sir Isaac's arguments. In the same period, Dr Aaron L. Patkin, a prominent Melbourne barrister and author of some note, who had left Russia in 1920, published another anti-Isaacs pamphlet, *Zionism: Sober or Extreme?* (1942). After Harris's death in 1944, the paper changed its editorial policy.

An anti-Zionist cartoon, Australian Jewish Outlook, *September 1947*

A new anti-Zionist paper in Perth, the *Australian Jewish Outlook*, supported Sir Isaac Isaacs's advocacy for a bi-national state for both Arabs and Jews, which the *Outlook* called 'practical Zionism'. With the creation of the Jewish State in 1948, these conflicts came to an end.

The general press was far from sympathetic to the Zionist cause. Most news on Palestine came 'either from or through London' and was supportive of British policies in Palestine. The *Sydney Morning Herald* was highly critical of the partition decision, while the populist *Bulletin* and sensation-mongering *Smith's Weekly* were even more pro-British and anti-Zionist. *Smith's* published a sensational claim in 1947 that Major Michael Comay, who had come to meet Australia's political leaders and seek their support for a Jewish state, but had addressed a Youth Aliyah Appeal, was raising funds to support terrorism. The Jewish community, represented by vice-president of Youth Aliyah, Dr Fanny Reading, took the paper to court for libel. Since no legislation prohibited group libel and Dr Reading was not mentioned by name, Mr Justice Herron found for *Smith's Weekly*, but he deferred payment of costs, indicating his sympathy with the Youth Aliyah libel claim.

Support for Zionism increases

Attitudes changed significantly with the events of the 1930s and the Holocaust. Nazi racist theories led journalist Eric Baume, an assimilated Jew, to declare as early as 1936:

> Hitler had given the Jews of every country in the world a startling lesson of what not to do.
> He has indicated that even in a violently anti-Semitic country it is better to be a Jew courageously than to avoid or seek to avoid the menace of anti-Semitism by the often attempted movement towards assimilation . . . The Jew who is ashamed of being a Jew has no place not only in the Jewish community but anywhere in the world . . .
> The answer to Hitler's challenge does not lie in wild talking or empty vain threats. The challenge to every Jew can only be answered by the thought of the Zionist movement.[16]

The mass influx of European immigrants between 1938 and 1961 brought an even stronger commitment to Zionism. As victims of anti-semitism, they were keenly aware of the need for a Jewish homeland to provide a refuge from persecution. They also brought their own experience of European Zionist organisations.[17]

Zionist leadership was strengthened in the 1930s and 1940s, mainly by Eastern European Jews – led by Max Freilich and his close friend, Horace B. Newman, in Sydney, and Samuel Wynn, Dr Aaron Patkin, Solomon Wertheim and Joseph Solvey in Melbourne. Many refugees joined the Zionist leadership ranks. Visits by Zionist emissary Dr Bension Shein in 1933 and 1938 increased support for Zionism, as did that of Shlomo Lowy, Jewish National Fund emissary, who arrived in September 1939 and remained until the end of the war, due to the disruption of shipping. For the first time, Australian Zionism had a professional leadership, and Lowy's 'zeal and devotion' contributed to the growth of the Jewish National Fund.

Palestine Committees were formed in 1941 to attract influential Jews and non-Jews to support the Zionist cause. Bishop Charles Venn Pilcher, an Anglican bishop who strongly supported Zionism, chaired the Sydney committee. In Melbourne, the Pro-Palestine Committee included the premier, lord mayor and Catholic archbishop, with Professor H. A. Woodruff as chairman. Such non-Jewish support helped to raise the status of Zionism.

By 1945, a new understanding of Zionism was emerging in Australia. The Stone/Isaacs controversy had benefited the movement, since 'out of the welter of ideas and the widely publicised exchanges between Sir Isaac Isaacs and the leaders of the community, the Zionist image grew in prestige and importance'.[18]

Evatt and the State of Israel

Under the leadership of Dr Herbert Vere Evatt, Australia played a central role in the establishment of the State of Israel. Australia was one of the eleven nations constituting the United Nations Special Committee on Palestine, which recommended either partition or the creation of a unitary state. In the Committee's vote on these proposals, Australia abstained on Evatt's instructions. Following this, an Ad Hoc Committee on Palestine was formed, with all the member states of the United Nations represented. Dr Evatt, who had hoped to become chairman of the United Nations General Assembly but had been defeated by Dr Oswaldo Aranha of Brazil, was invited to chair the Ad Hoc Committee, which voted on the two proposals on 25 November 1947. A majority of 25 voted for, with 13 against and 17 abstentions, including New Zealand and some South American countries. In the four days before the crucial General Assembly vote, New Zealand was lobbied to change its position, and Evatt requested the United Nations Secretary-General, Trygve Lie, to ask the chairman, Aranha, to persuade the Latin American countries to support partition because, as he urged, 'the choice now is between a complete washout and a positive solution'.[19] A two-thirds majority for partition was required, and each vote was vital. On 29 November, 33 member nations, including Australia, supported the proposal, 13 opposed and 9 abstained. Resolution 181 created two states – Arab and Jewish – with Jerusalem to be under international control.

On Evatt's return to Australia, he was given a tremendous ovation at a dinner for over 400 people organised by the Zionist Federation. All speakers paid tribute to his contribution to the historic decision. Bishop Pilcher complimented Dr Evatt's 'typically Australian feat of horsemanship in bringing home 57 refractory steeds'.[20] When the United States sought to overturn the decision by proposing a trusteeship for Palestine in early 1948, Evatt strongly opposed their change of mind, insisting that 'the decision of a competent international conference should be accepted after there has been a full and fair debate, and a settlement has been reached'.[21] Evatt continued to be highly critical of British policy. The British sought to bypass Evatt, restricting a full exchange of information because of his pro-Zionist stance.[22] When United Nations Mediator, Count Folke Bernadotte, recommended in 1948 that the Negev be ceded to the Arabs and restrictions imposed on Jewish immigration to Israel, Australia again objected strongly.[23]

David Ben Gurion declared Israeli independence on 15 May 1948, and the new country was faced with an existential struggle. The British government placed pressure on Australia not to recognise the new state immediately, and diplomatic relations were not established until 29 January 1949, when Australia extended both *de facto* and *de jure* recognition, even though Britain had extended *de facto* recognition only.[24] Evatt served as chairman of the United Nations General Assembly when Israel was admitted as a member. In a letter to Evatt in May 1949 Aubrey (Abba) S. Eban, Israel's representative to the United Nations, acknowledged Evatt's key role in the United Nations.[25]

The 1967 and 1973 wars

Any remaining suspicion of Zionism was overcome by the 1967 and 1973 wars between Israel and the Arabs. Throughout the Jewish world, there was a spontaneous and immediate response to the 1967 crisis, and the Australian community was no exception. In Melbourne, 7000 of a community of 34 000 attended a public rally called at the outbreak of the fighting, and 2500 attended a youth rally in the same week.[26] In Sydney, over 6000 people crowded into the Central Synagogue and its surrounds. In both cities, hundreds of Jewish youth volunteered to go to Israel.[27] A 1967 study of Melbourne Jewry found that most people interviewed reacted with a sense of deep emotional upset, listening to the news much more often and seeking social contacts with family and Jewish friends.[28] Those Jews who were assimilated or were not active in communal organisations were, in the main, just as affected. These feelings were reinforced by the Yom Kippur war of 1973.[29]

Identification with Zionism

The major Zionist organisations are associated with fundraising. They include the United Israel Appeal, which holds an annual appeal for money to assist in the integration of immigrants into Israel. In Australia, it has a federal structure, with a president elected from the state bodies. The Jewish National Fund (JNF: Keren Kayemet) raises money throughout the year through blue boxes, tree planting for *simchot* (festive occasions such as weddings and barmitzvahs), and larger functions. With the large number of blue boxes placed in Jewish homes throughout Australia, the JNF was described in 1946 as 'the most comprehensive Jewish organisation in the Southern Hemisphere'.[30] It continued to expand its activities after the war, and is still one of the most broadly based Jewish organisations in Australia. Women's International Zionist Organisation also raises funds, and is at the forefront of cultural and educational endeavours.

By 1945, Australian Jewry had developed a framework for the administration of Zionist activities that has remained largely unaltered. After the war, the Zionist Federation of Australia worked to assist in the growth of the Zionist youth movements and to encourage immigration to Israel (*aliyah*). The Federation affiliated with the World Zionist Organisation and sent representatives to the Zionist Congresses, held in Palestine/Israel every four years. Max Freilich was appointed a member of the Actions Committee of the World Zionist Organisation in November 1952, in recognition of the growing status of the Australian Zionist movement.[31] Since then, a number of Australian Zionist leaders have held such positions, with immediate past president, Mark Leibler, and present president, Dr Ron Weiser, being examples.

The Zionist movement's two-tiered system of elected representation and administration followed a similar pattern to that of the Executive Council of Australian Jewry and the Boards of Deputies. For most of its history, its headquarters alternated every four years between Sydney and Melbourne, while regular biennial conferences were held to discuss matters of policy. This system of rotation meant that it had neither a permanent general secretary nor administration and this, combined with large distances, complicated its administration.

Mark Leibler established an office in Melbourne in the 1980s, under the leadership of executive director, Haya Mond, who retired after fifteen years in 2002. Leibler served as president for a record twelve years, from 1982 to 1994. The first female president, another Melburnian, Ann Zablud, succeeded him, followed in 1996 by Sydney-based Dr Ron Weiser. When the Federation moved to Sydney in 1996, Dr Weiser decided it was time to create a permanent secretariat, and retained the office in Melbourne.[32]

At the state level, the various Zionist organisations are co-ordinated by Zionist Councils, which function in Victoria, New South Wales, Queensland, South Australia and Western Australia. The Zionist Councils are affiliated to the state branches of the United Israel Appeal,

Mark Leibler (right) and Dr Ron Weiser, next to Israeli President, Moshe Katzav, and his wife, and Ambassador Nati Tamir and his wife, at a Sydney community function in March 2005

the Jewish National Fund, Women's International Zionist Organisation, Youth Aliyah, and other Zionist organisations such as the Friends of the Hebrew University, Magen David Adom (Israeli Red Cross), Aid for Israel, Ezra and the National Council of Jewish Women. The prewar Jewish refugees established most of these organisations during the 1930s. The Zionist Councils have a very broad base of representation, with affiliate membership very similar to the Executive Council of Australian Jewry, including the schools, synagogues and main social and cultural organisations.

Zionist education and youth work is central to Zionist endeavours. The initial concept that all Zionists should move to Israel (known as *aliyah* – literally 'going up') quickly proved Utopian, because Western Jews enjoyed a comfortable lifestyle and were unwilling to uproot themselves. Few Jews from Western countries heeded Ben Gurion's call to settle in Israel, and Zionist leaders had to readjust their philosophy to accommodate the continued existence of diaspora Jewry. Before the creation of Israel, intensive Jewish education sought to increase support for Zionist aims and purposes. Since 1948, Jewish education has aimed at uniting the diaspora with the State of Israel. The Zionist youth movements, still largely based on political ideologies which pre-date 1948, continue to educate and to facilitate *aliyah*. These include Habonim-Dror (the 'Builders', Labor Zionist), Betar

(Revisionist, today associated with Likud), Bnei Akiva (literally 'Sons of Akiva', religious Zionists), HaShomer Hazair ('Youthful Guardians', extreme left-wing Zionists) in Melbourne, Netzer (Progressive) and Hineni ('I am here', modern, religious Zionists) which recently started at Central Synagogue, Sydney, and has spread to Melbourne. The various youth movements are combined in an umbrella organisation, the Australian Zionist Youth Council, which alternates its headquarters between Melbourne and Sydney. From its inception, Machon L'Madrichei Hutz L'Aretz (Institute for Jewish Leaders from Abroad) has been the most important training programme for the future leadership of Australian Jewry. By 1996, of the 770 youth leaders participating in Machon from across the diaspora, over 100 were Australians.

Australia–Israel relations

The story of the relationship between the Australian government and the Jewish state is a complex one, which has been recently analysed by Dr Chanan Reich in a book entitled *Australia and Israel: An Ambiguous Relationship*.[33] Despite the ambiguities in the official relationships, and specific tensions over the years, the overall sense within Australian Jewry is that since the days of Dr Evatt, Australia has been extremely supportive of the Jewish state, whilst also advocating the two-state solution to the Palestinian problem.

Jewish communal leadership has worked to influence successive Australian governments to follow a pro-Israel line. Officially, the Jewish community has always taken a non-political stance, supporting whichever political party was in power. However, particularly in Melbourne, there has always been strong support for the Australian Labor Party, stemming from the socialist background of many Eastern European Jews. Individual leaders such as Saul Same and Isador Magid have raised significant funds for the Labor Party. Whilst this connection was important in the 1940s, the position taken by Labor Party leaders later proved controversial.

During the twenty-three years of conservative government, Australia supported Israel, but with the election of Labor leader Gough Whitlam, in December 1972, the policy changed.[34] He opened a new chapter in Australian diplomatic history by recognising the People's Republic of China, focusing more on the Asia-Pacific region, building bridges with Third World countries, and moving away from reliance on the United States. Whitlam repeatedly claimed that he was following an 'even-handed' policy in the Middle East, but he was seen as modifying the previous pro-Israel Liberal policy to one of neutrality, which at times leaned to the Arab position. This drawing back from Israel manifested itself in a range of decisions, including Australia's voting patterns at the United Nations and moves to establish an Arab League Office in Australia, as well as creating contacts with the Palestine Liberation Organization and permitting its representatives to visit Australia. Lobbying by members of the Lebanese community, including businessman Reuben F. Scarf, together with the oil crisis after the 1973 Arab–Israeli war, contributed to the government's change of policy. Before the 1974 election, a communal breakfast was held in Melbourne to try to clarify Whitlam's stance on Israel. During the questions, Whitlam lost his cool, and stated 'You people are hard to please'.[35] He later complained that the Jewish community was trying to blackmail him.

Malcolm Fraser's election in 1975 restored the pro-Israel policy. The picture changed again with the election in 1983 of Bob Hawke, an ardent supporter of Israel. However, Hawke's period as prime minister proved to be turbulent. ECAJ president, Isi Leibler, who worked closely with Hawke on Soviet Jewry, experienced disappointments on a number of occasions when Australia voted against Israel in the United Nations. This sense of disappointment was heightened when Paul Keating assumed leadership. With the return of a Liberal government under John Howard in December 1995, Australia returned to its traditional support of Israel.

Israel advocacy

In response to growing left-wing anti-Israel feelings, the Zionist Federation of Australia, in partnership with the Executive Council of Australian Jewry, formed Australia–Israel Publications in August 1974, with Sam Lipski and later Michael Danby running the office. The *Australia/Israel Review* began publication under the joint chairmanship of Robert Zablud, a former president of the State Zionist Council of Victoria and the Victorian Jewish Board of Deputies, and Isador Magid, a leader of United Israel Appeal in Victoria. Sam Lipski stepped down in 1982, and Dr Colin Rubenstein was appointed as chair of the editorial committee, a position he retains. The *Review*'s circulation of 3600 in 1986 increased to 5000 by 2002. Isi Leibler and Richard Pratt formed the Australian Institute of Jewish Affairs in 1984, with the aim of sponsoring research and discussion into issues relating to the Jewish community. Over the years there was tension between these two bodies, but after Isi Leibler settled in Israel in 1995, they amalgamated. The resultant Australia/Israel & Jewish Affairs Committee, currently led by Mark Leibler,[36] is now the main Jewish public advocacy body in Australia.

7
TRANSFORMATION OR DISAPPEARANCE?

In 1945 a Jewish demographer, Joseph Gentilli, predicted that by the twenty-first century, almost no Jews would be living in Australia. This prediction has proved to be totally false because of the influx of immigrants, particularly of the survivors after World War II. In the immediate post-war years, Australian Jewry experienced a transformation in every aspect of community life.

Diversification of religious life

The religious structure of Australian Jewry is very different from that in the United States. Until 1933, Australian Jewry was very assimilated and conservative, tending to be 'more British than the British'. This was reflected in the early 'cathedral synagogues' established in Sydney and Melbourne, which maintained a 'high church atmosphere'.[1] Most Australian Jews considered themselves Australians of the Jewish faith, and distinctive religious practices, such as the observance of dietary laws or the wearing of a skullcap, were poorly maintained. The derivative nature of Australian culture, reflected in the Jewish community, resulted in a limited and conservative response by Australian Jews to the nineteenth-century challenges of modernisation. In the period when religious change predominated in North America, with the development of Reform and Conservative Judaism, the various Jewish communities in Australia developed a uniform reaction – the Anglo-Jewish form of modern orthodoxy – which remained rigid and standardised.

All this changed with the pre- and post-World War II Jewish immigration, which radically altered the face of Australian Jewry and diversified Jewish life (see Appendix 1). Progressive Judaism was first established with the creation of Temple Beth Israel in Melbourne in 1931. However, the movement began to flourish only after 1936, with the appointment of Rabbi Dr Herman Sanger, German born and Oxford educated, whose charismatic presence attracted many of the newcomers, particularly from Germany, Czechoslovakia and Hungary, as well as people who were disenchanted with traditional Judaism. Sanger visited Sydney in 1938 and established the Temple Emanuel, which also grew rapidly under the leadership of Rabbi Max Schenk, an American born and trained rabbi. Temple Emanuel attracted many of the German and other Central European refugees who settled in Sydney immediately before the outbreak of war. Reform Judaism was established later in the smaller centres, and there are Reform temples or services in all centres of Jewish life in Australia.

Similarly, Haredi (literally 'in awe', referring to ultra-orthodoxy) Judaism developed in this period. The Adass Israel was established in both Sydney and Melbourne during the 1940s. Habad (acronym for the Hebrew words *'hochmah, binah, da'at'* – wisdom, understanding and knowledge)[2] became a highly visible and influential movement, and today much of the rabbinical leadership in Australia is Habad-trained. The first Habad Yeshiva was established in a Jewish agricultural settlement at Shepparton in 1948, moved to Melbourne in 1951 and then spread to Sydney. Unlike modern orthodoxy, it is a fundamentalist movement that has revived many old traditions, the most obvious being long beards and earlocks for men, and long black coats and black hats, the traditional Hassidic garb. Based on piety and learning, the growth of the Habad movement in Australia is testimony to the vision and influence of Rabbi Menachem Mendel Schneersohn, the movement's late rebbe in New York. Since 1980, a large number of Habad centres and synagogues have been established in Melbourne, Sydney and Perth.

Sephardi immigrants, described as a 'minority within a minority', sought to preserve their own unique liturgical and cultural tradition by establishing Sephardi congregations, first in Sydney and later in Melbourne. These congregations, which represent national origins from Baghdadi/Indian to Egyptian to Moroccan, have often splintered. In addition, the number of mainstream synagogues greatly increased in the 1950s, and again from 1980 to 2000. Together with this came the building of the first Sydney communal mikvah in 1942, located in Bondi, and an improvement in Kashrut facilities, which previously had operated with inadequate standards.

In the early post-war years, the percentage of Jews in Australia who considered themselves as 'strictly orthodox' was very small. Many survivors rejected their religious upbringing after the Shoah. For them, God had died in Auschwitz. Yet, some of their children and grandchildren have returned to a more religious life. Exact demographic information exists only for Melbourne, in John Goldlust's 1992 study, but these findings, which indicate a move to greater religious observance, are fairly representative of the rest of Australian Jewry.[3] Based on religious self-description, 6 per cent of respondents identified themselves as 'strictly orthodox', 33 per cent were 'traditional religious', 15 per cent were Liberal/Reform, 43 per cent were 'Jewish but not religious', 1 per cent was opposed to religion and 2 per cent chose something else. On balance, the respondents felt that they were more religious at the time of the survey than they had been a few years earlier. In addition, the 'strictly orthodox' group was younger than the other groups, and the vast majority had attended a Jewish day school. This would seem to indicate a strengthening of religious commitment among Australian Jews.

The Melbourne survey also provided information about levels of Jewish ritual and practice. On the whole, synagogue attendance was fairly minimal, with only 9 per cent of respondents attending once a week or more. The majority attended services on High Holydays (46 per cent), and only 6 per cent never attended synagogue. As could be expected, the respondents' religious self-description was reflected in their synagogue attendance, with those who defined themselves as 'strictly orthodox' attending synagogue most frequently.

Anecdotal accounts indicate that these figures are relevant for Sydney Jewry. The largest synagogue in Sydney, Central Synagogue, was burnt down in 1994 as a result of an electrical fault. There was an acrimonious debate about how large its replacement should be, with some members arguing for a smaller, less expensive complex. A general meeting voted in favour of the larger complex. The new synagogue can seat 2000 members, but on a regular Saturday morning, only about 200 congregants attend. During the High Holydays, it is full to capacity.

Goldlust showed that for orthodox services, men attended more often than women, but for Liberal/Reform services the reverse was true. This reflects the differing role of women in orthodox and reform services. In terms of choice of synagogue, 16 per cent attended the strictly orthodox service (Yeshiva, Habad, Adass, Mizrachi and Katanga), 59 per cent mainstream, 21 per cent Liberal and 1 per cent

Sephardi, so that synagogue attendance does not reflect religious self-description. Family, friends and location influenced choice of place of worship. It is interesting to note that non-observant Jews, almost 50 per cent of Melbourne Jewry, most frequently chose to worship in orthodox synagogues (65 per cent), with 12 per cent worshipping in ultra-orthodox synagogues and only 15 per cent choosing a progressive service. Thus, synagogue affiliation tends to follow family patterns rather than strictly orthodox rules.

Most Australian Jews can best be described as non-practising orthodox, since they tend to join orthodox synagogues and send their children to orthodox schools, define themselves as Jewish but not religious, and observe some rituals. The most common practice (84 per cent) was attendance at a Passover seder. Next came barmitzvah (literally 'son of commandments', the ceremony marking a boy's religious maturity, aged thirteen), with 79 per cent of all boys being barmitzvah, although only 27 per cent of girls had a batmitzvah (literally 'daughter of commandments', the equivalent ceremony, aged twelve). While 71 per cent undertook some form of Shabbat observance, only 7 per cent observed Shabbat strictly. Yom Kippur was observed at some level by 72 per cent of respondents, with 54 per cent fasting every year, a further 7 per cent usually fasting and 12 per cent sometimes fasting. With Kashrut (dietary laws), 48 per cent observed some of the laws but, as with Shabbat, only 7 per cent kept Kashrut strictly. Another commonly practised Jewish observance was placing a mezzuzah on the front door, with 74 per cent doing so. Although the survey does not include information on circumcision, this is perhaps the most observed of all the Jewish rituals.

The diversification of religious life after 1945, and the strengthening of orthodox practice, is one illustration of how the refugees and Holocaust survivors enriched the community. It was a transformation, and while only 6–7 per cent are strictly orthodox, they provide the community with a strong core, which radiates outwards.

Changes in Jewish education

One of the most distinctive features of Australian Jewry is the strength of its day school movement. The first modern moves to establish a Jewish day school took place in Sydney during World War II, and the North Bondi Jewish Kindergarten and Day School was established in August 1942. Its founding principal was a young German rabbi, Elchanan Blumenthal, who found refuge in England before the war only to be rounded up and sent as an internee to Australia on the *Dunera* in 1940. After his early release he went to Sydney, where he initiated the Jewish day school movement with the help of a leading Sydney philanthropist, Abraham Rabinovitch. The *Hebrew Standard of Australasia* reported his speech at the official opening in February 1943:

> The reason why in this solemn moment of consecrating the new school, he recalled to mind and also wished to recall to mind of those present, the saddest reality of the present time, the unspeakable agonies of European Jewry. Let us sadly remember them, all those who over there on the other side are experiencing the full brunt of mysterious Jewish suffering and all centres of Jewish learning are lying in ruins.[4]

However, the two founders of the kindergarten and school conflicted, and Rabbi Blumenthal departed for Melbourne at the beginning of 1944. As he later recalled, 'Whereas I strove to achieve a scope which would include the entire community for each group of Sydney Jews, Rabinovitch was thinking of a separate parochial institution limited to people of his persuasion [strictly orthodox Jews]'.[5] The school, later named Moriah, thus remained tiny, with less than a hundred students until the 1960s.

The first communal Jewish day school, Mount Scopus College, was created in Melbourne in 1947. The idea of establishing a Hebrew day school had first been proposed by Benzion Patkin in 1933.[6] He intensified his campaign after 1945, but faced obstacles including the fear that the segregation of Jewish children would lead to increased antisemitism, and that pupils would be unable to mix within the general community once they left school.[7] Zelman Cowen, later to be governor-general of Australia, argued in a letter published in the *Australian Jewish Herald* on 2 March 1945 that a Jewish day school 'will tend to isolate the Jewish population as a separate national group within the community'.[8] Cowen later changed his mind on this.

The establishment of Mount Scopus was a milestone in the transformation of Melbourne Jewry from its anglicised orientation to cultural pluralism. From its beginnings in February 1949, the school was an unqualified success. The school council had planned for an enrolment of 90, but the school opened with 120 children. It expanded rapidly and, at its peak in the 1980s, was the largest private Jewish day school in the diaspora, with 2800 students.

Mount Scopus College, Melbourne, in the 1950s

Dr Hans Ruskin, chairman of the Education Committee of the Victorian Jewish Board of Deputies, outlined in 1958 the reasons for the school's success:

(a) The re-establishment of the State of Israel which has given Jews in all countries a new pride and interest in all things Jewish
(b) The stream of immigrants who have greatly suffered because of their faith, and desire their children to become conscious and educated Jews
(c) The fact that by clever but dignified propaganda of Jewish education, it has gradually become fashionable and 'the proper thing to do'
(d) Endeavours to make Jewish teaching more attractive by furnishing brighter schoolrooms, employing enthusiastic teachers, and introducing modern and appealing curricula.[9]

The school quickly reached high scholastic standards, and in 1957 it obtained 'the highest marks of any High School in Victoria'.[10] Academic success was important for Mount Scopus's development because Jewish parents are career-oriented.

The success of Mount Scopus encouraged the growth of other Jewish day schools. It reflected the need and possibility for diversity of educational aims across the entire spectrum of Jewish religion and culture. Yeshiva College for boys was founded in 1951 and Beth Rivka for girls in 1955. The Adass Israel School, founded in 1952, met the needs of the ultra-orthodox community. The modern orthodox Zionist Mizrachi movement established its day school, Yavneh College, in 1959, and today it is a primary and high school called Leibler-Yavneh College.

Jewish kindergartens also grew rapidly in Melbourne. The first, Bialik, was established in Carlton in 1942, with Hebrew classes after school and on Sunday mornings for school-aged children. Its founders were Eastern European Jews, some of whom had lived in Palestine before emigrating to Melbourne. Under the guidance of Israel Kipen,[11] Bialik developed into a day school, Bialik College, in 1963. In many ways, Bialik is unique because from its inception it was a secular, Hebrew-based school, as distinct from the purely religious schools that previously had prevailed in Australia. It is the second largest Jewish day school in Melbourne. A Yiddish primary school, the Sholem Aleichem School, opened in 1975, based on Bundist principles of secular Yiddish culture. The Reform Jewish day school, King David College, was founded in 1978.

Initially, the success story of the Melbourne day school movement was not mirrored in Sydney, due to the different nature of the two communities and aggravated by personality clashes. After the war, the North Bondi Jewish Day School and Kindergarten expanded slowly, and in January 1953 opened as a primary school on a newly acquired campus in Bellevue Hill. Renamed Moriah College, its enrolment remained tiny. An attempt to create a community-based school modelled on Mount Scopus, the King David School, opened in 1958, also failed – and, following Rabinovitch's death in 1964, the two schools amalgamated in 1968. The day school movement in Sydney was hampered by a number of factors. Some members of the Jewish community felt that Moriah's benefactor and president for twenty-one years, Abraham Rabinovitch, was too authoritarian, and that he stifled Moriah and prevented a community school from developing.[12] In addition, many parents were apprehensive of the effects of segregating their children in Jewish schools, and were deeply concerned about academic standards.

The rapid expansion of the Jewish day school movement began in the 1970s. One decisive factor was the strengthening of Jewish identity following the 1967 and 1973 Arab–Israeli wars. Another was the adoption of multiculturalism as official government policy, whereby separate ethnic and religious schools became more acceptable. Cutbacks in public-sector funding were producing a general sense of disaffection with state schools, with a resultant increase in private school enrolments. Federal government funding for private schools facilitated the expansion of Jewish schools. New waves of immigration from the Soviet Union and South Africa provided more students.

Educational leadership was also important. Harold Nagley was appointed principal of Moriah College in 1965, and under his leadership the school forged ahead. Academic success followed suit, and in 1977 three girls were in the top ten in the state, with one being the top girl. Outstanding matriculation results have continued, with Moriah ranked as the top school in New South Wales in 2004. The school moved to a new campus at Queens Park in 1994, and has continued to expand. Moriah College is now the largest Jewish day school in Australasia, with an enrolment of close to 1800 students.[13]

In Melbourne, student numbers at Mount Scopus College have declined significantly, whilst enrolments at Bialik College increased substantially in the 1990s. During that decade, total Jewish day school enrolments decreased, particularly at the primary level, even though the proportion of Jewish children in private schooling has increased. The 2001 Census showed that only 23 per cent of Jewish children attended government schools, compared to 77 per cent of the general population. Of those in private schools, 66 per cent attended Jewish primary schools but only 55 per cent attended Jewish secondary schools.[14]

Most of the younger members of Perth Jewry in the 1950s were second- and third-generation Australians who lacked a firm grounding in Judaism. For a few, the answer to this problem and to growing intermarriage lay in establishing a Jewish day school. With support from the Seeligson Trust, a free school, the Seeligson kindergarten, opened its doors in 1958.[15] One year later, eleven children enrolled in the first class of the Carmel Jewish Day School, which added a new class each year. The school purchased land from the Maccabean League at Mount Lawley and built its own premises in 1963, and it has grown to become a bastion of Jewish life in Perth. A junior high school was established in 1973, and in 1978 the senior high school was inaugurated 'due to the enthusiasm of the pupils themselves'.[16]

The success of Carmel School lies partly in the community's geographical concentration in and around Mount Lawley. One controversial issue is the school's admission policy. Initially, it had no formal policy, but financial support from the Seeligson Trust was dependent on the school only accepting children who were Jewish from the orthodox perspective. In the 1990s, the school board stressed an open admissions policy, but reaffirmed that the school was orthodox and, whilst attendance at all religious activities was compulsory, children who were not Jewish according to orthodox Jewish law could not participate in some ceremonies, such as a boy being called to read from the Torah. Parents of a child at the school took legal action in the Equal Opportunity Tribunal in 1996, but the judge's decision in September 1999 vindicated the school's position.[17]

Part-time Jewish education continued to be provided by the Jewish education boards in the various states and, in the smaller Jewish centres such as Adelaide, Brisbane, Canberra, and Newcastle, Hebrew classes are offered through the local synagogue and/or temple. In Melbourne, the work of the United Jewish Education Board was supplemented by various synagogue Talmud Torahs. An interesting innovation was the Jewish Secular Humanistic School on Saturday mornings, starting in 1992 – and the Education Board developed a 'radio cheder'.[18] In Sydney, by the mid-1950s, the New South Wales Board of Jewish

Education provided part-time education for 1590 children through right-of-entry classes, and 814 children at Talmud Torahs and Sunday Schools.[19] It also offered a correspondence programme. The Board has continued to expand, introducing Hebrew as an elective subject into government primary and secondary schools in the late 1980s. Other innovations include the informal education programme through the Jewish Student Network, which includes a Sabbath experience for Jewish children living in rural areas. Overall, part-time Jewish education suffers from inadequate hours, the lack of suitably qualified teachers and the difficulty that the students usually have varying levels of knowledge, which cannot easily be catered for.[20]

Social and cultural institutions

Australian Jewry's social and cultural institutions range from B'nai B'rith and the National Council of Jewish Women to Kadimah in Melbourne, which sponsors Yiddish culture, and the Hakoah Club in Sydney, which began as a sporting club but became the community's main social and cultural meeting point thanks to its central location in Bondi and excellent modern premises. The Australian Jewish Historical Society was founded in Sydney in 1938, with its journal starting in 1939, and in 1953 a section was formed in Melbourne.

Jewish cultural life has benefited from the growth of multiculturalism in Australia, particularly during the 1970s. Under the Labor government of Gough Whitlam, the Minister for Immigration, Al Grassby, recommended the establishment of ethnic broadcasting stations. The scheme was finally implemented in 1975, and since then the Jewish community has been served by radio 2EA in Sydney and 3EA in Melbourne, which together broadcast in over fifty community languages. The Jewish community languages are Hebrew, Yiddish and English, and there are three to four hours of broadcasting each week. However, at present there is no Jewish community television service.

The Shalom Institute in Sydney plays an interesting role. It started as a Jewish residential college at the University of New South Wales in 1973. Today it is a key centre for adult education and for student and young adult activities. The latter include initiatives to enable young adults to meet prospective partners, such as 'Table for 8' ('It's not a date, it's Table for 8!') and Rendezvous holiday trips organised for singles between twenty-five and forty years. A body called Network coordinates a large number of affiliated young adult groups, and the J-Net Calendar of monthly activities is mailed out to 3000 households.[21] The

7 TRANSFORMATION OR DISAPPEARANCE?

At the opening of the Sydney Jewish Museum in November 1992, the founder, John Saunders, stands in front, third from the right.

Shalom Institute has also been involved with communal and leadership development over the years.

Holocaust museums were developed in both Melbourne and Sydney in the 1980s, to sponsor Holocaust remembrance and education. In Melbourne, the Jewish Holocaust Museum and Research Centre was opened in Elsternwick. The Sydney Jewish Museum was opened in 1992, dedicated to the Holocaust and Australian Jewish history and located in the historic Maccabean Hall. It has been described as 'a landmark event'.[22] The opening of these museums, as well as the Melbourne-based Jewish Museum of Australia, marked the 'beginnings of a museum culture for Australian Jewry'.[23]

Jewish cultural and intellectual life flowered in the second half of the 1980s. It was fostered by the Australian Institute of Jewish Affairs, which sponsored visits to Australia of leading Jewish thinkers and scholars. The bicentennial activities in 1988 – the Melbourne Arts Festival and the Sydney exhibition *Old Songs in a New Land* at Hyde Park Barracks, as well as tours by the Australian Jewish Historical Society in Sydney throughout 1988 and publication of the first comprehensive histories of Australian Jewry – all provided a new focus and awareness of local Jewish history and cultural identity.[24] The publication in 1989 of a new quarterly journal, *Generation*, was a 'sign that the post-war Australian-born generation of Jewish writers and intellectuals is beginning a more active search for its own distinctive voice', but publication ceased in December 2000.[25] The *Australia/Israel Review*, established in the 1970s, continued to be an important publication, and the longest serving community paper, the *Australian Jewish News*, celebrated its centenary in November 1995.[26]

Philanthropic and welfare institutions also expanded. As the number of Jewish immigrants decreased, the Jewish Welfare Societies gradually shifted their activities to include a host of services covering the aged, unemployed, sick, mentally ill, orphans and others. In the 1990s they changed their name to Jewish Community Services, and in 1999 became Jewish Care. The Jewish Social Services Council of Victoria was established in 1960 through the co-ordination of the Victorian Jewish Board of Deputies, and Sydney Jewry opened a Jewish Hospital, Wolper.

The Sir Moses Montefiore Home for the Aged in Sydney resumed its Hunter's Hill site after the war, and facilities have been constantly upgraded. In the last two decades the Home has purchased properties for aged care in Sydney's eastern suburbs, where most of the Jewish community resides. Similarly, in Melbourne the Montefiore Homes for the elderly have greatly expanded with constant rebuilding projects, while the Emmy Monash Home for the Aged was established by Holocaust survivors to provide for elderly people who were unable to gain admission to the Montefiore Homes.[27] The Welfare Society established blocks of flats for the elderly. In Perth, work by the Council of Jewish Women resulted in the Maurice Zeffert Home for the Aged being opened in 1959. Its facilities now include a nursing home, operating theatre and the Sir Zelman Cowen Retirement Village. While Adelaide Jewry briefly opened an old age home, it was closed due to financial problems.

Countering assimilation

While these developments in the broad canvas of Australian Jewish life have transformed Jewish identity, there is much debate as to whether the changes in Jewish education and religious life are sufficiently strong to counter the effects of assimilation. The high proportion of children in Jewish schools is a significant achievement. In 1957, communal leader Abe Troy wrote this about plans to open a Jewish day school in Perth: 'I should like to indulge in a bit of fantasy, though, as Herzl said, if you will it, it need not be a dream, and this is the possibility of having a Jewish primary day school'.[28] This dream was realised, and the school eventually catered for kindergarten to year 12. Coincidentally, the title of Moriah College's history is 'If you will it, it is no dream'.[29] The early founders of the movement would, indeed, be surprised at its success. The present generation of Jewish children are much more knowledgeable about Hebrew and Jewish Studies than their parents' generation.

A major motivation in creating full-time Jewish schools was to counter assimilation. The success of the day school movement in this area is subject to much debate. Two major studies in Melbourne found that while the ultra-orthodox schools, and particularly the girls' school, Beth Rivka, were successful in fostering a strong Jewish identity, this was not the case for the other schools, whose students sometimes became disillusioned with their Jewish Studies. Schools needed to develop a more professional approach to the teaching and learning of Hebrew and Jewish Studies, particularly in the areas of curriculum and professional development. Since no further research has been undertaken, it is difficult to draw definitive conclusions on this issue. Dr Oswald Tofler has analysed the intermarriage figures in Perth by comparing students from Jewish primary and secondary schools with those who did not attend Jewish schools. He stressed that whilst his findings were not definite, the data seems to indicate that Jewish high school education does have a favourable effect in countering intermarriage.[30] Other important factors, such as the home environment, involvement in a Jewish youth movement, visits and study in Israel, and the peer group also need to be investigated.

Overall, the profile of Jewish religious and Zionist identification remains strong, even though recent demographic studies indicate a significant increase in intermarriage amongst the younger generation, who are also marrying later and in some cases choosing not to have children. Despite its declining birth rate, Australian Jewry is one of the few diaspora communities that is increasing in size as a result of continuing immigration.

8
JEWISH WOMEN

The status of Jewish women is similar to the situation of women in all the 'Abrahamic faiths', including Christianity, and particularly orthodox Christianity. It is also not dissimilar to that of women in the general Australian community, a subject of much critical commentary by feminist writers. In the first half of the twentieth century, Jewish women played an innovative role both in Zionism and in fostering immigration from Europe through two important organisations, the National Council of Jewish Women (NCJW) and the Women's International Zionist Organisation (WIZO). More recently, key individuals have emerged as leaders in their own right, and Jewish women have played an active role in the feminist movement.[1]

Women and communal life

The main contribution of Jewish women before the 1920s was either as helpmates to their husbands or in philanthropic endeavours. In Jewish tradition, *'tzeddakah'* (charity) is seen as central, and here Jewish women quickly made their mark. One of the earliest Jewish charitable organisations created in Sydney was the Sydney Ladies' Hebrew Benevolent and Maternity Society, founded in 1844 to provide relief for distressed Jewish women.[2] The second women's organisation to be registered formally in Australia, it continued to function until 1981. In Victoria a similar organisation, the Hebrew Ladies' Benevolent Society, was founded in 1857. During the depression of the 1890s, other such charitable organisations run by women were established. In Sydney, these included the Jewish Girls' Guild, founded to engage in non-sectarian work, and the Help-in-Need Society, established in 1898.

The women who ran these societies were also active in the Montefiore Homes for the Aged, established in Sydney in 1880 and in Melbourne in 1885, and participated in non-Jewish charities such as the Red Cross. During World War I, the editor of a Sydney-based paper, the *Hebrew Standard*, referred to 'the many enthusiastic workers of the Jewish faith who identified with the Red Cross'. Some key women of this period were Ida Cohen (1867–1970) of Tamworth, who was officially recognised for her services to the Red Cross; Julia Levy (1886–1959), who arrived in Australia in 1935, having previously married a businessman and parliamentarian, Lewis Wolfe Levy (d. 1914); London-born Isabel Solomon of Adelaide, and Fanny Breckler (1877–1946) of Perth.

The most remarkable effort of Jewish women in Sydney in the nineteenth century was their assistance in the building of the Great Synagogue. A spectacular bazaar raised close to £5000, one-fifth of the total cost of the building.[3] After their initial input, women were not in evidence. They had no say in the synagogue's management, though a number of unsuccessful attempts were made to allow women to vote at its annual meetings. A Women's Auxiliary of limited membership was formed in 1936, and it was only in 1941, under the leadership of Bertha Porush that it was opened to all female members.

The example of the Great Synagogue reflected the general situation for women in Jewish communities throughout Australia. One exception was the Victorian Ladies Zionist League, Ha-Tikvah, which was established by Rose Altson in 1905, not as an auxiliary to a male counterpart but as an autonomous group. It operated for a number of years, and in 1908 resisted attempts to amalgamate with its male counterpart, the Victorian Zionist League. However, it fell on 'hard times' and petered out before World War I.[4]

The first move to organise Jewish women in a more formal way came with the creation of the Council of Jewish Women. This organisation was formed in Sydney in 1923 after Dr Fanny Reading (1884–1974) was inspired by the words of visiting American Zionist emissary, Bella Pevsner. Its initial ideals, which continue to influence Council philosophy, included loyalty to Judaism, support for Israel and service to all worthy causes – both Jewish and non-Jewish – in the fields of education and philanthropy, while endeavouring to further the interests and cater for the needs of women and children. Interstate branches had been established by the late 1920s, and in 1929 the first interstate

Dr Fanny Reading at her graduation in medicine, 1921

conference was held, leading to the creation of the National Council of Jewish Women.[5]

For many Australian Jews, Dr Fanny Reading was a household name. Born in Minsk, Russia, and emigrating to Australia as a child in the 1890s, she grew up in Ballarat, Victoria. After gaining her Diploma of Music in 1914, she studied medicine and graduated in 1921.

Dr Fanny Reading had a flair for organisation and has been described as 'a dreamer of great dreams with the courage to implement them even in the face of strong opposition'.[6] Like her gentile feminist colleagues of the inter-war years, she set about mobilising Jewish women at the grassroots level. Her concern with social welfare was summed up in the message she wrote personally on every conference programme, 'that the Council of Jewish Women stands above all things for the Law of Loving-kindness'.[7] Vera Cohen (1902–1994) took over the leadership from Dr Reading in 1955.

The NCJW national office moved to Melbourne in the late 1960s, following the election of Mina Fink (1913–1990). She had arrived as a young bride from Bialystok in Poland in the early 1930s, and worked untiringly as her husband Leo Fink's helpmate, assisting Jewish immigrants. After his death, she devoted her efforts to improving the status of women, acting as a bridge on feminist issues between her own pre-war generation and that of her daughter, who represented the new attitudes of professional women in the 1970s. Since then, NCJW leadership has alternated between Melbourne and Sydney.[8]

Another key organisation, the Women's International Zionist Organisation,[9] was founded in Sydney as Ivriah by Reike Cohen (1887–1964), a strong leader who was originally active in the NCJW.[10] As Marilyn Lake has commented, 'The history of Australian feminism was marked by a series of rivalries between strong women',[11] and the split between Cohen and Reading is evidence of this. Ethel Morris established the Melbourne branch of WIZO in July 1934, and in 1937 the Sydney-based Ivriah was renamed the Women's International Zionist Organisation. Ruby Rich-Schalit was elected the first federal president, a position that she retained for three years.

Ida Bension-Wynn from Canada was a key personality in the development of WIZO. A prominent Zionist leader, she first visited Australia in July 1938, and was responsible for creating a federal WIZO movement. She returned for a second visit in 1939, after which she married Melbourne winemaker and veteran Zionist leader, Samuel Wynn.[12] Since WIZO was better known in Europe than the NCJW, it attracted many key leaders from the European refugees, including people such

Josie Lacey, Margaret Gutman, Nina Bassat and Diane Shteinman with Ezer Weizmann (front) and Dr Philip Bliss in the background

as Sydney-based Hannah Kessler and Melbourne-based Dr Alice Benfrey. By the time of Ida Wynn's early death in 1948, Australian WIZO had a 4000-strong membership, making it one of the largest movements within the Jewish community.

Women's Zionist activities were further diversified with the establishment of Ezra in September 1939. Concerned primarily with improving maternity facilities in Palestine, Ezra was a response to the appeals for help of Rose Slutzkin, who visited Australia from Palestine with her daughter. Emunah, the religious women's Zionist organisation, was established more recently.

Organisations established after the war include the women's B'nai B'rith chapters, of which the Sydney chapter, established in 1945, was the first. Both the United Israel Appeal and, in New South Wales, the Jewish Communal Appeal created separate women's divisions.

More women entered the general leadership ranks after 1985. Eve Mahlab, who was involved in the Welfare Society in Melbourne, headed the 1986 welfare appeal, while in Sydney, Jewish Care is led by Eva Fischl. Janet Simons came through the ranks of the United Israel Appeal Women's Division to become vice-president of organisation. In Perth, Tirza Cohen served as president of the Council of Western Australian Jewry, while Ruth Holzman was president of the Australian

Capital Territory Council. In Melbourne, Zosia Mercer became president of the State Zionist Council of Victoria. Ann Zablud was elected chairperson of the Victorian Jewish Board of Deputies in 1987, and in 1995 was the first woman to head a federal organisation, the Zionist Federation of Australia. Diane Shteinman was elected president of the community's roof body, the Executive Council of Australian Jewry, in 1995.[13] Her Melbourne successor was lawyer Nina Bassat, the second woman and the first Holocaust survivor to hold this key position. As individuals, these women have made important contributions. Women have also been very prominent in what W. D. Rubinstein describes as the 'secondary level of Jewish leadership': they fill most administrative posts of the Boards of Deputies, State Zionist Councils, ECAJ and Zionist Federation of Australia. However, this is largely because community posts tend to be less well paid and have lower status than top positions in the corporate sector.

Women have also been active in Jewish cultural and education life. The Australian Jewish Genealogical Society was founded in Sydney by Holocaust child survivor, Sophie Caplan. In Melbourne, Beverley Davis served for many years as the honorary secretary of the Australian Jewish Historical Society; in Sydney, Louise Rosenberg was honorary secretary for twenty-five years and then honorary historian, while the position of honorary treasurer was filled by Phoebe Davis, followed by Miriam Solomon. Helen Bersten served as honorary archivist from 1979, whilst I was president from 1996 to 2004, when Sophie Caplan assumed the position. Women played a key role at both the professional and voluntary levels in the development of museums. At the Jewish Museum of Australia, whose director was Dr Helen Light, 90 per cent of the almost 400 active volunteers were women. Similarly, the Sydney Jewish Museum is dependent on volunteers, particularly Holocaust survivors, and again the majority are female. Many Jewish women work as volunteers in public institutions as well. In addition, women have been central to the development of Jewish education in schools, universities and in adult education in recent years.

Innovative responses

Jewish women have contributed to the community in a number of other areas, including immigration, Youth Aliyah, the establishment of convalescent and old age homes, public relations and sport. In many of them – particularly immigration and Zionism – women were innovative in their approach.

In immigration, women were more perceptive than men in recognising the need to escape from Europe. In her recollection of their departure from Nazi Germany in 1938, Betty Lipton commented:

> A woman sometimes has a sixth feeling. I had read all the *Stürmer* magazines and so on because I wanted to be in the picture about what was happening. So I said to my husband, 'You know, I think we will have to leave'. He said, 'No, you won't have a six-room apartment and two servants if we do that'. But I said, 'OK, then I'll have a one-room flat with you: but I want to be safe'. He wouldn't believe me. He was terribly afraid to emigrate.[14]

Eventually the family left Germany, thanks to Betty Lipton's vision, and this story was mirrored in many other families. The refugee women's lives changed more than those of the men. They had to learn to cope without domestic servants, and most worked together with their husbands to rebuild their lives. Often the men were unhelpful or even a burden. As one daughter remarked, 'My father talked a lot, but my mother seemed to do all the work'.[15]

Both the Council of Jewish Women and WIZO were very active in immigrant reception. The federal government introduced quota restrictions for European immigrants in 1928. While the male leadership welcomed these restrictions, Dr Fanny Reading asked:

> Who are we to say that we are pleased that certain immigration restrictions will be placed on the admittance of our brethren into our country? That we are glad that our task will be made lighter while our brethren languish for freedom and the right to live?[16]

Women met the refugees before the war and survivors after the war at the boats and planes, and helped them integrate into society.[17]

They were also concerned with the care of the sick and with providing convalescent facilities for Jewish people. In Sydney, the NCJW sponsored Wolper Hospital, one of the first organisations to have a female president, Lynn Davies. Similarly, the Maurice Zeffert Old Age Home in Perth started as an NCJW project due to the initiative of Edna Luber-Smith.

Another example of dynamic leadership by a woman was Youth Aliyah, founded in Germany in the early 1930s and introduced into Australia in 1938 by Friedl Levi, who was associated with the movement from its inception. For five years she travelled in Germany on fundraising tours, while also assisting children to escape. The Nazis imprisoned her in 1938, whereupon she and her husband, Dr H. G. Levi, a lawyer, decided to emigrate to Australia.

Women have also contributed to public relations. Journalist Caroline Isaacson was appointed Director of the Public Relations Bureau of the Victorian Jewish Board of Deputies in 1952. Evelyn Rothfield played an active role in this area, especially through her association with the Jewish Council to Combat Fascism and Anti-Semitism in the 1940s and 1950s, and through her work with NCJW. The Jewish press, a crucial institution in the community, has had a number of women editors, including three editors of the *Australian Jewish Times/News*: Eve Symon (1965–1980), Susan Bures (1983–1996) and Deborah Stone (2000–2003). After Eve Symon's retirement from the *Times*, she became chairperson of the Public Relations Committee of the New South Wales Board of Deputies, and shortly before her death was elected vice-president.

In recent years, women have been innovative in fostering interfaith activities. In Sydney, Josie Lacey was instrumental in the formation of the Women's Interfaith Network, which brings together all the major faiths in Australia. Peta Jones Pellach has also been active in this arena, and is part of the National Dialogue of the three major Abrahamic faiths: Judaism, Christianity and Islam.

In all these areas of innovation, women have been applying their desire for '*tikkun olam*' (repairing the world). For, as Israeli psychologist Amia Leiblich has written:

> boys and girls have entirely different approaches to moral dilemmas. Boys use the principle of justice, while girls' morality attempts to minimise hurt for everyone, to take responsibility over the other's lot and to care for his or her wellbeing.[18]

Whilst Leiblich cautions against generalisations, research seems to indicate that women's approach is more relational, reflecting concern for the care for others, rather than individualism. This gender difference seems to be reflected in the areas of innovation introduced by Australian Jewish women.

Women and religious life

The successful introduction of Progressive Judaism into Australia in the 1930s resulted from the efforts of a Melbourne widow, Ada Phillips (1862–1967), who came from a long-established Victorian Jewish family, the Crawcours. She attended a Progressive service in London in 1928 and, impressed with their approach, decided to establish the movement in Melbourne. She was supported by her two daughters, Isabella, a physician, and Millie, who became the first honorary secretary. From the beginning, women were accepted as equals in all facets of congregational life, including membership of the board of management.

Reform Judaism, at least in theory, offers full equality to women in both religious and lay leadership. The first female Liberal rabbi, American-born Karen Soria, was appointed assistant minister at Temple Beth Israel in Melbourne in 1981. Thereafter, two female rabbis were appointed in Sydney, while a number of female rabbis are active in communal life in Melbourne. Of these, two are Australian-born: Aviva Kipen of Melbourne and Jackie Ninio who, originally from Adelaide, was appointed to Sydney's Temple Emanuel in Woollahra.

In orthodox Judaism, the situation is much more complex. However, there have been important developments to increase opportunities for orthodox Jewish women within the religious framework. Most important of these is the establishment of Women's Tefillah (prayer) Groups, which also provide opportunities for Jewish learning. In addition, the difficult issues of the *get* (divorce) and marriage have been canvassed through petitions at both the national and international level, largely organised by the NCJW, with both Dr Geulah Solomon of Melbourne and Josie Lacey of Sydney playing key roles.

Prominence outside the community

Jewish women have, since the nineteenth century, played key roles not only in community charitable endeavours but also in the country's educational system, the professions, business, music, literature and the arts. Their story begins with Esther Abrahams, the Jewish First Fleeter.[19] Lysbeth Cohen used Esther Abrahams's name in the title of her study of Jewish women in New South Wales, which is to date the only substantial survey of the contribution of Jewish women in Australia.[20]

In the field of education, Jewish women have made significant contributions. Gladys Marks (1883–1970) was, in the 1920s, the first woman lecturer in the Faculty of Arts at the University of Sydney, and for a short time was acting Professor of French. Fanny Cohen (1887–1975) became headmistress of a select state school, Fort Street Girls' High School, and was a member of the Senate of the University of Sydney, while Sophia 'Zoe' Benjamin (1882–1962) founded the kindergarten movement and the Sydney Kindergarten Teachers' Training College.[21] Lillian Daphne de Lissa, a contemporary of Zoe Benjamin, was also a pioneer in kindergarten education.[22] Leah Kloot (1886–1962) came to Australia after World War I, having married a Jewish ANZAC (Australia and New Zealand Army Corps); during the Depression, she became the first president of the Victorian Association of Mothers' Clubs. More recently, Professor Bettina Cass served as Dean of the Faculty of Arts at the University of Sydney.

In politics and in the professions, especially law and medicine, there were a number of pioneering women. Dr Constance Ellis was the first woman to qualify as a doctor in Victoria, while a leading communal figure, Nerida Goodman (née Cohen), was the third woman to qualify as a barrister in New South Wales, and Mahla Pearlman was president of the New South Wales Law Association before becoming one of the first female judges in the state.

In public life, Julia Rapke (née Levi, 1886–1959), a teacher of public speaking, became one of the first female justices of the peace in 1928, as well as being vice-president of the National Council of Women of Victoria and president of the Victorian Women's Citizen Movement, Margaret Davis was the first Jewish woman member of parliament, in the New South Wales Legislative Council (1967–1978). Sydney-based businesswoman Stella Cornelius became well known for her work in peace and conflict resolution.[23]

Businesswomen who have made their mark include Helena Rubinstein, who began her outstanding cosmetics career in rural Victoria, producing creams to protect women's skin from the harsh Australian sun. Another Victorian, Poppy King, at first carved out a successful career in the cosmetic industry, but went bankrupt in the early 1990s. The remarkable Fanny Breckler (née Masel, 1877–1946) grew up in Perth. Widowed in 1912, with four children still in her care, she established her first shoe store, The Dainty Walk, in Perth, and then Betts and Betts and Cecil Brothers. Her firm was continued by her family, and was included in the *Business Review Weekly*'s 'Rich List' in 1986. Melbourne's Eve Mahlab was named Bulletin/Qantas businesswoman of the year in 1982.

Two of the pioneering contributors to music lived in New South Wales. Mirrie Hill (née Solomon), married to well-known composer Alfred Hill, composed more than 160 pieces. Esther Kahn also composed music, particularly in the 1930s, but her work was not adequately recognised.

The art world, like that of music and culture in general, was greatly enriched by refugee artists, who not only developed galleries but also became part of the art-buying public. One example is Holocaust survivor Judy Cassab, whose story is one of struggle, determination and dedication to establish herself as a leading figure in a new land. Born in Vienna, she returned to her family's native Hungary and married John Kampfner shortly before the outbreak of World War II. She spent the war years as an art student in Budapest and later, after the assumption of direct control by the Nazis, was disguised as a non-Jewish factory worker and separated from her husband in order to avoid deportation and death. Miraculously reunited after the war, and both sole survivors of their respective families, the couple emigrated to Australia in 1951. Initially, Cassab taught art to earn money to buy equipment, while her husband, a chemical engineer, struggled to build his career. Following her first exhibition in 1953, she developed a fine reputation, twice winning the prestigious Archibald Prize for portrait painting.

Theatre and ballet also benefited greatly from refugee actors, audiences and patrons. Gertrude Bodenwieser, a Viennese refugee who had served since 1926 as Professor of Dance and Choreography at the Austrian State Academy of Music and Performance, introduced modern dance to the Sydney stage in 1939.

In the literary field, journalist Zara Aronson is known for her work in Sydney and Melbourne; Nancy Keesing published a number of short-story collections and novels, and became chair of the Australian Literature Board; poet Judith Rodriguez and Holocaust poet Lily Brett are widely published. Yvonne Fein, daughter of Holocaust survivors, published a well-received novel, *April's Fool*, in 2001.

Some children of immigrants have chosen the medium of film to depict the Australian Jewish experience. Sandra Levy, who joined the Australian Broadcasting Commission in 1972, was appointed Director of Programmes in 2001. In 1984, she devised and produced a mini-series, *Palace of Dreams*, based on her family's experiences in Australia during the Depression years. Monique Schwartz produced a film about Jewish experiences in the inner-Melbourne suburb of Carlton, and in 2001 released *Mammadrama*, a study of the Jewish mother in film. Canadian Rachael Kohn has contributed to ABC radio programmes on religion, her current programme being *The Spirit of Things*. In 2005, the University of New South Wales awarded her an honorary doctorate in recognition of her contribution to religion and the media.

Sport is a central aspect of Australian culture, and Jewish women have contributed even there. Naomi Wolinski (1881–1969) became well known in Australia as a lawn bowls champion and administrator. Hannah Hart was instrumental in the 1925 beginnings of the interstate sport carnivals, and women have been active in Maccabi, the Australian Jewish sporting organisation that emerged from the interstate carnivals.

Feminism

Australia was one of the first countries to give women the right to vote, but Jewish women do not appear to have played a significant role in the suffrage movement, due both to its close connections with the Christian Temperance movement and to the Jewish community's patriarchal structures. Whilst both Vida Goldstein and Dora Montefiore had Jewish connections – Vida Goldstein's father was Jewish and Dora had married into the Montefiores, a well-known Sephardi family – neither was affiliated with the Jewish community.

In the inter-war years, feminists fought for greater equality and Jewish female leaders were directly involved. The most outstanding early feminist was Ruby Rich-Schalit (1888–1988). Born in rural New South Wales as the fourth of six children, her parents moved to Sydney, where she grew up with memories of the family entertaining on Friday nights: 'We used to stand in a row, introduce ourselves in rhyme and then put on a little play in costume'. She studied piano both in Australia and with Arthur Schnabel in Berlin and Raoul Pugno in Paris. Although she performed in London for a BBC Empire Concert, her father would not permit her to play professionally.

Rich-Schalit became involved in the women's movement in 1922 when she met Millicent Preston-Stanley, who was seeking election to parliament, and agreed to be her campaign secretary. The campaign failed, but Preston-Stanley later became the third woman elected to parliament. Rich-Schalit also became close to another leading Australian feminist, Jessie Street, whose (unsuccessful) election campaigns she co-ordinated. In 1926, she joined the Racial Hygiene Association (later the Family Planning Association), which educated women in sexual relations and the prevention of venereal disease.

These links established between Jewish and non-Jewish feminists led them to work together on many issues of equality during the second phase of Australian feminism, post 1920. Nerida Cohen assisted Jessie Street in her battle for equal pay for women, while Ida Wynn established a close relationship with Greta Hort, philosopher and principal of Women's College at the University of Melbourne. In the fight against government immigration quotas, Jewish women joined with liberal feminists such as Camilla Wedgewood and Jessie Street, both of whom were strong supporters of more liberal policies as well as of the establishment of a Jewish national homeland in Palestine.[24]

While NCJW leaders worked to upgrade their status, radical feminism did not appeal to most Jewish women, who gave priority to home and family. As Marlo Newton commented, the NCJW 'pursued a form of feminism which stressed the importance of women achieving within the context of the family and communal life . . . while opposing radical challenges to Judaism or the structure of the community'.[25]

A recent study by Barbara Bloch and Eva Cox of connections between Australian Jewish feminists and their Jewish identity shows a larger number of active Jewish feminists than has previously been acknowledged. A major factor in their attraction to the feminist movement was their sense of being 'an outsider in all its varied possibilities'. Bloch and Cox argue that Hannah Arendt's concept of the 'conscious pariah' is an appropriate way of understanding the women in their survey.[26] It is important to note that Professor Eva Cox (née Hauser), who was born in Vienna and lectures in the social sciences at the University of Technology, Sydney, herself played a leading role in the Women's Electoral Lobby, established in 1972. A more recent Jewish feminist is Sydney-born Elizabeth Grosz, an internationally recognised scholar in the fields of French feminist theory, cultural theory, psychoanalysis and the body. Her academic career has spanned the University of Sydney, Monash University (at the newly formed Institute of Critical and Cultural Studies) and Rutgers University, New York, where she is currently a professor in the Department of Women's and Gender Studies.

Conclusion

Despite significant advances over the last few decades, Jewish women in Australia do not enjoy full equality with their male counterparts. Since most take their domestic responsibilities seriously, full equality is definitely elusive. Women still bear the major responsibility for home and family, their traditional areas in Judaism. In addition, power, and community leadership, rest with those with money, who are mainly men. Efforts to foster women in leadership roles can be seen in the establishment of Women Power, a Sydney training ground for women. Perhaps the next generation of women will come fully into their own in Jewish communal leadership.

9
THE BROADER COMMUNITY

Since World War II, Jews have continued to make a substantial contribution to Australian society, particularly in business, the professions and the arts. Most Jewish immigrants embraced their new life in Australia. This was particularly true for the post-1945 refugee groups, including the survivors of the Holocaust and, later, the Hungarian and Egyptian 'escapees'. For all these groups, the greatest benefit was to live in a free, democratic society. They no longer feared that someone would knock on the door in the middle of the night with a pair of handcuffs.[1] This sense of security is attested to in numerous contemporary accounts. After the Chip Chase immigrant hostel was opened by the Jewish Welfare Society in 1950, one survivor wrote an article called 'On Coming Home':

> It is a very peculiar feeling. It is almost midnight. We are in the middle of a city with two million residents. We are in Sydney. We are in Australia. You who were born here or have been living here for many years, you might not understand these feelings. Though it is midnight, though it is just our second day in Sydney, we seem to be at home. Already we start to have the same sense of security as Australian citizens. We are beginning to share the confidence in their fellow citizens and in their country.[2]

Unlike many of the non-Jewish displaced persons who had escaped from countries behind the Iron Curtain, for Jewish refugees there was no thought of Australia as a temporary refuge. Most became loyal, grateful and permanent citizens of their new country.

The business world

Most Jews who arrived after 1945 brought few material possessions. They did, however, bring new industrial skills, and most reacted to the challenges of a new land with hard work, drive and enterprise. Australian Jewry is today a largely middle-class urban group, concentrated in Melbourne and Sydney. Whilst most newcomers enjoyed a moderate level of prosperity, there were some who were not able to re-establish themselves and lived in poverty. As with many other immigrant groups, they encouraged their children to achieve academic success, resulting in higher educational standards for the Jewish community than for the general Australian population.

Within this pattern of general economic achievement, there have been a number of Jewish immigrants whose entrepreneurial flair and business acumen have enabled them to achieve outstanding success in the financial world. Over the last twenty years, Jews have featured in the *Business Review Weekly*'s 'Rich List', the 200 wealthiest individuals and families in Australia. Between 20 and 25 per cent of these 200 names are Jewish business people, mostly immigrants or of immigrant background from Central and Eastern Europe, who 'started from scratch' in Australia. This is a remarkable contribution from a community that constitutes less than half a per cent of Australia's population.[3] The essence of this business success is the story of refugees, and children of refugees, who were highly motivated to create a new and more secure life for themselves in a land where they had found a haven from persecution.[4]

A number of factors help to explain the Jewish success story. Most important was the willingness to work hard, 'often seven days a week and sixteen hours a day to get somewhere',[5] usually with the assistance of their wives. Imagination was another central ingredient, as 'new products must be conceived, new ways of doing things conjured up, and ways around problems found'.[6] As a result of persecution and discrimination, Jews have tended to be innovators. This is highlighted by the Holocaust experience where, in the struggle for survival, it was often the young Jews who had the physical strength and ingenuity to stay alive. The number of Holocaust survivors who have made it to the top is a testimony to the human spirit and an ability to fight for life and security. Partnerships and helping one another, whether through family or friends, were also of considerable benefit. They allowed for a pooling of resources and talent, facilitated problem solving and allowed for sharing of responsibilities. The common ethnic heritage was also important, as partners could communicate easily. It is of interest to note that, in most of the successful partnerships, the two men came from the same national as well as religious background. In addition, the immigrants brought European know-how and maintained their contacts with Europe, often travelling abroad to stay abreast of the most recent developments.

In analysing the Jewish profile, a distinctive pattern emerges. Many of the Jewish businessmen listed in the *Business Review Weekly* gained their wealth from family businesses rather than from the traditional sources of Australian wealth, such as the banks, the pastoral industry and large public companies. Historically, Jewish businessmen have shied away from heavy industry because, as an uprooted and persecuted group, they have been unwilling to invest in fixed locations. The more mobile textile or fashion industry has predominated as the initial basis of wealth in many of the 'rags to riches' stories. This was especially true of the Polish Jews of Melbourne, who dominated the Flinders Lane 'rag trade', the *shmatter* business as it was called in Yiddish. Jews have been prominent in textiles partly as a result of historical trends. Under Islam, land and poll taxes levied against Jews contributed to their moving to urban centres, where they became the dyers, amongst other crafts. Under Christianity in medieval Western Europe, Jews could only be moneylenders or dealers in old clothes, whilst in Eastern Europe they became the middle class, including the tailors. When Jews emigrated, they tended to continue these traditional activities – particularly in the textile industry, because it was easy to purchase a sewing machine and set up in business. Later, many of these manufacturers made judicious property investments or became involved in property development. Other areas of Jewish activity included soft furnishings, smallgoods, catering and hotels, entertainment and publishing.

There are many similarities in the stories of successful Jewish entrepreneurs in Melbourne and Sydney, but important differences are reflective of the two communities. In Melbourne, most of the entrepreneurs originated in Eastern Europe and arrived either as part of the Polish immigration in the late 1920s and 1930s, as did the family of Visyboard magnate, Richard Pratt, or as survivors after the war. In Sydney, on the other hand, most were Central European Jews, largely Hungarian born. These national differences have produced different economic patterns, since the Melbourne-based Polish Jews have, in the main, been heads of private companies, while the Hungarian Jews became heads of public ones.

In Sydney, the property company Westfield Holdings began with the business partnership of Slovakian-born Frank Lowy and Hungarian-born John Saunders, who changed his name from Jeno Schwarz. Both were penniless Holocaust survivors who met when Saunders was running a delicatessen shop at Town Hall railway station and Lowy was delivering smallgoods to him. They started Westfield with a small shopping centre opposite Blacktown station in Sydney's western suburbs. Their knowledge of several European languages made the complex a great success in a largely migrant area.[7] From these small beginnings, the company grew. In 1987, the partnership dissolved; Lowy has now developed Westfield into an international company with shopping malls in Australia and the United States.[8]

Many businessmen have been concerned to put something back into the country that has given them so much. Marc Besen is one example:

> You've got to set an example. To give financially and to give your time and effort. If you are successful then you find yourself taking a lot from around you. My motivating force – and I know that this is going to sound hackneyed – is to put back into the community.[9]

The Besen Foundation that he established distributes funds each year for Australian research projects. Other entrepreneurs have contributed to art, music and opera, as well as to academic and charitable institutions. Frank Lowy, for example, established a think tank in his name in 2002, to celebrate his fiftieth anniversary in Australia by giving back something of real value to the country that had given him so much.

Academia and the professions

In Judaism, the Torah – the Five Books of Moses – is seen as the will of God, so Torah study is elevated as a religious duty and is seen to be as important, if not more so, than prayer. This stress on study resulted in a high level of literacy and a veneration of scholarship over the millennia. A second-century rabbinic statement claimed that 'the world is sustained by the breath of school children'. This focus on the importance of learning has in modern times been transferred from religious to secular studies. As Jews suffered persecution and expulsions, they held to the sense that intellect and knowledge were always portable.

This Jewish intellectual tradition is evident in Australia. To name the Jews who have contributed to Australian universities would result in a very long list, but some of the best known are Professors Robert Manne, Peter Singer, Henry Mayer and Sol Encel.

Medical practitioners were among the refugees who arrived both before and after the war. In most cases they had to retrain, which was easiest in New South Wales, where they could requalify by undertaking the final three years of medical studies at the University of Sydney. However, the British Medical Association, the forerunner of the Australian Medical Association, was concerned about competition from foreign doctors, and in 1938 introduced a quota of only eight foreign doctors to be registered annually.[10]

Initially, the quota was not a problem. However, thirteen doctors, all of whom had survived the Holocaust, enrolled at the University of Sydney after the war and completed their studies in 1950. In that year, two foreign doctors had registered on the basis of outstanding medical qualifications, so that only six more could be registered. All thirteen filed into the offices of the Medical Board, wrote their names on pieces of paper that were put into a hat, and the first six names to be pulled out were registered. The remaining seven doctors had to wait until the following year. This episode created an uproar. Clarrie Martin, the New South Wales Attorney-General, described it as 'an example of a throwback to sheer intellectual barbarism' of which 'the State of New South Wales should be eternally ashamed'[11] – and in the end the quota was removed.

Most of the refugee doctors worked as general practitioners, since their specialist qualifications, with few exceptions such as psychiatry, were not recognised. In the second generation, however, Jewish medical graduates have made significant contributions in many fields. They include leading immunologist, Professor Ron Penny, who came from Poland to Sydney in 1937 as a young child. Dr Jack Hansky, also from Poland, came to Melbourne in 1939 when he was seven years old, and made a significant contribution in the field of gastroenterology, especially in relation to acid secretion in ulcer disease. Holocaust survivor, Dr Leopold Dintenfass, arrived in Sydney in 1950 and completed a Master of Science degree. As a pioneer of research into arthritis, he was invited by the United States Space Centre to undertake research into the joint problems of astronauts, and this led to a lifelong involvement in the medical problems of space travel.

Australian architecture was challenged by the innovative approach of refugee architects. Harry Seidler became one of Australia's foremost architects and a pioneer of modern construction techniques. He was born in Vienna in 1923 and, after the Anschluss of Austria in March 1938, was sent by his parents to London. During the war years he was interned and deported to Canada where, after his release, he studied architecture. After the war, Seidler's parents emigrated from Britain to Australia, and he joined them in 1948. His creations include Sydney's Australia Square complex.

The Jews who have made contributions to legal practice are too numerous to list, and since 1945 there have been many outstanding law academics and judges. One of the most outstanding was Professor Julius Stone, the son of a Russian Jew who fled the pogroms in the 1890s and settled in England. Born in Leeds in 1907, Stone's brilliant mind helped him to overcome poverty and complete a law degree at Oxford. He then won a scholarship to Harvard where, on completing his doctorate, he taught as an associate professor. After returning to England and then serving for a period as Dean of Law at Auckland University College, he was Challis Professor of International Law and Jurisprudence at the University of Sydney for thirty years, then Professor of Law at the University of New South Wales. Others who have played leading roles in academia and the public service include Professor Louis Waller, who was Dean of Law at Monash University and Victorian Law Reform Commissioner, and Justice Ronald Sackville, Dean of Law at the University of New South Wales (1972–1985), Chairman of the New South Wales Law Reform Commission (1981–1984) and now a Federal Court Judge.[12]

The most outstanding legal academic has been Sir Zelman Cowen, who was born in Melbourne in 1919, also the offspring of Russian Jews. He received a Rhodes scholarship to Oxford, but interrupted his studies to join the Australian navy and only took up his scholarship at the end of the war. At Oxford, he completed a degree in civil law and became a Fellow at Oriel College. He was appointed Professor of Public Law at the University of Melbourne in 1950, and served until 1967 as professor and dean. He was knighted in 1967 in recognition of his contribution to law and education. His academic career included vice-chancellorship of New England University (1967–1970) and Queensland University (1970–1977). He was appointed as Governor-General following the furore over Gough Whitlam's dismissal as prime minister by Sir John Kerr, and his healing approach, deep humanity, distinguished legal mind and quiet, unassuming manner helped to restore prestige to the office. When he retired in 1982, he became Provost (President) of Oriel College, his old Oxford college.[13]

Professor Zelman Cowen became Australia's second Jewish governor-general in 1977

Gordon Samuels, a well-known barrister and judge in New South Wales, served as Governor of New South Wales, retiring in 2000. Jim Spigelman, son of Holocaust survivors (and cousin of Art Spigelman, well known for his book *Maus*), was appointed Chief Justice in 2000. He has been at the forefront of major human rights campaigns, and speaks openly about his Jewish heritage. Spigelman is not the only Jewish lawyer who has been prominent in the area of human rights. Judge Aaron Levine, born in Sydney in 1910 of Russian parentage, made a landmark judgment in the 1970s, allowing abortion. Two other names stand out: Marcus Einfeld, son of Labor politician Sydney David Einfeld, in Sydney, and Ron Castan in Melbourne. Both Einfeld and Castan have been leading advocates of the rights of indigenous Australians, with the former leading the Commonwealth investigation into Aboriginal deaths in custody.

The armed forces: World War II

As in World War I, young men and women throughout Australia immediately enlisted, making a total of 3870 Jewish service personnel. The most outstanding soldier of this period was Major-General Paul Cullen, son of Sir Samuel Cohen; he changed his name in case he was captured. Since 1945, Cullen has had an outstanding record of community service, notably as president of Austcare. Other leading soldiers included Brigadier Joseph Steigrad, a Sydney surgeon; Dr Stanley Goulston, another medical practitioner and one of the 'Rats of Tobruk'; and Peter Stuart Isaacson, who became an ace pilot and was awarded the Distinguished Flying Medal. Jews were also active on the home front, and the Sydney Jewish community erected a Monash Recreation Hut in Hyde Park for all servicemen, to be staffed by volunteers from the Council of Jewish Women. This was a departure from World War I, when Jews would not have established a separate facility.[14]

Political life

The extent of Jewish involvement in politics has declined, especially since the 1980s. Participants have largely been on the Left, reflecting the Jewish concern for humanitarian issues and justice. Probably the outstanding figure in the Australian Labor Party has been Sydney Einfeld. Born in 1909, his attraction to the ALP was a natural outcome of his desire to work for the 'little people who really needed a champion'.[15] He was elected to the federal seat of Phillip in 1961, but was defeated in 1963. In 1965, he succeeded another Jewish Labor politician, Abe Landa, who represented the state seat of Bondi from 1930 to 1932 and again from 1940 to 1965. Landa had been appointed to London as New South Wales Agent-General, and Einfeld held Bondi until 1971, then Waverley until 1981. He served as Deputy Leader of the Opposition from 1968 to 1973 and Shadow Minister for Consumer Affairs. Following the election of the Wran government in 1976, he became Minister for Consumer Affairs and Cooperative Societies. He was Minister for Housing from 1978 until 1980, and remained Minister for Consumer Affairs until his retirement in 1981. He assumed the latter position at the age of sixty-eight, and introduced significant legislation, the effects of which are felt today. He brought in fair trading laws, the Contracts Review Act (1980), 'use by' dates on all perishable food, regulation of second-hand car sales and real estate transactions, and price regulation of staples such as milk, bread and petrol, and established the Consumer Claims Tribunal to dispense affordable and prompt justice. Einfeld kept in the top drawer of his desk a list of the eighteen promises he had made during the campaign, and worked his way through each item until he had fulfilled all those promises. This action undoubtedly contributed to his reputation on both sides of politics as one of the most effective ministers of contemporary times. After his retirement at the age of seventy-two, he became a radio commentator on consumer affairs.[16]

Other New South Wales politicians included Max Falstein; Sir Asher Joel, who represented the Country Party in the Legislative Council from 1957; Paul Landa, a nephew of Abe Landa, who was a minister in the Wran government with Einfeld; and Margaret Davis, also in the Legislative Council. In Melbourne, Sir Archie Michaelis was in the Legislative Council; and Baron David Snider (Liberal, 1955–1966), Walter Jona (Liberal, 1962–1984 and a Cabinet minister) and David Bornstein (Labor, 1970–1975) were all members of the Legislative Assembly in the post-war years.

In the 1970s and 1980s, Jewish parliamentarians included Joe Berinson, who was a minister in the Whitlam government and later moved to state parliament; Dr Moss Cass and Barry Cohen, who both served as Minister for Arts and the Environment in the Hawke government; and Liberal Senator Peter Baume, who was Minister for Education in the Fraser government.

The number of Jews in both state and federal parliament has plummeted since the mid-1980s. Michael Danby was elected in 1998 to the House of Representatives as the Labor member for Melbourne Ports, which has a higher percentage of Jews (28 per cent) than any other electorate. He is the only Jew in federal parliament. As journalist Mark Dapin commented of Melbourne Ports, 'There are more wealthy people who vote Labor than anywhere else in the country, because of an influx of affluent, liberal media workers; because of a vestigial socialist tradition among the comfortable Jews of Caulfield;

and because of Danby'.[17] After a number of years as head of the ALP state office, Eric Roozendaal entered the New South Wales upper house in September 2004, becoming the fourth Jewish federal or state parliamentarian across Australia. In his inaugural speech he paid tribute to 'a kind Dutch policeman [who] hid a little Jewish seven-year-old boy, his four-year-old sister and mother for 15 months. That seven year old was my father. In those 15 months, he never saw daylight'.[18] For a list of Jewish parliamentarians, see Appendix 1.

There are a number of reasons for the dramatic decline in the number of Jewish parliamentarians. Jews had spread across country districts during the nineteenth century, and many were elected to represent those areas. When Jews later concentrated in Sydney and Melbourne, there were only a couple of electorates where they formed an electorally significant group: around St Kilda and Caulfield in Melbourne and the eastern suburbs in Sydney. Whereas Jews were initially motivated to become involved in the political processes to show their gratitude for the British democratic system, by the twentieth century they were engaged in other areas of endeavour, such as the law and medicine. Other, and larger, ethnic groups have now entered the political fray, making entry into politics more competitive.

Political allegiances have also changed. While most Jews standing for parliament have been members of the ALP, support for the Liberal Party has increased since the late 1960s. This is due to a number of factors, including the impact of multiculturalism, which has made diversity acceptable; the tendency of the Jewish middle class to follow the general socio-economic voting pattern and vote Liberal; and the tendency of Jews who escaped from communist rule also to support the Liberal Party. In addition, a perception that the ALP has taken a less supportive position on Israel since the Whitlam years has contributed to its diminishing support. As former Liberal Party member and parliamentarian Peter Baume wrote, 'Jews' votes have increasingly gone to the Liberal Party while Jewish political activism has not'.[19]

The arts

The arts have benefited at every level from the contribution of Jews – as performers and artists, as sponsors and financial donors and as audiences. Non-Jewish actor and director Hayes Gordon acknowledged this contribution as follows:

> It would seem that Australia has much to be thankful for in the dislocation of people as a result of Hitler's war. While it was undoubtedly painful perhaps beyond measure to witness great cultures burnt with their books, yet so many Europeans were able somehow to salvage a measure of this cultural wealth, and bring it with them to their new home on this vast Pacific island. They came at a time when Australia was crying out to find itself. And coming with a fresh outlook, it was often the newcomer who saw what needed to be done, and how.[20]

Indeed, Jewish newcomers have played a key role in transforming Australian society from a cultural backwater to a cosmopolitan multicultural society.

Performance of classical music grew rapidly between 1939 and the early 1950s. Musica Viva, which is one of the world's largest non-profit private societies sponsoring chamber music, was formed during the war. It was started by a small group of refugee musicians in Sydney, including Richard Goldner and Theo Salzman, and was supported by a committee of refugees that included enthusiasts such as Rudi Ernst, Fred Wenkart and Charles Berg. Cecile Selby, a Viennese refugee, opened her Warrawee home for rehearsals and even provided players with a place to live. In its early phase, Goldner was the moving spirit behind Musica Viva. While still classified as an 'enemy alien', he was questioned by the local policeman about his employment. Goldner replied cryptically that 'my former profession is now my hobby and my former hobby is now going to be my job'.[21] The policeman was perplexed, but Goldner did just that. He turned his ability as an inventor into a living, and his previous profession, as a first viola player in Simon Pullman's chamber ensemble in Vienna, became his hobby – in reality an obsession.

After the war, the state symphony orchestras established by the Australian Broadcasting Commission benefited from the talents of Jewish players and conductors. These included Viennese-born Henry Krips, who was musical director and conductor for the ABC in Perth and later in Adelaide; violinist Samuel Helfgott, who joined the Sydney Symphony Orchestra; and pianist Werner Baer, who became musical director of the ABC in New South Wales. Others in the musical scene included composers George Dreyfus, Felix Werder and Larry Sitsky. Dreyfus, a bassoon player with the Melbourne Symphony Orchestra, is best known for his compositions for television programmes such as the ABC's *Rush* and *Power Without Glory*. Other well-known musicians include pianist Isadore Goodman, piano accordionist Herbie Marks,

Tommy Tycho and Rachel Valler and, more recently, pianist Simon Tedeschi and classical guitarist Slavor Gregorian.

Jewish writers Judah Waten and David Martin were among the first to depict the Australian immigrant experience. They wrote in both English and Yiddish. Waten's *Alien Son* (1952) was the first such work. This exchange between the writer's father, who wanted to take his family to a Jewish play, and a blacksmith, Mr McGonty, highlights the cultural differences between established Australians and foreign Jewish immigrants:

> A bewildered expression spread over Mr McGonty's face. What was the man talking about? To make matters worse, he found it hard to understand his English. Father's speech contained such a remarkable mix of Yiddish, Russian and Hebrew words suitably, as he thought, adorned with English endings, that even I found some difficulty in following every word. But at least I knew before hand that it was all about the theatre.
>
> At last with my aid Mr McGonty understood that Father was going to some sort of foreign performance or other. He averted his eyes from us, but he couldn't conceal his sudden distrust. His black fingers fidgeted with his belt. It was as though the strange legends and superstitions that cling around every Jew had suddenly come to his mind.[22]

Three Yiddish writers added to multicultural literature in a country that was largely monolingual until World War II. Pinchas Goldhar was the pioneer, arriving in Australia in 1928 and settling at first in Shepparton, Victoria. Herz Bergner arrived in Melbourne shortly before the war and published his best-known novel, *Between Sea and Sky*, in 1947. After the war, renowned Yiddish essayist and critic Yehoshua Rappaport came to Melbourne from Shanghai, and continued to publish essays and literary criticism in Yiddish.

A second generation of writers, mostly children of Holocaust survivors, has sought to write about their parents' experiences and the lost world of Polish Jewry. In this group are Mark Baker, whose *Fiftieth Gate* (1997) won a number of prizes and has become a secondary school text; poet Lily Brett; and short-story writers Serge Liberman and Arnold Zable. Zable's work epitomises not only the old world but also the vibrancy of the new life in post-war Carlton. Recently, many survivors have written their memoirs and, while these vary in quality, some are powerful, have won prizes and will be an important record for future generations. Elliot Perlman, a young Melbourne barrister, has written two successful novels, and his first, *Three Dollars* (1998), was released as a film in 2005. Perlman's books are works of social realism with universal themes, and he has been described as representing the new generation of Australian writers.

Major visual artists include Judy Cassab, Sali Herman and Louis Kahan, and Jews have developed galleries and been part of the buying public. Yosl Bergner, who eventually settled in Israel, had a significant influence on Australian art in the 1930s and 1940s.

Theatre and dance have been enriched by Jewish refugees, whether as actors and audiences or as patrons, such as Sydney furrier Bernhard Hammerman. The theatre scene in Australia before 1945 was parochial. In Sydney, for example, there were only two main theatres in 1947, the Theatre Royal for musicals and the Minerva, which began with serious productions but soon faced difficulties. Serious theatre gained strength in the 1950s through, for example, the Independent Theatre, which was founded by Doris Fitton and supported in part by the Jewish refugee community. Gertrude Bodenwieser introduced modern dance into Sydney, and the city's Kleine Wiener Theater (Viennese Theatre, 1941–1985), which presented plays in German in the Viennese style, was one of the first ethnic theatres.[23] Child refugee, the actor Henri Szeps, is best known for his role in the ABC television comedy, *Mother and Son*. One of a number of Jews who have contributed to cinema in Australia was the early pioneer Sir Bernard Freeman, who founded the Australian subsidiary of Metro-Goldwyn-Mayer and, as managing director, built up the staff from three to a thousand, and built and renovated theatres and drive-ins after 1945.

An interesting and controversial Jewish personality in the entertainment world was Roy Rene, who was born Harry Van der Sluys (later spelt Sluice) in 1892, the fourth of seven children. His career spanned the first half of the twentieth century. Apart from his theatre performances, especially with comedian, writer and producer Nat Phillips as 'Stiffy and Mo', he was best known for his performances after the war in the Colgate-Palmolive radio shows. Mo played on his Jewish background throughout his career, with pork jokes and big noses being a staple part of his routine. These undignified jokes, together with his comic makeup – whitened face, painted black beard, sidewhiskers, two 'Vs' of moustache, and blackened eyebrows – evoked the displeasure of the Jewish communal leaders of the time, who feared it would promote antisemitism.[24] Yet his routines were part of a well-established English tradition, and a deliberate copy of the well-known East End Jewish comedian whose name he had assumed.

'Mo' in his renowned make-up

Restaurants and food

Jewish immigrants were among the first Europeans to introduce a more cosmopolitan flavour to Australia's dining tables. Pre-war cafes and restaurants had been, on the whole, uninspiring places – with grilled lamb chops or steak, fried eggs and bacon being the staple menu. The immigrants brought espresso coffee, Viennese patisseries and a wide range of European foods. Perhaps the most colourful of the many leading restaurateurs was dentist Walter Magnus who, like Richard Goldner, transformed his pre-war hobby – his love of good food – into his profession. He also became a patron of the arts, particularly by assisting aspiring artists, and his large form has been immortalised by William Dobell, whose portrait of him hangs in the Australian

National Gallery. The European cuisine was later enriched by Sephardi Jews from India and Egypt, and by Israeli chefs, who have introduced Middle Eastern foods such as felafel, humus and tahina.

Conclusion

The radical changes in post-war Australia have resulted from a mix of the many post-war ethnic groups. Pre-war Jewish refugees were the forerunners of this transformation from a cultural backwater into a vibrant multicultural society. The contributions of Jewish refugees and survivors has been further reinforced by more recent waves of immigrants from South Africa, the former Soviet Union and Israel.

10
RECENT IMMIGRANTS

Australian Jewry is one of the few diaspora communities that is growing in size – growth entirely due to immigration rather than to natural increase. Three main groups have been emigrating to Australia since the 1960s: South Africans, Russians and Israelis. In 2004, a survey was carried out for the Jewish Agency of these three groups, based on data from the Australian Bureau of Statistics 2001 Census, a quantitative survey and qualitative interviews.[1]

From South Africa

The group from South Africa has had the most significant impact on Australian Jewry. According to the 2001 Census, 10 473 Jews had been born in South Africa but, allowing for under-counting of 20 per cent, the number is likely to be closer to 14 000–15 000.[2] The first immigrants, 13 families, arrived in 1948, having determined that life under the antisemitic Prime Minister Dr Daniel Malan would be untenable. The second wave, some 47 families, came in the early 1960s after the Sharpeville massacre. A third, more substantial wave occurred after 1975, following the Soweto riots. In the last five years of apartheid, to 1990, emigration again increased, and was maintained until 1995. South African immigration has decreased slightly since then, but many are still coming, largely because of the high level of crime and a sense of insecurity. As one new arrival commented, 'I lost six friends and acquaintances in the period before emigration. Dad's best friend was killed last year . . . there is a sense of hopelessness in the future of the country because of the crime situation. Funeral after funeral wears you down'.[3]

In 2001, South Africans constituted 12.5 per cent of all Jews living in Australia – 58 per cent in Sydney, 26 per cent in Melbourne and 13 per cent in Perth. Within each of these cities, their demographic profile is quite distinct. In Sydney, most settled in the north, mainly in St Ives, although recent data indicates a shift to the eastern suburbs. In Melbourne, there was a rapid growth of Jewish population in the Doncaster/Templestowe areas in 1987–1991, but since 1997 there has been a marked shift to the more traditionally Jewish South Caulfield.[4] In Perth, Jews born in South Africa, who constitute 26 per cent of the total Jewish population, have spread out from Mount Lawley into cheaper northern suburbs including Dianella, Coolbinia, Noranda and Yokine. South African immigrants, together with their Australian-born children and grandchildren, have doubled the size of Perth Jewry from around 3000 to over 6000, with the main group arriving after 1987. As one Perth communal worker said, 'Thank God for the South Africans. I grew up in a small community. They've enriched it.'[5]

The South African Jews have, like all immigrants, faced a difficult phase of transition. When they arrive they feel unsettled, often having left family and friends behind, and there are differences between Australian and South African Jewish and general society. But after initial difficulty, most have settled in well and only a handful have sought assistance from Jewish Care. In Perth, the main role of Jewish Care in the early 1980s was lending household goods until theirs had arrived, and providing short-term accommodation, initially in a rented flat. Later, the government agency Homes/West enabled Jewish Care to purchase a strata villa, which was later replaced by a house closer to Carmel School and synagogues.

Generally speaking, South Africans cannot get a visa to emigrate to Australia without a job, and over 70 per cent visit Australia before making up their minds to leave – which is quite remarkable when compared with other immigrant groups. The Jewish Agency survey indicates that 72 per cent of Jewish immigrants have a university degree, and thus they are the best educated, most highly skilled and most affluent immigrant group ever to come to Australia. Since most are professionals, they have settled into a similar professional and social environment and, even though many doctors and lawyers have had to requalify, they have been able to readjust to life in Australia.

South African Jews arrived with a strong sense of Jewish identification and a very low intermarriage rate. The survey showed that 80 per cent see tradition as the most important element, with 70 per cent also listing religion. On the scale of one to ten, 76 per cent ranked themselves at five for religiosity. Most have integrated well within the general Australian community, with 92 per cent seeing Australia as their home and feeling comfortable with the Australian way of life. About a quarter have visited South Africa over the last five years. Their level of Jewish observance has tended to decrease in Australia, but most have retained strong links with South African family and friends in Australia and also feel at home in the local Jewish community.

They are a more homogeneous group than Australian Jewry as a whole, as almost all families had their origins in Lithuania, indeed from within 200 kilometres of each other. This uniformity of background is reflected in the dialect of Yiddish that they speak, in food traditions, and in synagogue rituals and management. A choir is a key feature of synagogue worship in South Africa, which has a strong musical tradition of *hazanut* (liturgical music). South African congregations are also much more uniform, with the rabbi's authority not easily questioned. This is very different from Australian congregations, particularly in Melbourne, where each congregation is a little *shtiebl* (small prayer group or congregation, usually meeting in private homes) to itself, and there are a number of Betei Din (rabbinical courts) and no strong communal discipline.

In Melbourne, South African immigrants have contributed to the formation and strengthening of synagogues. After 1987, they bolstered the Northern Suburbs Shule in Doncaster, and around 60 per cent of the 450 families were ex-South African. This number declined to around 200 families after the shift to South Caulfield. The Central Shule (known affectionately as the 'Zulu Shule') opened in South Caulfield in 1998, growing out of an association between Ian Harris and Yitzhak Riesenberg, a Habad rabbi. It developed from a small minyan held in private homes to the opening of a new synagogue in 2003 – whose attendance represents the South African religious commitment. Thus, it is packed on Friday night but Saturday morning has difficulty getting a minyan, since most South African Jews still drive and carry out normal activities on Shabbat. Its service is modelled on the Johannesburg synagogues, with a male choir of fifteen mainly singing music from South Africa. Blake Street, established in 1996, is another new and smaller congregation. The well-established congregations, such as St Kilda Hebrew Congregation, have also attracted

South Africans. St Kilda's chief minister, Rabbi Philip Heilbrun, estimates that about a quarter of the congregation's members are, like himself, South African expatriates.

In Sydney, South Africans have made significant contributions to established congregations such as South Head Synagogue and Central Synagogue, as well as to the newly created congregations of Kehillat Masada and Habad in St Ives. In addition, the Jewish Learning Centre, established to strengthen traditional Judaism in Sydney, has been funded and largely supported by South African expatriates. This Centre assisted a congregation of young adults, Ohr Hadash, which has a high proportion of South Africans and opened its premises in Bondi in 2003.

In Perth, two new congregations were started, largely as a result of the South African immigration. The Northern Suburbs Congregation, also known as the Noranda Shule, was set up in 1987 and built its own synagogue in 1992. The Dianella Shule also operates as a *Beth Midrash* (study centre) and, while not specifically South African, about 60 per cent of its participants are ex-South Africans.[6] Perth Hebrew Congregation, the oldest congregation in Perth, has also benefited, with a number of South Africans joining the synagogue board over the last decade.

The Progressive congregations have been less affected by the South African immigration, as Reform Judaism is not strongly part of the South African Jewish tradition. In Sydney, Rabbi Richard Lampert (1977–2004) of North Shore Temple Emanuel was born in South Africa and was known to some South African immigrants who joined his Chatswood congregation. In Melbourne, some South Africans have joined Temple Beth Israel and taken on leadership roles; but this has not happened in Perth's Temple David, which is facing difficulties.

The South Africans brought with them a strong belief in the day school movement, a product of an ethnic cohesiveness strengthened by apartheid, which encouraged groups to stay 'segregated'. They have supported the established Jewish schools so that, for example, about one-third of the students at Mount Scopus College are now ex-South African, while in Perth, Carmel School has high South African student numbers. Carmel sends a team annually to South Africa to recruit new families, a policy also followed by Mount Scopus, Melbourne, and Masada, Sydney. By the late 1970s, South Africans constituted over half the student body of Masada College on Sydney's North Shore, and this has increased to about 80 per cent. In 1981, it opened its high school in St Ives, which developed to a peak of 800 students.

Roy Steinman at a Moriah College prize giving in 2002

But the shift to the east has, since 1995, caused enrolment problems. In Melbourne, the Doncaster Habad School established at the North Eastern Jewish Centre reached its peak with 120 students in 1990, but the departure of many South Africans led to the school's closure in 2000. In the early years, the newcomers did experience some adjustment problems – especially at Masada College, where the Australian children felt they were outnumbered. South Africans have provided Jewish Studies and Hebrew teachers and educational leadership, notably Roy Steinman, principal of Moriah College in Sydney, and Hilton Rubin of Mount Scopus College.

Jewish communal life has been enriched by the South Africans. They joined the National Council of Jewish Women and in Melbourne formed a special Mitzvah Group, which has helped with programmes for the Russian Golden Age Club. They have also brought their own food traditions. In Sydney, they have enriched kosher food outlets, and a number of South African shops in Melbourne and Sydney sell traditional fare such as *biltong*. The Jewish Male Choir, founded in Melbourne by Rabbi Ronald Lubofsky, is now largely ex-South African, as is its conductor, Brett Kaye, and choirmaster, Myron Blecher.

Whilst South African support of Zionism was strong, with 89 per cent of respondents to the Jewish Agency survey donating to Israel, it is felt in both Sydney and Melbourne that their contribution to Zionist fundraising is less than their numbers would warrant. In contrast, the more established South African Jews in Perth are seen as vital to Zionist activities in the community. Thus, South Africans have tended to be more involved with *shul* (synagogue) and school, and less involved with the Jewish Board of Deputies and the Zionist organisations.

The contribution of the South African Jews has enriched Australian Jewry. They have joined established synagogues and schools, and in Melbourne and Perth have established their own synagogues. They have brought new traditions in choral music, and have strengthened kosher facilities because of their support of traditional Jewish life. But they have also created disaffection, as they are seen by many Australian Jews as being arrogant and dominating, having taken over the leadership of established institutions by removing the local leadership, or having founded their own to the detriment of existing structures.

Russian migration

It is very difficult to determine the exact number of Jews who emigrated to Australia after the collapse of the Soviet Union. The 2001 Census shows 6404 Russian Jews, constituting 7.6 per cent of the overall Jewish population. However, the number sponsored by Jewish organisations is much greater.

There have been two distinct waves of immigration. The first occurred between 1971 and 1981, when the Soviet government responded to demands to permit family reunion in Israel. Soviet Jews received permission to emigrate to Israel only, but once they left the country, many (called '*noshrim*') opted to go to other Western countries. In Australia, they were classified under the humanitarian immigration programme between 1982 and 1987. Emigration from the Soviet Union plummeted after 1982, restarted in 1987 with *glasnost*, and was transformed into mass emigration after the collapse of the Soviet Union in 1989. The numbers coming to Australia have greatly declined since 1997, because most Russian Jews no longer qualify for the humanitarian programme. Dr Nikolay Borshevsky has estimated that about 30 000 Russian Jews have arrived in Australia since 1971.[7] While it is clear that many are lost to the community, the Census number of 6404 is probably significantly less than the actual number.

Most Russian Jews who chose Australia rather than Israel did so because of the 'pull' factors of a 'better future for the family' and the need to 'join family and friends'. Immigration in the 1970s was in some ways easier, because those who left knew that they could never go back and that their future lay here. Those who arrived after 1989, knowing that they could go back, have less incentive to succeed in Australia. However, the Jewish Agency survey shows that 87 per cent consider Australia home, and most have abandoned their ties with Russia.

As with the South Africans, Russian Jews also have specific settlement patterns. Nearly all settled in Melbourne and Sydney, with two-thirds choosing Melbourne. The elderly and less well off are concentrated in areas where they receive government housing, such as East St Kilda in Melbourne and Woolloomooloo and Surry Hills in Sydney. Overall, they need the greatest level of assistance on arrival. Vladimir Dubossarsky, who arrived in 1977, described the difficulties:

> We arrived not from another country or planet, but from a different constellation. There have been no parallels with the Soviet system in human history . . . We were robots programmed to work, act in a certain way . . . The government was uncaring, even an enemy and we developed skills of survival unmatched in the world.[8]

Jewish Welfare assisted Russian immigrants in Melbourne, Sydney and Perth from the late 1970s. A number were elderly: old age pensioners who did not speak English, faced financial problems, and had difficulty negotiating government services. Russian speakers were employed to overcome the linguistic barriers; English classes were organised within the community, often taught by volunteers; and an employment bureau operated to assist the Russians to find jobs. Despite these efforts, Russian Jews felt that they were not well catered for by the local community. As Dubossarsky put it, 'Australian Jews were not prepared to accept us . . . we are alien to them and they are alien to us'.[9] This sense of alienation from the established community is not a new phenomenon and is well documented for previous waves of immigrants to Australia.

The Russian language, combined with the common experiences of living under Soviet rule – including restrictions on Jewish life, opposition to connection with Israel, and antisemitic discrimination – have been uniting factors for all Russian Jews. These factors have also affected the nature of Jewish identification, with most Russians seeing themselves as Jewish on the basis of birth, nationality and antisemitism. This pattern of identification is explained by people's experiences in the Soviet Union, where they knew they were Jewish only from the 'J' stamped on their identity cards, which acted as internal passports and controlled all activities. The 'J' indicated ethnic origin and resulted in discrimination.

Most Russian Jews arrived in Australia with almost no knowledge of Judaism. Those who affiliated as Jews have increased their Jewish observance, and given that they had not been permitted to practise Judaism openly, this is understandable. Some who were not circumcised undertook *brit milah*, either before or after they arrived. The Russians are very family-oriented and have created a strong social network, tending to marry amongst themselves. One of the religious problems is that there are many mixed marriages where non-Jewish spouses are reluctant to convert or to provide their children with a Jewish environment. A minority of non-Jewish spouses have converted and been married according to Jewish tradition, usually through the Habad movement.

While many Russian Jews are not affiliated with any group within the Jewish community, organisations have been formed to cater for their needs and overcome the language barrier. At the urging of the late Lubavitch rebbe, Menachem Mendel Schneersohn, Rabbi Yoram Ulman returned to Sydney in 1986 to create an organisation for Russian Jews named Friends of Refugees of Eastern Europe (FREE). Its members 'started from scratch'. They rented premises known as Habad House in Bondi, where many Russian Jews live. High Holyday services at the Hakoah Club attract as many as 2000 people. In Melbourne, New York Habad rabbi, Eliozer Gorelik, established the Russian Jewish Community Centre in 1980. He started with 50 families, and through hard work and outreach activities has attracted around 1700 families. Rabbi Gorelik worked with Jewish Care to meet Russian immigrants at the airport, find them accommodation, produce a Russian newsletter and help them send their children to a Jewish school. Baruch Shapiro, a young rabbi, joined him in 1998. They are now rebuilding the synagogue and hope to expand facilities to include a child-care centre and a preschool. Reform Judaism was not known in the Soviet Union, so most Russian Jews support the orthodox synagogues in Melbourne and Sydney, led by Habad rabbis. However, a number of their children attend the Progressive schools, King David in Melbourne and Emanuel in Sydney.

In the early years, Russian Jews sent their children to Jewish schools because they received subsidies, but could no longer do so when these subsidies decreased. In Melbourne, many children go to state primary schools in Gardenvale, St Kilda, Caulfield and Brighton and, at secondary level, to Brighton High School and McKinnon College. Whilst the United Jewish Education Board provides scripture classes, there is a real concern that these children will be lost to the community.

Social activities are very important for Russian Jews. In Melbourne, the Shalom Association was formed in 1979, as a community base for Russian immigrants. Shalom worked closely with Jewish Care in the 1990s to welcome and absorb the newcomers. It also started a monthly newspaper in Russian called *Shalom*, and later a bi-monthly newsletter, *Menorah*. Shalom initially operated at Kadimah in Elsternwick, but Jewish Care provided an excellent venue in St Kilda from 1994. In addition, the Jewish Community Council of Victoria, under the presidency of Nina Bassat, set up a task force for the integration of Russian Jews. It operated for six years, providing educational and social facilities, with two executive members from Shalom, Rimma Sverdlin and Vladimir Tsivlin, being particularly active. Rimma Sverdlin has also worked on a voluntary basis with the three Golden Age Clubs run by the National Council of Jewish Women. Participants come to share meals, with the gatherings providing them with a social framework as well as a link to Judaism. The Association of Former Inmates of Nazi Concentration Camps & Ghettos from the Former Soviet Union deals with restitution questions, and provides cultural functions.

In Sydney, the Russian Jewish community is not as well organised. The Association of Jewish Engineers, which is a member of the Jewish Board of Deputies, is indicative of the highly educated nature of Russian Jews. Many of the engineers, scientists and other professionals had been part of the Soviet intelligentsia. There is also a small group of World War II veterans, and Golden Year Clubs run through Jewish Care.

Those Russian Jews who rediscover their Jewish identity in Australia feel a strong connection to Israel. As Roman Mirkus, president of the Shalom Association, expressed it:

> For years we have been creating our activities to reflect Jewish life, and there is no doubt that members of our community feel much more strongly about Israel as a country than they do about the synagogue which is something that is very foreign to many Russian Jews.[10]

Sydney Jewry held one of the largest-ever pro-Israel demonstrations in April 2002, with an estimated attendance of 5000–10 000. It was very noticeable that a large number of Russian Jews were present.[11]

From Israel

The exact number of Israelis living in Australia is subject to conjecture. The 2001 Census lists 6574 immigrants from Israel, of whom 3886 are Jews born there. This would constitute only 4.6 per cent of the total Jewish population, but anecdotal evidence suggests a much higher figure. Many Israelis arrive as backpackers and then seek ways to remain in Australia, and would not list themselves as Jewish in the Census.

While there has been immigration from the State of Israel since its creation in 1948, the main wave started after the 1982 Lebanon war, which provoked the first open dissent within Israeli society. Dissent was heightened by the 1987 Intifada, and then by the al-Aqsa Intifada of September 2000, and emigration from Israel increased. Whilst most Israelis are attracted to Australia because of what is perceived as its 'better climate, lifestyle and political stability' and 'better future for the family', the political situation in Israel is an important factor.

There are three main Israeli groups. Some have come because they have met and married an Australian citizen (either Jewish or non-Jewish). Others are couples who have left Israel as a result of dissatisfaction. Yet others have come on a short-term basis and stayed permanently.

Whilst 49 per cent of Israeli-born Jews live in Victoria and 35 per cent in New South Wales, 16.1 per cent live in the smaller states, including 7.1 per cent in Western Australia and 6.3 per cent in Queensland. In the major cities, they tend not to live in or near areas of Jewish concentration. In Western Australia, they live in Perth, near the coast, and in Fremantle; in Melbourne, they live in Bentleigh and East Bentleigh, and in or near the Dandenong Ranges at Bayswater, Ferntree Gully and Lysterfield, and some live in the rural city of Ballarat; and in New South Wales, they are also dispersed. It is estimated that of about 1000 Jews living in and around Byron Bay, 300 are Israelis.[12] Reasons for Israelis not living in areas of high Jewish concentration include expense and lack of a sense of belonging to the Jewish community.

Many Israelis are well educated, although a number are at the lower end of the socio-economic scale. Most identify on a national basis as Israelis rather than on the basis of religion, and many are unaffiliated with any Jewish group. While they have settled in Australia, a large minority (37 per cent) still see Israel as their home. Those who maintain their national identity visit Israel regularly, on average once every five years, and speak Hebrew in the home. Those who have chosen to identify as Jews tend to observe more religious rituals than they did in Israel, probably because there are fewer ways in Australia to identify culturally.[13] Among those Israelis who live near a synagogue, 70 per cent attend some services; attendance by those who do not live near a synagogue is very low.

Religious facilities have been created in the last five years to meet the needs of Israelis in both Melbourne and Sydney. In Melbourne, Belgium-born Habad rabbi, Motty Liberov, established the Israeli Synagogue, called HaMerkaz Shelanu (Our Centre) – a secular name – in 1998. The Centre developed quickly, and in 2004 the community purchased a new building in Elsternwick. Rabbi Liberov is almost the only observant Jew at services, yet for the closing service (Ne'elah) on Yom Kippur, up to 700 Israelis come to hear the shofar blown. Israelis participate in the two main post-biblical festivals in particular – Purim and Chanukah – and on Purim the Centre attracts up to 1000 participants. Daily after-school Hebrew classes are held at the Centre, for which 216 students were registered in 2004. In addition to formal Hebrew studies, the Centre organises youth activities and camps. The number of Israelis in Sydney is smaller, but Rabbi Dadon runs weekly services at Bondi.

Some Israelis support Jewish day school education, but much less so than the South Africans and Russians. At Mount Scopus College in Melbourne, the Director of Jewish Studies estimates that there are only about a dozen pupils whose parents are both Israeli, although more have one Israeli parent. Some children attend the Melbourne Yiddish School, Sholem Aleichem, because it is cheaper and does not have a Zionist or religious ideology, and in both Melbourne and Sydney, some secular Israeli parents choose the Progressive schools, King David and Emanuel, because they are not orthodox.

The Israelis have a strong cultural link with Israeli singing and dancing and the Hebrew language. Hebrew is fostered through language programmes on the government-sponsored ethnic radio station, SBS – in Sydney with Nitza Lowenstein and in Melbourne with Yehuda Kaplan. In Melbourne, a number of groups have been formed to cater for the needs of Israelis. These include HaMerkaz HaIsraeli, Haverim and, for women, Tarbuth (National Council of Jewish Women) and a special Women's International Zionist Organisation group, WIZO Amit, which has about 200 members. About eight years ago, Menachem Khoen formed HaMerkaz Israeli (The Israeli Centre) with the assistance of Mordechai Yedid, then the Israeli consul-general. They started to commemorate Yom HaZickaron (Remembrance Day for Israelis killed during the War of Independence and other wars). The first commemoration attracted around 400 people, and this has become an annual feature, expanding to Sydney as well.[14] The State Zionist Council of Victoria established Haverim in 2003, with the assistance of Dr Dvir Abramovitch, lecturer in Modern Hebrew at the University of Melbourne. Haverim's activities have attracted up to 800 participants.[15] In Sydney, the main Israeli cultural group is Kesher, established through the Jewish National Fund and organised by Aviva Kogus. This group initially met in private homes and the Hakoah Club, but then started to meet at the Jewish Folk Centre Hall in Bondi Junction, and recently Aviva Kogus became president of the Jewish Folk Centre.

Overall, there is a sense that only a small proportion of Israelis are involved in Zionist activities, mainly through the Jewish National Fund. One Melbourne respondent feels that most Israelis who are not orthodox feel 'we have done our best for Israel in the past',[16] while many are not in the position to donate and feel that the community is only interested in wealthy Jews.[17]

Israeli-born Jews are the only one of the three new immigration groups whose rate of intermix, defined by intermarriage, is above 10 per cent.[18] In de facto relationships, the intermix rate is 45 per cent, with Israeli men more likely to enter an interfaith relationship. These figures, combined with their geographical dispersion and low membership of Jewish groups, indicate that the Israelis are the most likely to lose their Jewish identity. However, in a post-modern world where people have multiple identities and undertake various journeys during their lives, it is impossible to generalise. As one respondent to the Jewish Agency survey had found, it was only after the birth of his daughter that he reconnected to his Jewish roots through Hebrew: 'I wanted to give her something unique, and that was the Hebrew language with its culture of literature, music and even film'.[19]

Conclusion

The three main immigration groups have in various ways both intensified and diluted Jewish life. The South Africans have contributed significantly to the local community's religious, educational, social and welfare structures, whilst those Russians and Israelis who have affiliated have become more observant. The Jewish Agency survey shows that for an overwhelming majority of all three groups (90 per cent), being Jewish is important to them. This can be seen with the rapid growth of synagogues in Melbourne, Perth and Sydney since 1980 (see Appendix 1).

At the same time, dilution is evident. It is clear from communal data that many immigrants are not identifying as Jews once they integrate into the general community, and it is not possible even to speculate about these numbers. This dilution can also be seen in the decline in day school levels since 2000. While a loss of 152 students out of over 10 000 is small, it is significant given the increasing Jewish population in Australia, and is a cause for concern.

CONCLUSION

Australian Jewry is a vibrant community, confident of its role in a multicultural society and highly regarded within international Jewry. It has maintained its particular profile in terms of geographical concentration, family structures, education levels and employment. Its rich religious, educational, cultural and ethnic life, and its strong organisational structure, serve as a model for other ethnic communities. Nevertheless, concerns about the rise of antisemitism, and the pressures of assimilation, both challenge this positive picture.

Population distribution

Ninety per cent of the community continue to be concentrated in Melbourne and Sydney. In Melbourne, 51.4 per cent of the Jewish population live in the southeastern Glen Eira municipality (including Bentleigh, Caulfield, Caulfield South and Elsternwick), which has been described as Victoria's 'Jewish hub'.[1] This population increased between 1996 and 2001. Jews also live in the neighbouring municipalities of Stonnington (including Glen Iris, Malvern, South Yarra and Toorak) and of Port Phillip (including Balaclava, Elwood, Port Melbourne and St Kilda), whose populations have also increased since 1996. In the Manningham municipality (including Doncaster and Templestowe), Jewish population has further declined. Analysis of 2004 Census data shows that 40 per cent of Melbourne's Jews have moved since the 1996 Census: 31.4 per cent from another district in Victoria and 6.3 per cent having arrived as immigrants. In Sydney, 63 per cent of all Jews live in the eastern suburbs, in the municipalities of Waverley, Woollahra and Randwick, and Bondi has the highest concentration. The second highest concentration (22 per cent) is in the north, around St Ives, which is a very popular area for the South African immigrants. Only 5 per cent of Jews in New South Wales live outside Sydney.[2]

This geographical concentration is very important in understanding Jewish identity. In order to lead a Jewish life, it is necessary to live close to Jewish facilities such as schools, synagogues and kosher food outlets. Research has shown that those Jews who live outside the areas of Jewish concentration are more likely to abandon their Jewish ties.

Age and fertility

Australian Jewry has a higher proportion of elderly people. In Sydney in 1996, 9000 of the 40 000 Jews were over sixty, and 2400 were more than eighty years old. In Melbourne, it has been estimated that nearly a third of the community is over sixty, and this proportion is increasing. This pattern is due to low fertility rates, longer life expectancy, the movement of the baby boomers of the 1940s and 1950s into the older age group, and the social assimilation of younger groups.

Conversely, younger age groups are under-represented, even though the conventional family structure of married couples with children is slightly higher than in the general community (in Melbourne it is 56.6 per cent compared to 51.6 per cent). Jewish fertility rates have been lower than in the general community and, although the community experienced a post-war 'baby boom', it was smaller than in other religious groups. There has been much debate on Jewish fertility trends. Walter Lippmann has argued that the Jewish birth rate peaked in 1951 and has been in decline since that date. On the other hand, in their study of 1961, 1966 and 1971 Census figures, Encel and Buckley have shown that fertility rates rose for Jewish women aged between twenty and forty years – because they were less affected by the war years and because of a middle-class trend towards larger families. Today, fertility is declining, just as it is in Australian society generally. This decline is likely to continue, with couples more likely to have smaller families, to postpone having children, and to choose either not to marry or not to have children.[3]

Economics and education

Post-war Jewish immigrants made rapid economic and social progress and integrated quickly within the general Australian society. Their occupational patterns diverge widely from those of the general population, and are typical of Jewish communities across the world. In Melbourne in 1991, 37 per cent of men and 16 per cent of women were in business or self-employed. A high proportion was in the professions, particularly men and women born in Australia.[4]

The Census figures for 1996 and 2001 indicate that the Jewish community continues to be highly affluent, with the young being particularly well off – over 50 per cent of the youth earn in excess of $62 000 per annum, which is a very comfortable income.[5] In Melbourne, where only 4.7 per cent are unemployed, nearly two-thirds of Jewish workers are employed in one of the three highest-status job categories: professionals (37.9 per cent, compared to 19.2 per cent of the general population), associate professional (12.3 per cent) and managers and administrators (13.4 per cent). Conversely, only 5.9 per cent are tradespersons, labourers and related workers, compared with 20.4 per cent of the general population, and there are almost no agricultural workers.

The economic success of Australian Jewry is reflected in their housing. In Melbourne, about three-quarters of the Jewish population own or are in the process of purchasing their own home, and only 20 per cent live in rental accommodation. The high proportion living in apartments or flats (20.3 per cent compared to 11.9 per cent of the general population) may reflect the higher proportion of the elderly in the community.

The affluence enjoyed by most Australian Jews reflects their high level of education. Compared to their non-Jewish neighbours, more have received some form of post-secondary education. The 1991 Jewish Agency survey in Melbourne found that 20 per cent of respondents had either a trade qualification or some tertiary training, while a further 46 per cent had tertiary qualifications, 32 per cent had undergraduate qualifications and 14 per cent had postgraduate qualifications. Education continues to be an important part of the daily lives of Jews, and the 2001 Census figures for Melbourne Jewry show more than one-quarter enrolled in some educational institution. Over half have some tertiary qualification, and 34 per cent have university qualification – which is significantly higher than in the general population, where only a quarter have some form of tertiary qualification.[6] The numbers of men and women with undergraduate qualifications are very similar, and a higher proportion of men have postgraduate qualifications (17 per cent compared with

10 per cent of women).[7] These findings reinforce the pattern of rising educational standards among Australian Jewry that was indicated in earlier studies.[8]

Despite the economic success of most Jews, the notion that there are no poor Jews is not correct. Pockets of disadvantage do exist, mainly among the elderly, often Russian Jews, surviving on a pension; the increasing number of women living on their own; and single-parent families. The 2001 Census shows that in Melbourne, 4.4 per cent of Jews had a weekly income of under $200, compared with 4.6 per cent of the general population. Overall, however, post-war Jewish immigrants have established themselves very successfully within the Australian society.

Intermarriage

There is considerable debate as to whether the community is again facing a dramatic increase in intermarriage. Some demographers use the Census statistics for the whole Jewish population, while others focus on the younger generation and extrapolate from their intermarriage rates into the future. According to the 1991 Goldlust study, intermarriage rates in Melbourne are still low. Overall, it was 9 per cent (although 7 per cent of respondents did not reply), and higher for men (11 per cent) than for women (6 per cent). Interestingly, the 40–49 age group had the highest intermarriage rate (14 per cent). These findings were confirmed by the 1996 Census figures, which give an overall intermarriage rate of 15 per cent for Australian Jewry, one percentage point higher than in 1991. The rates for Melbourne were significantly lower than for Sydney, reflecting the different nature of the two communities, while the smaller and more isolated communities had a much higher rate of intermarriage.[9] In contrast, a Jewish Communal Appeal study of Sydney in 1999 presented a much less positive picture, arguing that the Census figures are deceptive and that intermarriage rates are increasing dramatically in the younger age group.

The Sydney study claims that the portion of young people with a non-Jewish partner is one-third of those individuals studied. In addition, while there are fewer non-married couples in the Jewish community than in the general community, a very high proportion of those couples are mixed (74 per cent) and they tend to live away from the main Jewish centres.[10] This indicates that these couples are perhaps reluctant to make their relationship official by marrying outside the faith. The children of those who have moved away from Jewish centres are less likely to be brought up as Jews.

The number of couples in mixed marriages was found to be much lower in areas of Jewish concentration. Thus in Bondi, where the highest concentration of the state's Jewish population lives (12 per cent), only 10 per cent of couples are in mixed marriages. In contrast, in country New South Wales, where only 5 per cent of Jews live, intermarriage is extremely high (84 per cent). Even in one city, there can be a very wide variation of levels of assimilation. The vast majority of Sydney's Jews live in centres where all the community facilities are readily available, and their intermarriage rates are relatively low (around 14 per cent). However, as the bonds of Jewish identification weaken, and Jews move away from the community centres, the incidence of assimilation and intermarriage increases. There is no doubt that this is the case with a growing number of younger people in the Australian Jewish community. The Sydney study found that 'overall, about 47 per cent of children in mixed marriages were listed as Jewish'.[11] Thus, while Encel and Buckley found in the 1970s that even where the non-Jewish partner did not convert, the children were often raised as Jewish, by the 1990s the proportion of such children being raised as Jewish is still significant, but may have decreased.

Marrying out of the faith is a very emotive issue within the Jewish community, especially for Holocaust survivors. Many parents are strongly opposed to their children dating a non-Jew, let alone marrying one, as they fear loss from the faith. *In Duty Bound*, a play written by Jerusalem-born Ron Elisha and first produced in 1979, highlights the resulting tensions.

An important question concerning Jewish world leaders is what factors mitigate against intermarriage. The Melbourne study found that people are more likely to intermarry if they do not attend a Jewish day school and if they classify themselves as Jewish but not religious. It also found that the group with the highest proportion of intermarriage was the most recent wave of immigrants (1986–1991).[12] This can largely be attributed to immigrants from the Soviet Union, where many Jews had intermarried over the years. Among South African Jews, on the other hand, intermarriage is fairly uncommon. The higher rate of intermarriage among Russian Jews is evidenced in the intermarriage rate of 40 per cent for Jews in the Sydney suburb of Waterloo, where a high proportion of them live.[13] While the demographic figures may be inconclusive, anecdotal evidence supports the Sydney findings. The rate of inter-dating appears to be high, and will probably lead to an increase in intermarriage. In addition, young people in general are tending not to get married, or are marrying later in life. Thus, the prognosis for the future of Australian Jewry is guarded.

Melbourne/Sydney differences

No matter what index of Jewish identification and communal commitment one selects, Melbourne Jewry has always, since 1945, registered on a much higher level. This has held true for Jewish day schools attendances, Yiddish culture, funds raised for Israel, participants in long-term youth leadership programmes in Israel, and the number of students in *yeshivot*. However, over the last two decades Sydney Jewry has strengthened its communal structures, and the gap has narrowed.

A number of factors account for these differences. An important one is immigration patterns. After 1945, Melbourne Jewry attracted a much higher proportion of Polish Jews, while Sydney, as a more cosmopolitan city, attracted more assimilated immigrants from Central Europe – countries such as Germany, Austria, and especially Hungary. These immigration trends produced institutional differences. While Melbourne Jewry had about 20 Landsmannschaften (organisations of former residents of various towns and cities in Poland and the Ukraine) with a Federation of Landsmannschaften, Sydney Jewry had none. The spectrum of Jewish day schools in Melbourne reflects the wide range of Jewish identification in Poland between the wars.

Other historical and local conditions help account for the differences. Jewish life in nineteenth-century Melbourne was already more diverse. This was due to the fact that Melbourne was founded later, and by free settlers, so that the community 'seemed to have begun on a higher Jewish note, and attracted more of the intensely Jewish immigrants and ministers from the start'.[14] Melbourne's history of higher church attendance, and its stronger intellectual traditions, were also important factors. Geography played a role, in that Melbourne's colder climate discouraged outdoor activities, while the external beauty of Sydney led to a more materialistic and hedonistic approach to life.

The recent narrowing of the gap between the two communities can be seen in a number of areas. Only 17 per cent of Jewish children attended Jewish day schools in Sydney in 1970, compared to over 50 per cent in Melbourne. Today, the figures are 62 per cent in Sydney and 66 per cent in Melbourne. Melbourne traditionally raised double the amount raised in Sydney for the United Israel Appeal and emergency Zionist funds, even though the difference in the size of the two communities is not great. Yet over the last decade that has changed dramatically, and Sydney now raises almost the same amount as Melbourne.

The fabric of Sydney's Jewish life has strengthened for a number of reasons. In Melbourne, there is no central communal fundraising organisation, making joint communal and long-term planning difficult, while in Sydney a co-ordinated body, the Jewish Communal Appeal (JCA), also undertakes communal planning. The JCA was formed after the Six Day War in 1967, when local fundraising was disrupted by a decision to hold an emergency United Israel Appeal. While initially the JCA struggled to achieve communal acceptance, the picture has changed dramatically in recent years. A young, dynamic leadership group has taken the organisation to higher levels of communal giving. The JCA has given the community a new sense of unity, and the rigorous processes of its allocation committee have allowed for more logical planning in the use of community funds. Partly because of its more secure funding base, the community's umbrella body is far stronger and more effective in maintaining communal discipline than its Melbourne counterpart. Another major consideration is that South African Jews have injected energy into Sydney's Jewish life, not just in numbers but also in terms of Jewish commitment.

Melbourne Jewry is still very much the more dynamic and vital of the two communities. It has, however, faced more difficulties in terms of communal cohesion, and it is faced with stronger internal division. It will be interesting to chart the effect that the structural changes made by Sydney Jewry will have on the future wellbeing of the community. The question is, which is more important for long-term Jewish survival – communal unity or pluralistic 'richness'?

'New antisemitism'

During the first Gulf War, Gerry Levy, Sydney-based president of the New South Wales Jewish Board of Deputies, received an urgent call that the North Shore Temple had been set on fire. He rushed over to find the synagogue's rabbi standing outside with the Torah scrolls in his arms and one building completely gutted. As a young boy, Levy had been in Germany during Kristallnacht, the Nazi pogrom of November 1938, when the synagogue of his hometown, Magdeburg, was burnt down and his community violently attacked. On that January day in 1991, he felt he was reliving these events and found the experience extremely traumatic.[15]

With the 1990–1991 Gulf War came a spate of attacks against Jewish institutions across Australia. Over a three-month period in Sydney, arsonists attacked five synagogues, a quarter of the total number. In Melbourne, the first arson attack occurred on the Jewish kindergarten in Doncaster, while a bomb threat was made against the Palais Theatre in St Kilda during a Jewish solidarity rally there. Other anti-Jewish manifestations included desecration of Jewish graves, and hate letters prophesying the coming of the 'Fourth Reich', in which Jews would be incarcerated in concentration camps like the 'Auschwitz holiday camp'. Bottles and eggs were hurled from passing cars at individuals walking in Melbourne streets. Following these events, Australian Jewry realised that much greater security was required, and the Community Security Groups came to play a more visible role.

With the failure of the 'Oslo Accords' and the outbreak of the al-Aqsa Intifada between Israel and the Palestinians in September 2000, attacks against the Jewish community increased. In September 2000, the synagogue in Roscoe Street in Bondi was attacked by arson, while anti-Israel graffiti were daubed on the Illawarra Synagogue in Sydney's south and a gasoline bomb was thrown into the Succah (a tabernacle built during the festival of Succot) of a rabbi in Bondi. The Canberra Jewish Centre was fire-bombed four times between September 2001 and September 2002. Individual Jews, particularly men wearing skullcaps, were physically attacked, and communal leaders received death threats. Violence and Jew-hatred were evident in pro-Palestinian public rallies. In Sydney in March 2000, over 2000 protestors marched to the United States Consulate, where Israeli and US flags, and posters of Israeli Prime Minister, Ehud Barak, were burnt. These events created fear and anxiety amongst Australian Jewry. Anti-Jewish attacks reached a peak in 2002 when at a Sydney rally in April, a banner proclaimed 'They crucified the king of peace so what do you expect?'.[16]

The Executive Council of Australian Jewry monitored the level of antisemitism. Since October 1989, Jeremy Jones has compiled annual reports documenting incidents, as well as activities of groups and individuals responsible for purveying antisemitism in Australia, such

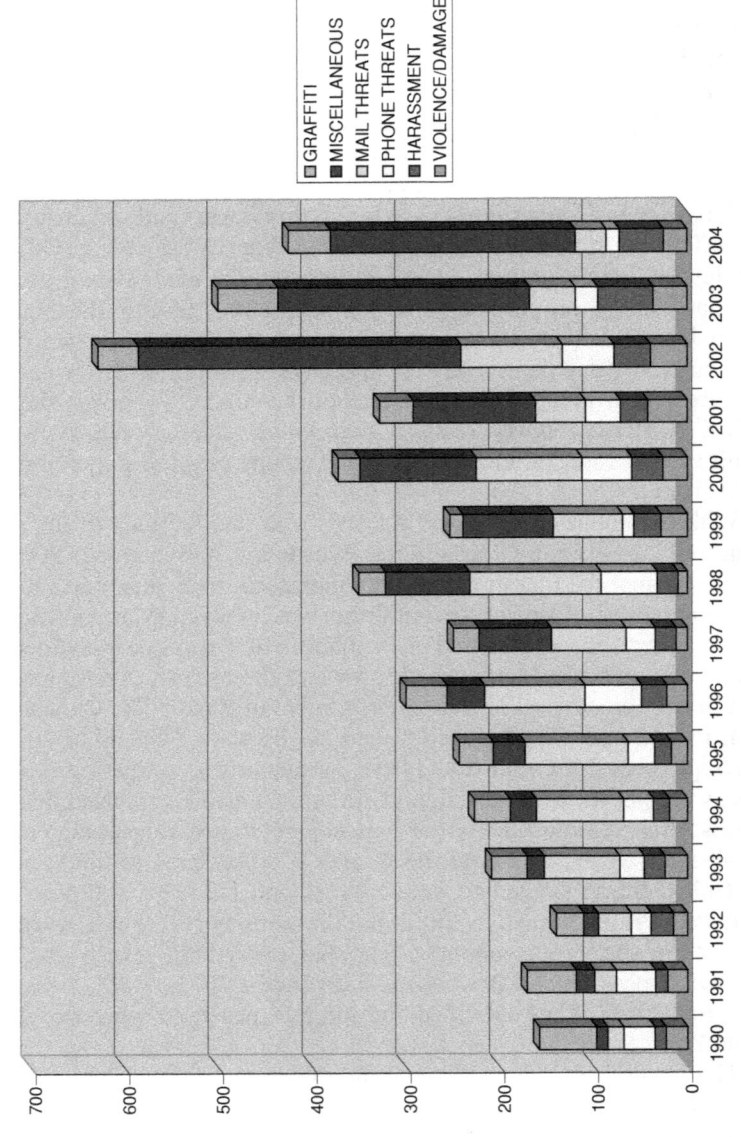

Graph showing the increase of antisemitic episodes since 1990 (ECAJ, Report on Antisemitism, 2004).

as Dr Fredrick Toben of the Adelaide Institute and Olga Scully in Tasmania.[17] These incidents include abusive emails, graffiti such as 'Bomb the Jews', threatening mail and reports of telephone threats, verbal harassment and abuse, including the bullying of Jewish children at school by some Muslim children, and actual physical violence against individuals and institutions. The majority of such attacks are anonymous, so it is difficult to determine who is responsible. In his introduction to the 2002–2003 survey, Jones notes that there were 'over 500 reports of anti-Jewish violence, vandalism, harassment and intimidation'. He presents a graph, showing that since 11 September 2001, the number of incidents has almost doubled, with 63 per cent of such attacks occurring in New South Wales.[18]

Telephone intimidation and hate letters have decreased since 1995, but hate emailing has been growing rapidly. Online media, including email and websites, are the area of greatest concern today. As Jones points out, 'individuals with time on their hands are able to reach a variety of audiences quickly and inexpensively'.[19] The medium used by antisemites may be new, but their messages are not. They continue to propagate the traditional anti-Jewish stereotypes, ranging from 'the international Jewish conspiracy' and 'the Jewish/Nazi analogy' via Holocaust denial to 'Mystical Jewish Power'. They promote the myth that Australian Jews influence public policy through their wealth and business connections, and label Jews as 'un-Christian' and Judaism as 'anti-Christianity'.[20]

While there were fewer physical attacks on Jewish institutions directly associated with the 2003 war in Iraq, these events certainly increased anti-Jewish feelings on university campuses, as left-wing, anti-war and anti-globalisation groups criticised Israel and the United States for their roles in the war. Dina Porat, head of the international centre for research on antisemitism at Tel Aviv University, argues that whilst more traditional attacks such as desecration of cemeteries and arson attacks against synagogues have decreased since 2001, the number of physical attacks against individual Jews have increased, and such activities are much harder to monitor. This has also been the Australian Jewish experience.

Most recently, the court case in Perth against Jack Roche, a Muslim convert, and Shannon Mark Post, an associate of the white supremacist Australian National Movement led by Jack van Tongeren, a far-right national extremist, highlighted the danger faced by Jewish institutions and individual Jews in Australia. Roche was planning to attack prominent Jewish leaders such as Rabbi Joseph Gutnick, as well as the

Israeli embassy.[21] Post was arrested for desecrating a synagogue in Menora with swastikas and slogans, including 'Hitler was right' and 'Jews out'.[22] To date, no arrests have been made for any of the arson attacks against the Jewish community.

It is important to note that in the same period, Muslims in Australia and elsewhere have also suffered abuse. During the first Gulf War there were attacks on Australian Muslims, and women wearing the *hijab* were the major targets. After the Al Qaeda attack on the World Trade Center in New York on September 11, 2001, members of the Arabic community again suffered abuse, and arson attacks were made on mosques. The worst incidents occurred in Queensland, where two Brisbane mosques, in Holland Park and Kuraby, were damaged by fire.[23] After the Bali bombings in 2002, attacks against Muslims in Australia again increased.

There is much debate as to whether the cause of these attacks against the Jewish community has been due to radicalised Islamic fundamentalism or the resurgence of extreme right-wing movements. The largest extreme right-wing organisation in Australia is the Australian League of Rights. Directed by Betty Luks in Adelaide, it publishes its weekly newsletter, *On Target*, as well as *New Times* and *Social Creditor*. The League maintains links with other far-right organisations, such as the Australian National Action, the Australian National Socialist Movement and the National Alliance, and builds ties with members of more recent organisations, such as Pauline Hanson's One Nation party. One Nation representative, Graeme Campbell of Western Australia,[24] had close associations with the League, which supports anti-immigration groups and Holocaust deniers such as Melbourne lawyer, John Bennett. The Citizens' Electoral Councils centred in Melbourne are part of the network of Lyndon la Rouche, American antisemite and conspiracy promoter.[25] There are also a number of small, radical 'Identity' churches, which claim to be Christian but emphasise the idea of white supremacy, with Jews being portrayed as evil. All these groups have in recent years increased their use of the Internet to spread their message of hate.[26] Another new phenomenon is hate music, which advocates racism and violence. The best-known band is 'Fortress' in Melbourne, which sells its music from three Internet sites.[27]

Robert Wistrich, world authority on the history of antisemitism,[28] points to Muslim antisemitism as a decisive factor in the rise of antisemitism in the world today. He argues that the 'vast output of anti-Semitic literature in the Arab and Muslim world' has 'become increasingly apparent as the anti-Semitic virus has taken root in the body politic of Islam to an unprecedented degree'.[29] Anti-Jewish publications can also be found in Australia.

In Australia, a number of anti-Jewish articles have appeared in the Arabic press, such as *An Nahar*, since the late 1970s. In September 1979, *An Nahar* claimed that the firing of shots into the car of a prominent Sydney Arab could have been due to 'hidden Zionist fingers'. The New South Wales Jewish Board of Deputies took legal action during the 1980s following the publication in *An Nahar* of extracts from the *Protocols of the Elders of Zion*, and again in 1992 and 1993 because of two offensive articles drawing on New Testament anti-Judaism. The first, 'Let His Blood Be Upon Us and Upon Our Children' by Michael Haddad, was published on 16 July 1992, and the second, 'A Discourse on Zionism and Christianity' by Hani-El Turk, on 6 May 1993. Haddad argued that the 'Hebrew state' was established through 'killing and expelling the Arab original residents from their homes at the hands of the international Zionists and criminal gangs' and that the 'presumed holocaust was disproved' because the idea of the Holocaust is 'to blackmail the world physically for generations to come'. He also referred to the 'Zionist holocaust against the Arabs' and made accusations of Israeli prostitutes 'committing adultery inside the Church of Resurrection in Jerusalem, the yard of the Al Aqsa Mosque' and other holy Christian and Muslim places. Following mediation, *An Nahar* eventually published a 'Correction' in August 1993, in which it admitted that both articles were 'derogatory to the Jewish faith and a vilification of the Jewish people'.

The Jewish community took legal action against the Sydney Arabic-language paper, *Al-Moharrer Al Arabi*, in 1994. It had published an offensive article entitled 'Blood for Zion's Unleavened Bread', accusing Jews of ritual murder. Referring to the Goldstein massacre in Hebron in February 1994, the author, Taleb Shaheen, charged that shedding 'Muslim blood is justifiable' for Jews, who were depicted as followers of a religion that finds it 'easy' to murder 'hundreds of human beings and even the entire human race'. Following action by the New South Wales Board of Deputies, the paper's editor, Morris Tadros (an Egyptian Christian), offered an apology.[30]

During the 1980s, the Jewish community was also concerned about the activities of Sheikh Taj Eldine El-Hilaly, Imam of the Lakemba mosque and, since 1989, Mufti of Australia. He entered Australia in 1982 on a three-month tourist visa that was later extended. The Minister for Immigration, Chris Hurford, decided in 1987 to deport Hilaly

Peter Wertheim (right) and Jeremy Jones, a leading figure in combating recent antisemitism, being interviewed during the trial of Dr Toben

because of his 'deep-seated contempt for basic Australian values and attitudes', but Hurford's successor, Mick Young, revoked the order. In 1988, the *Australian Jewish Times* highlighted an antisemitic speech by Hilaly at the University of Sydney entitled 'Islam and Judaism: Can They Co-exist?'. In this speech, Hilaly labelled Jews as 'the underlying cause of all wars threatening peace and security of the whole inhabited earth'. He also claimed that Jews 'try to control the world through sex, then sexual perversion, then the promotion of espionage, traitory and economic hoarding'.[31] Despite objections from Jewish leaders, no action was taken, and in September 1990 the newly appointed Minister for Immigration, Gerry Hand, granted Hilaly permanent residency.[32]

Since September 11, Muslim radicals have intensified their attacks on Jews both overseas and in Australia. At the time of the attack, Hilaly stated that he doubted that Muslims were involved.[33] He has continued to make controversial statements, such as praising the actions of suicide bombers.[34] While in Lebanon in 2003, he is purported to have said: 'Don't be surprised if one day you hear the *Muezzin* calling for prayer and saying *Allah Akbar* (Allah is Great) from the top of the White House. September 11 is God's work against oppressors'.[35] Hilaly claims he was mistranslated, or, as an article in the *Sun-Herald* put it, 'Lost in Translation'.[36] As elsewhere, radical Islam in Australia is growing. This is evident in the activities of the Sydney-based Islamic Youth Movement and its publication, *Nida'ul Islam*,

Both anti-Zionists and antisemites are quick to compare Israeli policies with those of Nazi Germany. At a major event of the United Israel Appeal at Darling Harbour in Sydney in 2004, anti-Israel protestors stood with placards proclaiming that Israel was committing genocide, a completely inaccurate and unfounded accusation. Similar claims are also made at university forums. In 2002, Associate Professor Ghassan Hage of the University of Sydney and Dr John Docker of the Australian National University attempted to introduce a boycott of Israeli academics, singling out Israel alone for human rights abuses. The key question is to what extent this left-wing demonisation of Israel, together with the use of world conspiracy theories, contributes to the racist violence in Australia. There is no doubt that comparison of Israel with Nazi Germany and the fostering of Jewish world conspiracy theories do contribute to an atmosphere of hatred against all Jews, which helps to justify violence against them.

Present-day problems

Respondents to the 1991 Goldlust survey were questioned about what they considered to be the major problems facing the community. They had to limit their responses to three issues. Nearly one in three mentioned problems surrounding assimilation / intermarriage / loss of Jewish identity. Also of concern was the rise of antisemitism. The needs of Jewish youth, both educational and social, were also raised. Most students were 'turned-off' by religious programmes in Jewish day schools. By focusing on day school education, the community has tended to put all its eggs in one basket, especially in terms of funding.

A broader approach to Jewish youth is needed. While Sydney has started to meet the needs of the young adult community, there is still not enough being done to create post-university Jewish organisations. This is a very difficult age group to cater for. Most graduates disappear into the work force, and only reappear if they find a Jewish partner and have children whom they want to send to Jewish schools. It is even more difficult to meet the needs of Jewish adults who do not attend university, since they are a minority group. Conflicts over the Liberal/Orthodox divide were also raised, as was the Melbourne/Sydney divide, and the need to meet representatives of other minorities, including women, and gay and lesbian Jews. Class snobbery is a problem, particularly at the day schools, where children from wealthier homes often form an exclusive 'in group'. In canvassing Jewish women specifically, the survey found that the highest level of concern related to 'religious issues (not related to marriage)' (16 per cent), discrimination and equity in orthodox Judaism (16 per cent), conflicts around the 'traditional' women's role (14 per cent), and 'religious issues surrounding marriage and/or divorce' (12 per cent).[37]

Conclusion

Australian Jewry has, since 1945, been enriched by new waves of immigrants who have changed an isolated Anglo-Jewish community to a pluralist religious and ethnic group that is fully integrated into the general society. The community continues to attract immigrants, and is today the tenth largest in the Jewish diaspora. Its members enjoy full acceptance, despite the increase of antisemitism in recent years. Although located at the edge of the Jewish world, it is perceived to be a model for other Jewish communities in the diaspora, as well as for ethnic communities in Australia.

Appendix 1
SYNAGOGUES

MELBOURNE SYNAGOGUES

Pre 1930	1930–1945	1945–1960	1960–1980	1980–2005
Melbourne Hebrew Congregation, 1844	Temple Beth Israel, 1930	South Caulfield Hebrew Congregation, 1948	Rabbinical College Yeshivah Gedolah, 1966	Kollel Beth Hatalmud – Yehuda Fishman Institute, 1981
East Melbourne Hebrew Congregation, (1852 est. congr.) 1877	Caulfield Hebrew Congregation, 1940	Kew Hebrew Congregation, 1948	Sassoon Yehuda Sephardi Synagogue, 1977	Chabad Houses: Bentleigh 1986, Malvern 1987; Yotzei Rusia 1987; Ohel Devorah, 1993; Glen Eira 1999; Caulfield 2001
St Kilda Hebrew Congregation, 1872	Elwood Talmud Torah, 1940	Brighton Hebrew Congregation, (est. Southern District Hebrew Congregation 1948), 1952		Rambam Sephardi Congregation, 1980s
Stone's Shule, 1911	Brunswick Talmud Torah, 1940	Leo Baeck Centre, 1948 (in current premises since 1970s)		Beit Aharon Memorial Synagogue, (1980 est. congr.) 1987
Carlton United Hebrew congregation, 1912	Mizrachi Congregation, beginnings 1943, present form 1952	Yeshivah, 1949		Elsternwick Jewish Community (Fay Rockman Synagogue), 1992

(cont.)

(*cont.*)

Pre 1930	1930–1945	1945–1960	1960–1980	1980–2005
		Adass Israel, 1950		Kedem Synagogue, 1996
		Moorabbin and District Hebrew Congregation, 1951		Blake Street Hebrew Congregation, (est. congr. 1987), 1996
		Bentleigh Progressive Synagogue, 1952		Hamakom, 1996
		Burwood Hebrew Congregation, 1953		Hamerkaz Shelanu, 1998
		Caulfield Beth Hamedrash, 1950s (in current premises since 1975)		Kehilat Nitzan, 1999 (at current premises since 2002)
		North Eastern Jewish War Memorial, Doncaster, 1962		Central Shule – Chabad. (est. congr. 1998), 2003

SYDNEY SYNAGOGUES

Pre 1930	1930–1945	1945–1960	1960–1980	1980–2005
Great Synagogue, 1878	Mizrachi (Bondi Mizrachi), 1931	Kingsford/Maroubra, 1946	Cyril Rosenbaum Synagogue – Sir Moses Montefiore Home, 1964	Chabad Lubavitch House of Bondi Beach, 1986
Bankstown, 1912	Temple Emanuel, 1939	Parramatta, 1948		Kehillat Masada Synagogue, 1986
Central Synagogue, 1912	Northern Suburbs (North Shore Synagogue), 1940	Strathfield, 1949		Beit Menachem (Chabad House of the North Shore), 1989
Newtown Synagogue (Western Suburbs), f.1878, synagogue built, 1918	Adass Yisroel, 1943	South Head (South Head and District Synagogue), 1950		Bet Yosef (The Caro Synagogue), 1992
	Illawarra Hebrew Congregation (Southern Sydney), 1943	NSW Association of Sephardi (The Sephardi Synagogue), 1950		Ha Rambam, 1993
		Manly Warringah, 1952		Baba Sali, 1993–2003
		Coogee, 1952		Kehillat Moriah – The Hugo Lowy Synagogue, 1994
		Roscoe Street, 1955		Ohr Chadash, 1995
		Yeshivah, 1955		Dover Heights Shule, 1997
		Cremorne, 1956		JCC Chabad Double Bay, 1997
		Machzika Hatorah Congregation Inc, 1957		The Shtiebl – Chinuch Foundation, 2001
		North Shore Temple Emanuel, 1960		

PERTH SYNAGOGUES

Pre 1930	1930–1945	1945–1960	1960–1980	1980–2005
Perth Hebrew Congregation, 1894 (in current premises since 1974)		Temple David Congregation, 1952		Chabad House, 1987
				Beth Midrash of WA Inc (Dianella Shule), 1994
				Northern Suburbs Hebrew Congregation, Perth Inc – Noranda Shule, (est. congr. 1987) 1992

Appendix 2*
PARLIAMENTARIANS

COMMONWEALTH

Elias Solomon 1901–1903 WA
Vaiban Solomon 1901–1903 SA
Isaac Isaacs 1901–1906 VIC
Pharez Phillips 1901–1906 VIC
(Sydney) Max Falstein 1940–1949 NSW (ALP)
Sydney Einfeld 1961–1963 NSW (ALP)
Samuel Cohen 1962–1969 VIC (ALP)
Joseph Berinson 1969–1975 WA (ALP)
Moss (Moses) Cass 1969–1983 VIC (ALP)
Barry Cohen 1969–1990 NSW (ALP)
Richard Klugman 1969–1990 NSW (ALP)
Peter Baume 1974–1991 NSW (Liberal)
Lewis Kent (orig. Kapolnai) 1980–1990 VIC (ALP)
Michael Danby 1998– VIC (ALP)

NEW SOUTH WALES

Jacob Montefiore MLC 1856–1860, 1874–1877
Morris Asher MLA 1859–1860

---

* Hilary Rubinstein has produced two alphabetical lists of parliamentarians: 'Australian Jewish members of parliament 1849–present. A complete listing' in the *Australian Jewish Historical Society Journal*, vol. 10, part 4, 1988, pp. 295–316 with an addendum in part 6, 1989, p. 542. This was updated in Rubinstein, Hilary L., 'Appendix: Jewish Parliamentarians in Australia, 1849 to the Present', Levey, Geoffrey Brahm and Philip Mendes (eds), *Jews and Australian Politics*, Brighton, Great Britain and Portland, Oregon, USA, Sussex Academic Press, 2004, pp. 245–53.

Saul Samuel MLA 1859–1860, 1862–1872, MLC 1872–1880
Samuel Cohen MLA 1860
Maurice Alexander MLA 1861–1872
Samuel Emanuel MLA 1862–1864
Julian Salomons MLC 1870–1871, 1887–1899
Lewis Levy MLA 1871–1872, 1874, MLC 1880–1885
Joseph Raphael MLA 1872–1874
Harris Nelson MLA 1872–1877
Solomon Meyer MLA 1874–1876
Henry Cohen MLA 1874–1880, 1882–1885
Philip Myers MLA 1880–1881
Leyser Levin MLA 1880–1885
Charles Collins MLA 1885–1887, 1890–1898
Samuel Joseph MLA 1864–1868, MLC 1881–1885, 1887–1893
Solomon Hyam MLA 1885–1887, MLC 1892–1901
Simeon Phillips MLA 1895–1904
John Cohen MLA 1898–1919
Albert Collins MLA 1901–1910
Sir Daniel Levy MLA 1901–1937
Hyman Goldstein MLA 1922–1925, 1927–1928
Ernest Marks MLA 1927–1930
Abram Landa MLA 1930–1932, 1941–1965
Ernest Mitchell MLC 1934–1943
Leon Snider MLC 1943–1965 (Liberal, Country Party)
Asher Joel MLC 1958–1978
Morton Cohen MLA 1965–1968 (Liberal)
Sydney Einfeld MLA 1965–1981 (ALP)
Margaret Davis (nee Alexander) MLC 1967–1978 (Liberal)
Derek Freeman MLC 1973–1984 (Liberal)
Paul Landa MLC 1973–1976, MLA 1976–1984 (ALP)
Ian Cohen MLC 1995– (Greens)
Eric Roozendaal MLC 2004– (ALP)

VICTORIA

Sidney Ricardo MLA 1857–1859
Edward Cohen MLA 1861–1865, 1868–1877
Nathaniel Levi MLA 1861–1865, 1866–1867, MLC 1892–1904
Charles Dyte MLA 1864–1871
Jonas Levien MLA 1871–1877, 1880–1906

Ephraim Zox MLA 1877–1899
Benjamin Fink MLA 1883–1889
Benjamin Benjamin MLC 1889–1892
Joseph Sternberg MLC 1891–1928
Samuel Samuel MLA 1892 (Labor)
Emanuel Steinfeld MLC 1892–1893 (Federationist)
Isaac Isaacs MLA 1892–1901
Daniel Lazarus MLA 1893–97, 1900–1902
John Isaacs MLA 1894–1902
Theodore Fink MLC 1894–1904
Max Hirsch MLA 1902–1903
Henry Cohen MLC 1921–1937 (Nat., UAP)
Harold Cohen MLC 1929–1935, MLA 1935–1943 (Nat., UAP)
Archie Michaelis MLC 1932–52 (UAP, Liberal)
Baron Snider MLA 1955–1964, MLC 1964–1966 (Liberal)
Walter Jona MLA 1962–1984 (Liberal)
David Bornstein MLA 1970–1975 (ALP)
Marsha Thompson MLC 1999– (ALP)

Possible Jewish origin

Adolphus Goldsmith MLC 1851–1853
George Levey MLA 1861–1867
Albert Harris MLA 1883–1889, 1889–1904, 1904–1910

SOUTH AUSTRALIA

Morris Marks MHA 1857–1858
Judah Solomon MHA 1858–1860, 1871–1875, MLC 1861–1866
Emanuel Solomon MHA 1862–1865, MLC 1867–1871
Maurice Salom MLC 1882–1891
Saul Solomon MHA 1887–1890
Lewis Cohen MHA 1887–1893, 1902–1906 (Protectionist)
Vaiban Solomon MHA 1890–1891, 1905–1908 (Free Trader, Federationist)

WESTERN AUSTRALIA

Lionel Samson MLC 1849–1856, 1859–1868
Elias Solomon MLA 1892–1901 (Independent)

Mathew Moss MLA 1895–1897, MLC 1900–1901, 1902–1914 (Liberal)
Harry Boan MLC 1917–1918, 1922–1924 (Nationalist)
Charles Nathan MLC 1930–1934
Joseph Berinson MLC 1980–1993 (ALP)

QUEENSLAND

Jacob Horwitz MLA 1878–1887
Francis Kates MLA 1878–1881, 1883–88, 1899–1903 (Liberal)
Isidore Lissner MLA 1883–1893, 1896–1899
Louis Goldring MLA 1888–1893

Possible Jewish origin

Eugen Hirschfeld MLC 1914

TASMANIA

Joseph Cohen MHA 1860–1861
John Davies MHA 1861, 1862–1872

MHR – Member of the House of Representatives
MHA – Member of the House of Assembly
MLA – Member of the Legislative Assembly
MLC – Member of the Legislative Council

Appendix 3
HOSTELS,* 1945–1960

MELBOURNE

Hostel	Address	Date of purchase	Type of accommodation	Date of sale/reuse
Bialystoker Centre	19 Robe St, St Kilda	July 1947	Large house, bed and breakfast	–
Camberwell House	818 Bourke Rd, Camberwell	December 1947	Reception house. Accommodate up to 80 people. July 1955 renovated	–
A. S. Rose House	29 Herbert St, St Kilda	March 1949	Could accommodate over 30 people in 12 rooms. Bought with the assistance of the American Jewish Labor committee	Later self-contained flats for the elderly
Ziegelbaum House	885 Drummond St, North Carlton	September 1949	Purchased by Northern Suburbs committee; converted into medical centre, 1951	Sold 1954

(cont.)

* Accommodation provided by the Jewish community for Holocaust survivors as part of its migrant reception program. These hostels were funded largely by American Jewish organisations: the American Joint Distribution Committee (AJDC), the Hebrew Immigrant Aid Society (HIAS) and the Refugee Economic Corporation (REC).

(cont.)

Hostel	Address	Date of purchase	Type of accommodation	Date of sale/reuse
David Abzacs House	912 Drummond St, North Carlton	December 1949	Small house, bed and breakfast	1954 rented by the Peretz School
Coburg House	1 The Grove, Coburg	October 1949	Small house bought in the name of Mutual Enterprises	1956 registered as apartments for elderly
E. H. Komlos	238 McKean St, North Fitzroy	May 1950	10-roomed house	Sold July 1955
Kew House	73 High St, Kew	1950	Small house	March 1953 cleared to be sold
Warsaw Jewish Centre	466 Punt Rd, South Yarra	February 1951	Previously rented property at 192 Tooronga Rd, Tooronga. Large two-storey house	Mid 1955 – AJW & RS October 1957 society headquarters
Radomer Centre	—	—	Operated by the Radomer landsmannschaften	—
Frances Barkman Home	Maleela Ave, Balwyn	1947	Previously Larino children's home	Sold 1958

SYDNEY

Hostel	Address	Date of purchase	Type of accommodation	Date of sale/reuse
Chelsea Park	Baulkham Hills	1939	Bought as an agricultural training farm. Later used for temporary accommodation	Sold 1952
Chip-Chase; later Komlos	34 Greenwich Rd, Greenwich	March 1949	Large two-storey home. Full board provided	Sold 1965
Chatswood	32 Albert St, Chatswood	August 1950	Small house, bed and breakfast	Sold 1954
Waverley	29 Ashton St, Waverley	August 1950	Small house, bed and breakfast	Sold 1959
Greenwich	Greenwich Rd, Greenwich	March 1951	House with eight rooms to accommodate eight families, bed and breakfast	—

BRISBANE

Hostel	Address	Date of purchase	Type of accommodation	Date of sale/reuse
Welfare House	41 Lindon St, Dutton Park	November 1948	Could house up to 20 people	Sold 1952

NOTES

Introduction
1. Menasseh ben Israel, 'A Petition for the Readmission of the Jews to England November 13, 1655', in Jacob Marcus, *The Jew in the Medieval World: A Source Book*, New York, Harper Torch Books, 1965, p. 67.
2. David S. Katz, *Philo-Semitism and the Readmission of the Jews to England, 1603–1655*, Oxford, Clarendon Press, 1982, p. 243.
3. Freedman, *A Minority in Britain*, London, 1955, p. 24.
4. V. D. Lipman, *A Social History of the Jews in England, 1850–1950*, London, 1954, p. 121.
5. Ibid., p. 40.
6. For a more detailed discussion of these nineteenth-century movements, see Rutland, The Jewish Community in New South Wales, 1914–1939, pp. 1–11; Blau, *Modern Varieties of Judaism*, p. 185.
7. Elbogen, *A Century of Jewish Life*, p. 373.
8. Blau, *Modern Varieties of Judaism*, pp. 57–8.
9. Elazar and Medding, *Jewish Communities in Frontier Societies*, pp. 7–8.
10. In 1903 the Reverend J. H. Landau, minister at the Great Synagogue, Sydney, commented that 'it happens that the community as a whole is more English than the Jews of England', *Hebrew Standard of Australasia*, 6 November 1908.
11. Elazar and Medding, *Jewish Communities in Frontier Societies*, p. 10.
12. Medding, *From Assimilation to Group Survival*, p. 77.
13. Rutland, The Jewish Community in New South Wales, 1914–1939, p. 11.
14. National Council of Jewish Women, *Council Bulletin*, April 1955.
15. Elazar and Medding, *Jewish Communities in Frontier Societies*, see ch. 18.

1 Convicts and early settlement
1. Levi and Bergman, *Australian Genesis*, p. 91.

2 Nathan, 'The Benefits of a Conviction'.
3 Levi and Bergman, *Australian Genesis*, p. 148.
4 Bersten, *Jewish Sydney*, p. 18.
5 This belief in resurrection also explains Judaism's taboo on cremation or on touching any part of the body, so that autopsies are not permitted except in special circumstances. See Lamm, *The Jewish Way in Death and Mourning*, pp. 10–11, 228–33.
6 Levi and Bergman *Australian Genesis*, p. 152.
7 Bergman, 'The Bizarre Life Story of Mordecai Moses the Shammas of the York Street Synagogue'.
8 Forbes, 'Australia's First Synagogue at Bridge Street, Sydney', p. 161.
9 Levi and Bergman, *Australian Genesis*, p. 163.
10 Aron and Arndt, *The Enduring Remnant*, pp. 5–10.

2 Waves of migration

1 Kellerman (ed.),'Interesting Account of the Travels of Abraham Abrahamsohn', p. 484.
2 Hilary Rubinstein, *The Jews in Victoria*, pp. 57–8.
3 Ochert, 'History of the Brisbane Hebrew Congregation'.
4 Forbes, 'Jews of NSW and the Gold Rushes'; Bersten, 'Jews in Rural New South Wales'.
5 Spielvogel, 'The Beginnings of the Ballarat Hebrew Congregation', pp. 111–12.
6 Ibid., p. 16.
7 Rosenthal, *Formula for Survival*, p. 18.
8 See Fredman, 'Bendigo Jewry'; Kunz, 'Rev Isaac Friedman'.
9 Isadore Solomon, 'Geelong Jewry', p. 336. The exact date of the erection of the permanent synagogue is not known.
10 David J. Benjamin, 'The Sydney Hebrew Certified Denominational School', p. 248.
11 Geulah Solomon, 'Jewish Education in Australia', p. 223.
12 Harold Sackville, John Sackville: The Man and the Legend, nd (lent to the author by Justice Ronald Sackville), pp. 7–8.
13 Cited in Fletcher, 'The Victorian Jewish Community, 1891–1901: Its Interrelationship with the Majority Gentile Community', *Australian Jewish Historical Society Journal*, vol. 13, no. 5, 1978, p. 250.
14 For a detailed history of the Central Synagogue, see Jones and Lutman, *Orach Hayim*.
15 Ivany (Bach), The Kadimah, p. 8.
16 Interview with David Feiglin (Moshe Feiglin's son), Melbourne, July 1987.
17 Stedman, 'From Russia to Brisbane, 1913', pp. 21–2.
18 Ibid., p. 27.
19 For more information on Freedman, see Mossenson, *Hebrew, Israelite, Jew*, especially chs 5, 6, 7, 8; Zusman, 'Rabbi David Isaac Freedman'.

20 Apple, 'Rabbi Jacob Saphir and His Voyage to Australia'. For a translation from the Hebrew, by Rabbi Lieb A. Falk, of Saphir's book, *Eben Saphir*, giving an account of his visits to Australia and New Zealand, see *Australian Jewish Historical Society Journal*, vol. 1, no. 1, pp. 19–22, no. 2, pp. 43–50, 1939, no. 3, pp. 86–92, no. 4, pp. 116–20, no. 5, pp. 153–9, no. 6, pp. 192–7, 1940.
21 Ibid., p. 45.
22 Ibid., p. 91.
23 Ibid., p. 119.
24 Rutland, *Pages of History*, pp. 70–1, 193.
25 *Hebrew Standard of Australasia*, 23 August 1929.

3 A place in Australian society
1 *Sunday Times*, 24 December 1922.
2 Fletcher, 'The Victorian Jewish Community, 1891–1901', p. 229.
3 Price, 'Jewish Settlers in Australia'.
4 Fletcher, 'The Victorian Jewish Community, 1891–1901', p. 227.
5 Hill, 'The Jews of Perth'.
6 Fletcher, 'The Victorian Jewish Community, 1891–1901', p. 231.
7 Price, 'Jewish Settlers in Australia', p. 394.
8 *Jewish Herald*, 27 December 1895, cited in Fletcher, 'The Victorian Jewish Community, 1891–1901', p. 31.
9 Sackville, John Sackville.
10 Wynn, *The Fortunes of Samuel Wynn*, p. ix.
11 Cramp and Mackaness, *A History of the United Grand Lodge of Ancient Free and Accepted Masons of New South Wales*, p. 399.
12 *Ivriah*, vol. 1, no. 7, 1937.
13 Medding, *From Assimilation to Group Survival*, pp. 199–200.
14 Bennett, 'Sir Julian Salomons: Fifth Chief Justice', p. 105.
15 Forbes, 'Sir Julian Salomons, 1835–1909'.
16 Fredman, 'Some Victorian Jewish Politicians'.
17 Cited in Fletcher, 'The Victorian Jewish Community, 1891–1901', p. 240. They were T. Fink, E. L. Fox, A. Harris, I. Isaacs, J. A. Isaacs, D. B. Lazarus, J. T. Levien (Legislative Assembly), and N. Levi, J. Sternberg (Legislative Council).
18 See Gordon, *Sir Isaac Isaacs*; Cowen, *Isaac Isaacs*; *Australian Dictionary of Biography*, vol. 9, pp. 444–50; Fredman, 'Some Victorian Jewish Politicians' and 'Isaacs in Politics'.
19 For a more detailed discussion of Jews and Federation, see Harold H. Glass, 'Some Jews and the Federal Movement'; Forbes, 'The Federation of the Commonwealth and the Role of Australian Jews'.
20 Cited in Fredman, 'Isaacs in Politics', p. 107; *Australian Dictionary of Biography*, vol. 9, p. 446.
21 For a more detailed discussion, see Medding, *From Assimilation to Group Survival*, p. 235.

22 *Hebrew Standard of Australasia*, 1 November 1895.
23 Ibid., 28 July 1916.

4 The watershed years
1 The term 'natives' here refers to the first white settlers.
2 *New Citizen*, 15 October 1949.
3 Letter from G. M. Berger, *Sydney Jewish News*, 26 January 1945.
4 W. J. Thomas, 'When Do Refugees Become Citizens?', *New Citizen*, 15 April 1946.
5 *Daily Telegraph*, 9 May 1939.
6 *Sunday Sun*, 15 January 1939.
7 *Sydney Morning Herald*, 19 August 1948.
8 *Commonwealth Parliamentary Debates*, vol. 189, 27 November 1946, p. 661.
9 Ibid.
10 Blakeney, *Australia and the Jewish Refugees, 1933–1948*, pp. 294–6; *Commonwealth Parliamentary Debates*, vol. 189, 28 November 1946, pp. 744–55.
11 *Sydney Jewish News*, 10 January 1947.
12 See Abram Landa's speech, New South Wales Legislative Assembly, December 1946; *Council Bulletin*, January 1947.
13 *Melbourne Herald*, 28 January 1947.
14 Rutland, 'Postwar Anti-Jewish Refugee Hysteria'.
15 W. D. Rubinstein, 'Australia and the Refugee Jews of Europe, 1933–1954', and *The Jews in Australia*, vol. 2, pp. 57–69.
16 Markus, 'Jewish Migration to Australia, 1938–1947', pp. 293–4, 297; Bartrop, *Australia and the Holocaust, 1933–1945*.
17 Andgel, *Fifty Years of Caring*, pp. 3–11.
18 Bartrop, *Australia and the Holocaust, 1933–1945*, p. 78.
19 Bartrop, 'The Australian Government's "Liberalisation" of Refugee Immigration Policy in 1938: Fact or Myth?'.
20 'Declaration on German Treatment of Jews', letter dated 18 December 1942, Correspondence Files, Department of the Interior, CRS A433, item 45/2/6325, National Archives of Australia, Canberra.
21 Kwiet, 'Responses of the Australian Jewish Leadership to the Holocaust'.
22 Kwiet, '"Be Patient and Reasonable!" The Internment of German-Jewish Refugees in Australia'.
23 Patkin, *The Dunera Internees*; Pearl, *The Dunera Scandal*.
24 Wilton and Bosworth, *Old Worlds and New Australia*, p. 7.
25 Memo, 21 September 1944, 'Post-War Migration', National Archives of Australia, CRS A373, item 7786/89, pp. 10, 16.
26 Ibid., p. 9.
27 Ibid., pp. 10, 16.
28 Sluga, *Bonegilla*, p. 1.
29 Calwell, *How Many Australians Tomorrow?*.

30 Adolph C. Glassgold, Shanghai, to Walter Brand, 2 December 1948, ECAJ correspondence files, Box E30, Archive of Australian Judaica, Fisher Library, University of Sydney.
31 Rutland, *Edge of the Diaspora*, p. 407.
32 Tasman Heyes to Walter Brand, 10 June 1949, Victorian Jewish Board of Deputies, correspondence files, Box 6, La Trobe Collection, State Library of Victoria, Melbourne.
33 Benjamin. 'A Very Serious Influx of Jews', pp. 85–9.
34 *Sydney Jewish News*, 14 July 1939.
35 *Sydney Morning Herald*, 13 May 1939.
36 *Hebrew Standard of Australasia*, 27 July 1939.
37 Australian Jewish Welfare Society, Minutes, 31 March 1947.
38 Gill, *Interrupted Journeys*; Palmer, *Reluctant Refuge*.
39 Interview with Mina Fink, Melbourne, October 1984.
40 Golvan, *The Distant Exodus*.

5 Diverse voices

1 Rutland, *Edge of the Diaspora*, pp. 101–3.
2 *Sydney Jewish News*, 11 August 1944.
3 Secretary, Department of External Affairs, to Jewish Advisory Board, 5 July 1944, Box 17, 167C, Australian Jewish Historical Society Archives, Mandelbaum House, Sydney.
4 See, for example, letter from Sam Karpin, Bureau of Jewish Affairs, to Herbert I. Wolff, Advisory Board, requesting a meeting to be held, 22 June 1944, Box 17, File 176C, Australian Jewish Historical Society Archives, Mandelbaum House, Sydney.
5 *Sydney Jewish News*, 11 August 1944.
6 *Australian Jewish Herald*, 28 July 1944, p. 5.
7 *Sydney Jewish News*, 20 April and 15 June 1945.
8 Notice of Motion for Alteration of the Constitution, 1947, Victorian Jewish Board of Deputies, correspondence files, Box 6, La Trobe Collection, State Library of Victoria.
9 Victorian Jewish Board of Deputies, Minutes, 4 April 1955.
10 Ibid., 11 December 1955.
11 Robert Goot, Annual Report, New South Wales Jewish Board of Deputies, 16 March 1982.
12 For the crisis with Professor Hanan Ashrawi, see Levey and Mendes (eds), *Jews and Australian Politics*, pp. 215–30.
13 Robert Goot, Annual Report, New South Wales Jewish Board of Deputies, 16 March 1982.
14 Annual Report, New South Wales Jewish Board of Deputies, 14 December 1951.
15 Minutes of half-yearly conference, Executive Council of Australian Jewry, Adelaide, 9 February 1952, Archive of Australian Judaica, Fisher Library, University of Sydney.

16 *Sydney Jewish News*, 25 July 1952.
17 *Sydney Jewish News*, 11 December 1953.
18 Einfeld represented Australia in 1954; Ashkanasy in 1955 and 1956; Einfeld in 1957 and 1958; and Ashkanasy in 1959 and 1960.
19 Perlzweig to Ashkanasy, 6 July 1955, World Jewish Congress correspondence 1954–1956, Box E1, Archive of Australian Judaica, Fisher Library, University of Sydney.
20 See Claims Conference files, Boxes C1–C9, Archive of Australian Judaica, Fisher Library, University of Sydney.
21 Robinson to Einfeld, 4 December 1953, and Einfeld to Robinson, 29 January 1954, World Jewish Congress 1952–1954, Box E5, Executive Council of Australian Jewry correspondence files, Archive of Australian Judaica, Fisher Library, University of Sydney.
22 Statement on Balts: Notes on Bonegilla Camp, statements collected by the Council to Combat Fascism and Anti-Semitism, Dr Max Joseph collection, Archive of Australian Judaica, Fisher Library, University of Sydney.
23 Draft letter, H. E. Holt, Minister for Immigration, to E. W. Renouf, 19 January 1950, Department of Immigration correspondence files, CRS A445, item 271.2.4, National Archives of Australia, Canberra.
24 For Cabinet: Proposals re German Migration to Australia, German Migration, Department of Immigration, CRS A445, item 194/2/3, National Archives of Australia, Canberra.
25 An enormous amount has been researched and written about this episode with theses by Allan Leibler, David Rechter and Sara McNaughton, and a number of articles by Philip Mendes and Rodney Gouttman.
26 See Gouttman, 'The Sam Cohen Affair', p. 70.

6 Israel and Zionism
1 Walter Duffield, 'Administrative Report', Nineteenth Zionist Conference, Melbourne, 30 January–1 February 1960, p. 4, Archive of Australian Judaica, Fisher Library, University of Sydney.
2 Forbes, 'Palestine Appeals in the 'Fifties and 'Sixties'.
3 Apple, 'Rabbi Jacob Saphir and His Voyage to Australia'.
4 Crown, 'The Initiatives and Influences in the Development of Australian Zionism, 1850–1948', p. 315.
5 Rutland, *Edge of the Diaspora*, p. 87; and Hyams, *The History of the Australian Zionist Movement*.
6 Samuel Halperin, *The Political World of American Zionism*, Detroit, Wayne State University Press, 1961, p. 6.
7 *Australasian Hebrew*, 28 February 1896.
8 *Hebrew Standard of Australasia*, 26 April 1901.
9 Hyams, *The History of the Australian Zionist Movement*, pp. 15–17.
10 Israel Cohen, *The Journal of a Jewish Traveller*, p. 60.
11 Rutland, *Edge of the Diaspora*, p. 163.
12 Rutland, The Jewish Community in New South Wales 1914–1939, p. 93.

13 Hyams, *The History of the Australian Zionist Movement*, pp. 42–5.
14 Crown, 'The Initiatives and Influences in the Development of Australian Zionism', p. 312.
15 *Hebrew Standard*, 4 September 1941.
16 Horowitz (ed.), *The Dawn and the Rebirth of Palestine*.
17 Rutland, *Edge of the Diaspora*, p. 303.
18 Freilich, *Zion in Our Time*, pp. 196–7.
19 Tennant, *Evatt*, p. 219.
20 *Sydney Jewish News*, 26 December 1947.
21 *Sydney Jewish News*, 9 April 1948.
22 Reich, *Australia and Israel*; Piggott, 'An Ideal Betrayed'.
23 Reich, *Australia and Israel*, p. 25.
24 Ibid., p. 28.
25 Aubrey S. Eban, Israel Mission to the United States, to H. V. Evatt, 18 May 1949, copy in Executive Council of Australian Jewry Correspondence Files, 1948–1949, Box E17, Archive of Australian Judaica, Fisher Library, University of Sydney.
26 Taft, 'The Impact of the Middle East Crisis of June 1967 on Melbourne Jewry', p. 261.
27 Rutland, *Pages of History*, p. 145.
28 Taft, 'The Impact of the Middle East Crisis of June 1967 on Melbourne Jewry', pp. 250–1.
29 Taft and Solomon, 'The Melbourne Jewish Community and the Middle East War of 1973', p. 58.
30 *Sydney Jewish News*, 22 February 1946.
31 *Sydney Jewish News*, 21 November 1952.
32 Information from Dr Ron Weiser, email, 16 November 2003.
33 Key works on Evatt include: Adelman, 'Australia and the Birth of Israel'; Gouttman, 'First Principles'; Reich, *Australia and Israel*; Renouf, '*Let Justice Be Done*'.
34 Reich, *Australia and Israel*.
35 The full transcript is in Australian Jewry, vol. 78, Leibler Archive, Jerusalem.
36 See Hyams, *The History of the Australian Zionist Movement*, pp. 137–8.

7 Transformation or disappearance?
1 Elazar and Medding, *Jewish Communities in Frontier Societies*, p. 10.
2 Also known as Lubavitch, from the town in Eastern Europe where it developed.
3 See Goldlust, *The Jews of Melbourne*, pp. 116, 119, 120–1 for the statistics cited to the end of this section.
4 *Hebrew Standard of Australasia*, 25 February 1943.
5 Blumenthal, *Trials and Challenges*, p. 81.
6 Patkin, *Heritage and Tradition*, p. 5.

7 Medding, *From Assimilation to Group Survival*, pp. 100–1.
8 Patkin, *Heritage and Tradition*, pp. 54–5.
9 H. S. Ruskin, Chairman, Executive Council of Australian Jewry, Education Standing Committee Report for ECAJ Annual Conference, August 1958.
10 Ibid.
11 Kipen, *A Life to Live*.
12 Sophie Caplan, The Jewish Day School Movement in New South Wales.
13 Rutland, 'If you will it, it is no dream'.
14 Szwarc, The Jewish Community of Victoria, p. 132.
15 Mossenson, *Hebrew, Israelite, Jew*, pp. 177–80.
16 Tofler, *Forty Years On*, p. 58.
17 Ibid., pp. 27, 73, 143.
18 Ruth, Jewish Secular Humanist Education in Australia.
19 *Sydney Jewish News*, 27 August 1954.
20 Tofler, *Forty Years On*, p. 6.
21 Biennial Report, State Zionist Council of New South Wales, 2000, p. 65.
22 *Australian Jewish News*, Sydney edition, 20 November 1992.
23 Ibid.
24 Hilary Rubinstein, *Chosen*; Rutland, *Edge of the Diaspora* (2001); Hilary and W. D. Rubinstein, *The Jews in Australia* (1991).
25 *Australian Jewish Times*, 20 October 1989.
26 Rutland, *Pages of History*.
27 Rutland, *Edge of the Diaspora*, p. 355.
28 *The Maccabean*, February 1957, cited in Tofler, *Forty Years On*, p. 11.
29 Rutland, 'If you will it, it is no dream'.
30 Tofler, *Forty Years On*, p. 143.

8 Jewish women

1 Rutland, 'The Changing Role of Women in Australian Jewry's Communal Structure'.
2 Porush, 'Retrospect of a Century-Old Charity'.
3 Keysor, 'The Sydney Hebrew Ladies' Bazaar, 1875'.
4 Hilary Rubinstein, *The Jews in Victoria*, vol. 1, pp. 123–4.
5 Newton, *Making A Difference*.
6 Council of Jewish Women, Minutes, 27 July 1923.
7 Andgel, 'The Laws of Loving Kindness'.
8 Melbourne-born Sylvia Gelman was national president from 1973 to 1979; New Zealand-born Ray Ginsburg from 1979 to 1985; Romanian-born child survivor of the Holocaust, Malvina Malinek, from 1985 to 1991; Sydney-born Lynn Davies from 1991 to 1997; Melbourne-born Dr Geulah Solomon from 1997 to 2003; and Sydney-born Robyn Lenn from 2003.
9 Grove-Pollak (ed.), *The Saga of a Movement*.
10 Hyams, 'Women in Early Australian Zionism'.
11 Lake, *Getting Equal*.

12 Freilich, *Zion in Our Time*; Wynn, *The Fortunes of Samuel Wynn*.
13 See Korn (ed.), *Shades of Belonging*.
14 Foster (ed.), *Community of Fate*.
15 Kirchhof, 'From Germany and Austria to Australia'.
16 Council of Jewish Women, *Council Bulletin*, November 1928.
17 Rutland, 'Perspectives from the Australian Jewish Community', *Lilith: A Feminist History Journal*, II, 2002, pp. 87–101.
18 Amia Leiblich, 'Time, Place, Gender and Memory: From the Perspective of an Israeli Psychologist', in Judith Tydor Baumel and Tova Cohen (eds), *Gender, Place and Memory in the Modern Jewish Experience: Re-Placing Ourselves*, London, Valentine Mitchell, 2003, p. 273.
19 Bergman, 'Esther Johnston, The Lieutenant-Governor's Wife'.
20 Lysbeth Cohen, *Beginning with Esther*.
21 Lysbeth Cohen, 'Not Merely Housewives'.
22 Rosenberg, *Of Folktales and Jewish Folk in Australian History*, pp. 66–70.
23 Mitchell, *The Matriarchs*.
24 Carr-Gregg and Maclean, '"A mouse nibbling at a mountain"'; Wetherell and Carr-Gregg, *Camilla*; Rutland, 'The Jewish Connection'.
25 Newton, *Making A Difference*, p. 55.
26 Bloch and Cox, 'Mending the World from the Margins'.

9 The broader community
1 Rutland, *Edge of the Diaspora*, p. 257.
2 *Sydney Jewish News*, 11 August 1950.
3 Ruth Ostrow, *The New Boy Network: Taking Over Corporate Australia*, Melbourne, Heinemann, 1987.
4 Sam Lipski, 'Partisan', *Australian Jewish Times*, 21 August 1986.
5 *Business Review Weekly*, 15 August 1986, p. 79.
6 *Sydney Morning Herald*, 26 September 1984.
7 Brasch, *Australian Jews of Today and the Part They Have Played*, p. 177.
8 Margo, *Pushing the Limits*.
9 Ruth Ostrow, 'The Man from Sussan to Give Her a Facelift', *Business Review Weekly*, 15 August 1986.
10 Rutland, *Take Heart Again*.
11 New South Wales Legislative Assembly, *Parliamentary Debates*, 5 October 1950, p. 567.
12 Rutland, *Edge of the Diaspora*, p. 270.
13 Interview with Sir Zelman Cowen (taped), Sydney, 1986.
14 Pynt (ed.), *Australian Jewry's Book of Honour: World War II*.
15 Interview with Billie Einfeld, Sydney, 1988.
16 Rutland, 'The Hon. Sydney David Einfeld, AO'.
17 Mark Dapin, 'Man in the Middle', *Sydney Morning Herald* (Good Weekend section), 27 November 2004.

18 *Australian Jewish News*, 24 September 2004.
19 Peter Baume, 'Jews and the Liberal Party of Australia', in Levey and Mendes (eds), *Jews and Australian Politics*, p. 88; see also Sol Encel, 'Jews and the Australian Labor Party' and Peter Medding, 'Australian Jewish Politics in Comparative Perspective', in ibid., pp. 47–65, 240.
20 *Viennese Theatre* (pamphlet), Sydney, 1966, p. 12 (lent to the author by the late Karl Bittman).
21 John Dushak, 'Richard Goldner: Musician and Inventor', *New Citizen*, 15 June 1946.
22 Judah Waten, *Alien Son*, Sydney, Picador, 1993 [1952], p. 33.
23 Bittman (ed.), *From Strauss to Matilda*.
24 West, 'Roy Rene'; Obituary, *Sydney Jewish News*, 26 November 1954.

10 Recent immigrants

1 Rutland and Gariano, Survey of Jews in the Diaspora; report commissioned by the Jewish Agency Research and Strategic Planning Unit and Department for Jewish Zionist Education. This report underpins much of the analysis in this chapter.
2 All researchers in the field of Jewish demography argue that the use of Census data without adjustment leads to under-counting of the Jewish population by up to 25 per cent.
3 Gavin Quiet, Melbourne respondent, 17 February 2004, in ibid.
4 Szwarc, *The Jewish Community of Victoria*, pp. 16, 44.
5 Executive Director, State Zionist Council of Western Australia, 8 December 2003, in Rutland and Gariano, Survey of Jews in the Diaspora.
6 It has a membership of 89, of whom 40 are ex-South African, 34 Australian and 15 others, including Israeli and South American. Statistics provided by Lynne Goodman, Dianella Shule, 8 December 2003.
7 Borshevsky, Report of Visit to Australian Jewish Community.
8 Vladimir Dubossarsky, address to the Australian Jewish Historical Society, Sydney, 28 March 2004.
9 Ibid.
10 Interview with Roman Mirkus, Melbourne, 17 February 2004, in Rutland and Gariano, Survey of Jews in the Diaspora.
11 Dr Ron Weiser, email communication, 22 April 2004.
12 Oryana Kaufman, 'Byron's No Beach for Two Jewish Councillors', *Australian Jewish News*, 23 April 2004.
13 Dr Ron Weiser, email communication, 22 April 2004.
14 Interview with Melbourne respondent, 16 February 2004, in Rutland and Gariano, Survey of Jews in the Diaspora.
15 Dr Dvir Abramovitch, email communication, 5 March 2004, in ibid.
16 Interview with Melbourne respondent, 18 February 2004, in Rutland and Gariano, Survey of Jews in the Diaspora.
17 Group interview, Melbourne, 16 February 2004, in ibid.

18 Intermix means marriage to a non-Jewish partner who has not converted.
19 Interview with Roi Luberman, Sydney, 28 February 2004, in ibid.

Conclusion
1 Szwarc, *The Jewish Community of Victoria*, pp. 16, 43.
2 Eckstein, Sydney Jewish Community Demographic Profile, New South Wales, p. 8.
3 Ibid., pp. 11–12.
4 Goldlust, *The Jews of Melbourne*, p. 183.
5 Eckstein, Sydney Jewish Community Demographic Profile, New South Wales, p. 20.
6 Szwarc, The Jewish Community of Victoria, p. 141.
7 Goldlust, *The Jews of Melbourne*, p. 176.
8 Medding, *From Assimilation to Group Survivál*, p. 29; Encel and Buckley, *The New South Wales Jewish Community*, p. 95.
9 Gariano and Rutland, 'Religious Intermix'.
10 Ibid., p. 17.
11 Ibid., p. 18.
12 Goldlust, *The Jews of Melbourne*, pp. 88–9.
13 Eckstein, Sydney Jewish Community Demographic Profile, New South Wales, p. 18
14 *Sydney Jewish News*, 9 September 1953.
15 Rutland and Caplan, *With One Voice*, p. 262.
16 Jeremy Jones, 'Rallying Cries', *The Review* (Australia/Israel Jewish Affairs Council), vol. 27, no. 5, May 2002, p. 32.
17 For a summary of the Toben and Scully cases, see Jeremy Jones, Annual Report on Antisemitism, 2002–2003, pp. 57–63.
18 Ibid., pp. 17, 14, 15.
19 Ibid., p. 47.
20 Ibid., pp. 7–14.
21 See Martin Daly, 'Trial Cut Short as Roche Admits Guilt', *Sydney Morning Herald*, 29–30 May 2004, p. 4.
22 'Jailed for Race Hate Graffiti Spree', *Sunday Times*, 20 April 2005.
23 *Australian*, 15, 24 September 2001; *Sydney Morning Herald*, 24 September 2001.
24 Matthew Collins, 'Like a New Man? Pauline Hanson and Her Suitors', *The Review* (Australia/Israel Jewish Affairs Council), vol. 26, no. 8, August 2001, p. 13.
25 Jones, Annual Report on Antisemitism, 2002–2003, pp. 64–6.
26 Ibid., pp. 67–9.
27 Tzvi Fleischer, 'Sounds of Hate', *The Review* (Australia/Israel Jewish Affairs Council), vol. 25, no. 8, August 2000, pp. 14–17.
28 Wistrich, *Antisemitism*.
29 Wistrich, *Muslim Anti-Semitism*.

30 Rutland and Caplan, *With One Voice*, pp. 310–11.
31 Jeremy Jones, 'Right to Know: Unhappy "Gentleman's Agreement"', *The Review* (Australia/Israel Jewish Affairs Council), December 2001, p. 32.
32 Rutland and Caplan, *With One Voice*, pp. 290–1.
33 ABC TV, 12 September 2001, quoted in 'Briefings', *The Review* (Australia/Israel Jewish Affairs Council), vol. 26, no. 10, October 2001, p. 31.
34 Jeremy Jones, 'Right to Know', *The Review* (Australia/Israel Jewish Affairs Council), vol. 26, no. 12, December 2001, p. 32.
35 Sermon at Sidon mosque, Lebanon, 13 September 2003, quoted in Kerry-Anne Walsh and Sean Berry, 'Lost in Translation', *Sun-Herald*, 7 March 2004, p. 56.
36 Kerry-Anne Walsh and Sean Berry, 'Lost in Translation', *Sun-Herald*, 7 March 2004, p. 56.
37 Goldlust, *The Jews of Melbourne*, p. 245.

BIBLIOGRAPHY

Aarons, Mark, *Sanctuary*, Melbourne, Heinemann, 1989.
—— *War Criminals Are Welcome*, Melbourne, Black Inc, 2001.
Adelman, Howard, 'Australia and the Birth of Israel: Midwife or Abortionist', *Australian Journal of Politics and History*, vol. 38, no. 3, 1992, pp. 354–74.
Andgel, Anne, 'The Laws of Loving Kindness: A Tribute to Dr. Fanny Reading, Founder of the National Council of Jewish Women of Australia in 1923', *Australian Jewish Historical Society Journal*, vol. 19, no. 2, 1998, pp. 199–257.
—— *Fifty Years of Caring: The History of the Australian Jewish Welfare Society, 1936–1986*, Sydney, Australian Jewish Welfare Society / Australian Jewish Historical Society, 1988.
Apple, R., 'Rabbi Jacob Saphir and His Voyage to Australia', *Australian Jewish Historical Society Journal*, vol. 6, no. 4, p. 201.
—— *The Jews*, in Making Australian Society series, Melbourne, Thomas Nelson, 1981.
Armstrong, Diane, *The Voyage of Their Life*, Sydney, HarperCollins, 2001.
Aron, Joseph and Judy Arndt, *The Enduring Remnant: The First 150 Years of the Melbourne Hebrew Congregation, 1841–1991*, Melbourne, Melbourne University Press, 1992.
Bartrop, Paul, 'The Australian Government's "Liberalisation" of Refugee Immigration Policy in 1938: Fact or Myth?', *Menorah: Australian Journal of Jewish Studies*, vol. 2, no. 1, 1988, pp. 66–82.
—— *Australia and the Holocaust, 1933–1945*, Melbourne, Australian Scholarly Publishing, 1994.
Benjamin, David J., 'The Sydney Hebrew Certified Denominational School', *Australian Jewish Historical Society Journal*, vol. 4, no. 5, 1956, p. 248.

Benjamin, Rodney, 'A Very Serious Influx of Jews': A History of Jewish Welfare in Victoria, Sydney, Allen & Unwin, 1998, pp. 85–9.
Bennett, J. M. 'Sir Julian Salomons: Fifth Chief Justice', Royal Australian Historical Society Journal, vol. 58, 1972.
Bergman, G. F. J., 'Esther Johnston, the Lieutenant-Governor's Wife: The Amazing Story of a Jewish Convict Girl', Australian Jewish Historical Society Journal, vol. 6, 1966, pp. 90–122.
—— 'The Bizarre Life Story of Mordecai Moses the Shammas of the York Street Synagogue', Australian Jewish Historical Society Journal, vol. 8, no. 3, pp. 100–8.
Bersten, Helen, Jewish Sydney: The First Hundred Years, 1788–1888, Sydney, Australian Jewish Historical Society, 1995.
—— 'Jews in Rural New South Wales', Australian Jewish Historical Society Journal, vol. 13, no. 4, 1997, pp. 552–95.
Bittman, Karl (ed.), From Strauss to Matilda: Viennese in Australia, Sydney, Wenkart Foundation, 1988.
Blakeney, Michael, Australia and the Jewish Refugees, 1933–1948, Sydney, Croom Helm, 1985.
Blau, J. L., Modern Varieties of Judaism, New York, Columbia University Press, 1966.
Bloch, Barbara and Eva Cox, 'Mending the World from the Margins: Jewish Women and Australian Feminism', in Levey and Mendes, Jews and Australian Politics, pp. 145–59.
Blumenthal, Elchanan, Trials and Challenges, Jerusalem, Jerusalem Academy Publishing, 1994.
Borshevsky, Nikolay, Report of Visit to Australian Jewish Community, unpublished MS, 2001 (Zionist Federation of Australia, Melbourne).
Brasch, R., Australian Jews of Today and the Part They Have Played, Sydney, Cassell, 1977.
Calwell, Arthur, How Many Australians Tomorrow?, Melbourne, 1945.
Caplan, Sophie, The Jewish Day School Movement in New South Wales, MEd thesis, University of Sydney, 1974.
Carr-Gregg, Charlotte and Pam Maclean, '"A mouse nibbling at a mountain": The Problem of Australian Refugee Policy and the Work of Camilla Wedgewood', Australian Journal of Politics and History, vol. 31, no. 1, 1985, pp. 49–60.
Cohen, Israel, The Journal of a Jewish Traveller, London, John Lane, the Bodley Head, 1925.
Cohen, Lysbeth, 'Not Merely Housewives', Australian Jewish Historical Society Journal, vol. 9, no. 1, 1981, pp. 8–24.
—— Beginning with Esther: Jewish Women in New South Wales from 1788, Sydney, Ayers & James Heritage Bookshops / Australian Jewish Times, 1987.

Cowen, Zelman, *Isaac Isaacs*, Melbourne, Oxford University Press, 1962.
Cramp, K. R. and George Mackaness, *A History of the United Grand Lodge of Ancient Free and Accepted Masons of New South Wales*, Sydney, Angus and Robertson, 1938.
Crown, Alan D., 'The Initiatives and Influences in the Development of Australian Zionism, 1850–1948', *Jewish Social Studies*, vol. 39, no. 4, 1977.
Eckstein, Gary, Sydney Jewish Community Demographic Profile, New South Wales, 1999 (Jewish Communal Appeal archive, Sydney).
Elazar, Daniel J. and Peter Medding, *Jewish Communities in Frontier Societies: Argentina, Australia and South Africa*, New York, Holmes & Meier, 1983.
Elbogen, I., *A Century of Jewish Life*, Philadelphia, Jewish Publication Society, 1945.
Encel, S. and B. Buckley, *The New South Wales Jewish Community: A Survey*, Sydney, University of New South Wales Press, 1978.
Fletcher, Frank, 'The Victorian Jewish Community, 1891–1901: Its Interrelationship with the Majority Gentile Community', *Australian Jewish Historical Society Journal*, vol. 13, no. 5, 1978.
Forbes, M. Z., 'Palestine Appeals in the 'Fifties and 'Sixties', *Australian Jewish Historical Society Journal*, vol. 3, no. 7, 1952.
—— 'Jews of NSW and the Gold Rushes', *Australian Jewish Historical Society Journal*, vol. 12, no. 2, 1994, pp. 282–326.
—— 'Sir Julian Salomons, 1835–1909', *Australian Jewish Historical Society Journal*, vol. 13, no. 3, 1996, pp. 367–94.
—— 'The Federation of the Commonwealth and the Role of Australian Jews', *Australian Jewish Historical Society Journal*, vol. 15, no. 4, 2001, pp. 506–46.
—— 'Australia's First Synagogue at Bridge Street, Sydney', *Australian Jewish Historical Society Journal*, vol. 16, 2002, p. 161.
Foster, John (ed.), *Community of Fate: Memoirs of German Jews in Melbourne*, Sydney, George Allen & Unwin, 1986.
Fredman, Lionel, 'Some Victorian Jewish Politicians', *Australian Jewish Historical Society Journal*, vol. 4, no. 3, 1955.
—— 'Bendigo Jewry', *Australian Jewish Historical Society Journal*, vol. 4, no. 4, 1956, pp. 175–83.
—— 'Isaacs in Politics', *Australian Jewish Historical Society Journal*, vol. 5, no. 4, 1961, pp. 189–203.
Freedman, M. (ed.), *A Minority in Britain: Social Studies of an Anglo-Jewish Community*, London, Valentine, 1955.
Freilich, Max, *Zion in Our Time: Memoirs of an Australian Zionist*, Sydney, Morgan Publications, 1967.
Gariano, A. and S. D. Rutland, 'Religious Intermix: 1996 Census Update', *People and Place*, vol. 5, no. 4, 1997.
Gill, Alan, *Interrupted Journeys*, Sydney, Simon and Schuster, 2004.

Glass, Harold H., 'Some Jews and the Federal Movement', *Australian Jewish Historical Society Journal*, vol. 3, no. 6, 1951.
Glass, S. B., 'The Foundations of the Great Synagogue', *Australian Jewish Historical Society Journal*, vol. 5, no. 4, 1956, p. 170.
Goldlust, John, *The Jews of Melbourne: A Community Profile*, Melbourne, Jewish Welfare Society, 1993.
Goldman, L. M., 'The Early Jewish Settlers in Victoria and Their Problems', (No. 1) '1835–1850', (No. 2) 'After Separation 1851–1865', *Australian Jewish Historical Society Journal*, vol. 4, nos 7, 8, 1958.
Golvan, Colin, *The Distant Exodus*, Sydney, ABC Books, 1991.
Gordon, Max, *Sir Isaac Isaacs: A Life of Service*, Melbourne, Heinemann, 1963.
Gouttman, Rodney, 'First Principles: H. V. Evatt and the Jewish Homeland', in W. D. Rubinstein (ed.), *Jews in the Sixth Continent*, Sydney, Allen & Unwin, 1987.
—— 'The Sam Cohen Affair: A Conspiracy?', *Australian Jewish Historical Society Journal*, vol. 15, no. 1, 1999, pp. 69–79.
Grove-Pollak, F. (ed.), *The Saga of a Movement: WIZO 1920–1970*, Jerusalem, Women's International Zionist Organisation, 1970.
Hill, Roger, 'The Jews of Perth: A Socio-Geographical Analysis', *Australian Jewish Historical Society Journal*, vol. 8, no. 1, 1975, pp. 6–47.
Horowitz, Israel (ed.), *The Dawn and the Rebirth of Palestine* (pamphlet), Sydney, Jewish National Fund, 1936.
Hyams, Bernard K., *The History of the Australian Zionist Movement*, Melbourne, Zionist Federation of Australia, 1998.
—— 'Women in Early Australian Zionism', *Australian Jewish Historical Society Journal*, vol. 15, no. 3, 2000, pp. 441–9.
Ivany (Bach), Susan, The Kadimah: 1911–1961, BA Hons thesis, Department of History, Monash University, 1979.
Jones, Jeremy, Annual Report on Antisemitism, 1990–2004 (Executive Council of Australian Jewry archives, Sydney).
Jones, Melinda and Ilana Lutman, *Orach Hayim: A Way of Life—The Central Synagogue*, Sydney, State Library of New South Wales Press, 2000.
Katz, David S., *Philo-Semitism and the Readmission of the Jews to England, 1603–1655*, Oxford, Clarendon Press, 1982.
Kellerman, M. H., 'Contemporary References to the York Street Synagogue', *Australian Jewish Historical Society Journal*, vol. 4, no. 4, 1956.
Kellerman, M. H. (ed.), 'Interesting Account of the Travels of Abraham Abrahamsohn', *Australian Jewish Historical Society Journal*, vol. 7, no. 7, 1974.
Keysor, A. A., 'The Sydney Hebrew Ladies' Bazaar, 1875', *Australian Jewish Historical Society Journal*, vol. 2, no. 9, 1953, pp. 469–85.
Kipen, Israel, *A Life to Live: An Autobiography*, Melbourne, Chandos Publishing, 1989.

Kirchhof, Astrid, 'From Germany and Austria to Australia: Experiences of Jewish Women Refugees in the 1930s', *Australian Jewish Historical Society Journal*, vol. 15, no. 1, 2000, pp. 237–51.

Korn, Neer (ed.), *Shades of Belonging: Conversations with Australian Jews*, Melbourne, Harper Collins, 1999.

Kunz, E., 'Rev Isaac Friedman', *Australian Jewish Historical Society Journal*, vol. 6, no. 5, 1968, pp. 279–83.

Kwiet, Konrad, '"Be Patient and Reasonable!" The Internment of German-Jewish Refugees in Australia', in Konrad Kwiet and John A. Moses, 'On Being a German-Jewish Refugee in Australia', *Australian Journal of Politics and History*, vol. 31, no. 1, 1985, pp. 61–77.

—— 'Responses of the Australian Jewish Leadership to the Holocaust', in W. D. Rubinstein (ed.), *Jews in the Sixth Continent*, Sydney, Allen & Unwin, 1987, pp. 211–12.

Lake, Marilyn, *Getting Equal: The History of Australian Feminism*, Sydney, Allen & Unwin, 1999.

Lamm, Maurice, *The Jewish Way in Death and Mourning*, New York, Jonathan David, 1969.

Levey, Geoffrey Brahm and Philip Mendes (eds), *Jews and Australian Politics*, Brighton, UK, Sussex Academic Press, 2004.

Levi, J. S. and G. F. J. Bergman, *Australian Genesis: Jewish Convicts and Settlers, 1788–1850*, second edition, Melbourne, Melbourne University Press, 2002 [1974].

Lipman, V. D., *A Social History of the Jews in England, 1850–1950*, London, 1954.

Margo, Jill, *Pushing the Limits*, Sydney, Harper Collins, 2000.

Markus, Andrew, 'Jewish Migration to Australia, 1938–1947', *Journal of Australian Studies*, no. 13, 1983.

Medding, Peter, *From Assimilation to Group Survival: A Political and Sociological Study of an Australian Jewish Community*, Melbourne, Cheshire, 1968.

Mendes, Philip, 'The Jewish Council to Combat Fascism and Anti-Semitism: An Historical Re-appraisal' (in 2 parts), *Australian Jewish Historical Society Journal*, vol. 10, nos 6, 7, pp. 524–51, 598–615.

Mitchell, Susan, *The Matriarchs: Twelve Australian Women Talk About Their Lives*, Melbourne, Penguin, 1987.

Mossenson, David, *Hebrew, Israelite, Jew: The History of the Jews of Western Australia*, Perth, University of Western Australia Press, 1990.

Nathan, Howard T., 'The Benefits of a Conviction', *Australian Jewish Historical Society Journal*, vol. 13, no. 1, 1995, pp. 5–14.

Newton, Marlo L., *Making A Difference: A History of the National Council of Jewish Women of Australia*, Melbourne, Hybrid Publishers, 2000.

Ochert, Morris S., 'History of the Brisbane Hebrew Congregation', *Australian Jewish Historical Society Journal*, vol. 9, nos 6, 7, 1984, pp. 457–65, 509–521.

—— 'Dr. Fanny Reading v. Smith's Weekly', *Australian Jewish Historical Society Journal*, vol. 13, no. 2, 1996, pp. 308–42.
Palmer, Glen, *Reluctant Refuge: Unaccompanied Refugee and Evacuee Children in Australia, 1933–45*, Sydney, Kangaroo Press, 1997.
Patkin, Benzion, *Heritage and Tradition: The Emergence of Mount Scopus College*, Melbourne, Hawthorn Press, 1972.
—— *The Dunera Internees*, Sydney, Cassell, 1979.
Pearl, Cyril, *The Dunera Scandal*, Sydney, Angus and Robertson, 1983.
Perry, Roland, *Monash: The Outsider Who Won a War*, Melbourne, Random House, 2004.
Piggott, Leanne, 'An Ideal Betrayed': Australia, Britain and the Palestinian Question, PhD thesis, Department of History, University of Sydney, 2002.
Porush, I., 'Retrospect of a Century-Old Charity', *Australian Jewish Historical Society Journal*, vol. 2, no. 2, pp. 77–9.
—— *The House of Israel: a study of Sydney Jewry from its foundation (1788) and a history of the Great Synagogue of Sydney, the mother congregation of Australian Jewry, compiled on the occasion of its centenary (1878–1978)*, Melbourne, Hawthorn Press, 1977.
Price, Charles, 'Jewish Settlers in Australia', *Australian Jewish Historical Society Journal*, vol. 5, no. 8, 1964.
Pynt, Gerald (ed.), *Australian Jewry's Book of Honour: World War II*, Adelaide, Australian Federation of Ex-Servicemen and Women, 1973.
Reich, Chanan, *Australia and Israel: An Ambiguous Relationship*, Melbourne, Melbourne University Press, 2002.
Renouf, Alan, *'Let Justice be Done': The Foreign Policy of Dr H. V. Evatt*, Brisbane, University of Queensland Press, 1983.
Rosenberg, Louise, *Of Folktales and Jewish Folk in Australian History*, Melbourne, Printworthy, 2004.
Rosenthal, Newman, *Formula for Survival: The Saga of the Ballarat Hebrew Congregation*, Melbourne, Hawthorn Press, 1979.
Rubinstein, Hilary L., *The Jews in Victoria, 1835–1985*, Sydney, Allen & Unwin, 1986.
—— *Chosen: The Jews in Australia*, Sydney, Allen & Unwin, 1987.
—— *The Jews in Australia: A Thematic History*, vol. 1, 1788–1945, Melbourne, William Heinemann, 1991.
Rubinstein, W. D., 'Australia and the Refugee Jews of Europe, 1933–1954: A Dissenting View', *Australian Jewish Historical Society Journal*, vol. 10, no. 6, 1989, pp. 500–23.
—— *The Jews in Australia: A Thematic History*, vol. 2, 1945 to the present, Melbourne, William Heinemann, 1991.
Ruth, Julie, Jewish Secular Humanist Education in Australia, DEd thesis, University of Melbourne, 1997.
Rutland, Suzanne D., The Jewish Community in New South Wales, 1914–1939, MA Hons thesis, University of Sydney, 1978.

—— *Take Heart Again: The Story of a Fellowship of Jewish Doctors*, Sydney, Fellowship of Jewish Doctors / Australian Jewish Historical Society, 1983.
—— 'The Changing Role of Women in Australian Jewry's Communal Structure', in W. D. Rubinstein (ed.), *Jews in the Sixth Continent*, Sydney, Allen & Unwin, 1987, pp. 101–26.
—— 'The Jewish Connection', in Heather Radi (ed.), *Jessie Street: Documents and Essays*, Sydney, Redress Press, 1990.
—— 'The Hon. Sydney David Einfeld, AO: Builder of Australian Jewry', *Australian Jewish Historical Society Journal*, vol. 11, no. 2, 1991, pp. 312–31.
—— *Pages of History: A Century of the Australian Jewish Press*, Sydney, Australian Jewish Press, 1995.
—— *Edge of the Diaspora: Two Centuries of Jewish Settlement in Australia*, Sydney, Brandl & Schlesinger, 2001.
—— 'Perspectives from the Australian Jewish Community', *Lilith: A Feminist History Journal*, II, 2002, pp. 87–101.
—— *'If you will it, it is no dream': The Moriah Story*, Sydney, Playright Publishing, 2003.
—— 'Postwar Anti-Jewish Refugee Hysteria: A Case of Racial or Religious Bigotry?', *Journal of Australian Studies: Sojourners and Strangers*, no. 77, 2003, pp. 69–79.
Rutland, Suzanne D. and Sophie Caplan, *With One Voice: The History of the New South Wales Jewish Board of Deputies*, Sydney, Australian Jewish Historical Society, 1998.
Rutland, Suzanne D. and Antonio Carlos Gariano, Survey of Jews in the Diaspora: An Australian Perspective, report commissioned by the Jewish Agency Research and Strategic Planning Unit and Department for Jewish Zionist Education, 2005 (Zionist Federation of Australia archive).
Sackville, Harold, John Sackville: The Man and the Legend, Melbourne, 1979.
Sluga, Glenda, *Bonegilla: 'A Place of No Hope'*, Melbourne, Department of History, University of Melbourne.
Solomon, Geulah, 'Jewish Education in Australia', in John Cleverley (ed.), *Half a Million Children: Studies in Non-Government Education in Australia*, Melbourne, Longman Cheshire, 1978.
Solomon, Isadore, 'Geelong Jewry', *Australian Jewish Historical Society Journal*, vol. 2, no. 6, 1946, p. 336.
Spielvogel, Nathan Fredrick, 'The Beginnings of the Ballarat Hebrew Congregation', *Australian Jewish Historical Society Journal*, vol. I, no. 4, 1940, pp. 111–12.
Staedter, Joseph and Hans Kimmel, *Sydney's Jewish Community: Materials for a Post-War (II) History*, Sydney, 1953.
Stedman, Solomon, 'From Russia to Brisbane, 1913', *Australian Jewish Historical Society Journal*, vol. 5, no. 1, 1959.

Szwarc, Barbara, *The Jewish Community of Victoria: A Demographic Profile of the Jewish Community in Victoria Based on the 2001 Australian Bureau of Statistics Census* (CD Rom), Melbourne, Jewish Community Council of Victoria, 2004.

Taft, Ronald, 'The Impact of the Middle East Crisis of June 1967 on Melbourne Jewry: An Empirical Study', *Jewish Journal of Sociology*, vol. 9, no. 2, 1967.

Taft, Ronald and Geulah Solomon, 'The Melbourne Jewish Community and the Middle East War of 1973', *Jewish Journal of Sociology*, vol. 16, no. 1, 1974.

Tennant, Kylie, *Evatt: Politics and Justice*, Sydney, Angus & Robertson, 1970.

Tofler, Oswald B., *Forty Years On: A History of G. Korsunski Carmel School*, Perth, self-published, [2000].

Tydor Baumel, Judith and Tova Cohen (eds), *Gender, Place and Memory in the Modern Jewish Experience: Re-Placing Ourselves*, London, Valentine Mitchell, 2003.

West, John, 'Roy Rene', in Leonie Kramer et al. (eds), *The Greats: Heroes, Larrikins, Leaders and Visionaries: The 50 Men and Women Who Shaped Australia*, Sydney, Angus and Robertson / Channel Nine / *Bulletin*, 1986.

Wetherell, David and Charlotte Carr-Gregg, *Camilla: C. H. Wedgwood, 1901– 1955: A Life*, Sydney, University of New South Wales Press, 1990.

Wilton, J. and R. Bosworth, *Old Worlds and New Australia: The Post-war Migrant Experience*, Melbourne, Penguin, 1984.

Wistrich, Robert S., *Antisemitism: The Longest Hatred*, New York, Pantheon, 1991.

—— *Muslim Anti-Semitism: A Clear and Present Danger*, American Jewish Committee, 2002.

Wynn, Allan, *The Fortunes of Samuel Wynn: Winemaker, Humanist and Zionist*, Melbourne, Cassell, 1968.

Zusman, Nate, 'Rabbi David Isaac Freedman: An Enduring Legacy', *Australian Jewish Historical Society Journal*, vol. 16, no. 4, 2003.

INDEX

Aarons, Mark 73
Abrahams, Esther 12, 114
Abrahams, Rabbi Dr Joseph 82
Abrahamsohn, Abraham 22
Abramovitch, Dr Dvir 146
academia 123
Adelaide Institute 156
Adler, Chief Rabbi Dr Hermann 5, 9, 82
Adler, Dr Nathan Marcus 5, 9, 34
age and fertility 149
agricultural colonies 32, 38, 94
Alexander III, Tsar 29
Alexander, Professor Samuel 46
Alien Son (Waten) 131
Aliens Classification and Advisory Committee 60
ALP (Australian Labor Party) 54, 76, 90, 91, 127, 128
Altson, Rose 107
anti-refugee hysteria 51. *see also* refugees
antisemitism: by Melbourne Club 60; in Australia 30; in economic depressions 50; new 154; stereotypes and 56; towards Salomons 42; under Stalin 76
al-Aqsa Intifada (2000) 144, 155
Arab League Office 91
Arabs: anti-Zionism 83; Muslim antisemitism 159; Muslims in Australia 158; Negev 87; riots in Jerusalem (1929) 83

Arajs Kommando (Latvian Security Auxiliary Police) 73
Arendt, Hannah 118
armed forces 46, 127
Aronson, Zara 116
arson attacks 155, 158
art 45, 115, 132
the arts *see* social and cultural life
Ashkanasy, Maurice 70, 74, 76
Ashkanasy, Solomon 81
Ashkenazi Jews 2, 5, 11
Asia/Pacific diaspora communities 74
assimilation 9, 34, 104, 161
Association of Jewish Engineers 143
Association of New Citizens 71
Australia House (London) 59, 60
Australia/Israel Review 91, 104
Australia–Israel relations 90
Australian Broadcasting Commission 130
Australian Genesis (Levi and Bergman) 12
Australian Imperial Force 47
Australian Institute of Jewish Affairs 92, 103
Australian Jewish Chronicle 34
Australian Jewish Genealogical Society 111
Australian Jewish Historical Society 102, 103
Australian Jewish Times/News 113

INDEX

Australian Jewish Welfare Society (AJWS) 56, 62, 63, 67
Australian Jewry: characteristics 34; diversification of religious life 93; in nineteenth and early twentieth centuries 8
Australian League of Rights 158
Australian Medical Association 124
Australian National Action 158
Australian National Movement 157
Australian National Socialist Movement 158
Australian Natives' Association 51, 54
Australian Zionist Youth Council 90
Austria 57

Baer, Werner 130
Baillieu family 40
Baker, Dr Mark 131
Balfour Declaration 81
Ballarat Jewish community 27
Barak, Ehud 155
barmitzvah 96
Baron de Hirsch Memorial Aid Society 31
Bassat, Nina 111, 143
Basser, Sir Adolph 41
batmitzvah 96
Baume, Eric 85
Baume, Peter 128, 129
Ben Gurion, David 87, 89
ben Israel, Menasseh 3
Bendigo (Vic) 23, 28
Benfrey, Dr Alice 110
Benjamin, Sir Benjamin 43, 49
Benjamin, Sophia ('Zoe') 115
Bennett, John 158
Bension-Wynn, Ida 109
Berg, Charles 130
Bergner, Herz 131
Bergner, Yosl 132
Berinson, Joe 128
Bernadotte, Count Folke 86
Bersten, Helen 111
Besen, Marc 123
Bialik College (Melbourne) 100
bicentennial 103
Blashki, Phillip 40
Blaubaum, Rabbi Elias 23

Blecher, Myron 139
Blewitt, Graham 73
Bligh, Governor William 12
Blumenthal, Elchanan 96
B'nai B'rith 110
Boas, Isaac Herbert 62
Bodenwieser, Gertrude 116, 132
Boer War 46
Bolton, Ken 54
Bonegilla (migrant camp) 72
Bornstein, David 128
Borshevsky, Dr Nikolay 140
Bramson, Rabbi Isador 31
Brand, Walter 63, 65
Breckler, Fanny (1877–1946) 107, 115
Brett, Lily 116, 131
Britain: Anglo-Jewry 5, 8, 82, 93; British Board of Deputies 77; *Dunera* (ship) 58; Eastern European immigrants 30; Jewish life in England 2; London's East End 12, 132; Palestine 86
British settlers 15
Brodie, Rabbi Israel 82
Brodsky, Maurice 46
Broken Hill (NSW) 31
Bruce, Stanley 57
Bulletin 30, 56
Bundism 6, 7, 32
Bures, Susan 113
burial societies 14
Business Review Weekly's 'Rich List' 121
business world 38, 121
Byron Bay (NSW) 144

Calwell, Arthur A. 54, 60, 63
Campbell, Eric 50
Campbell, Graeme 158
Canberra Jewish Centre 155
Caplan, Leslie 73
Caplan, Sophie 111
care and convalescence 112
Carlton United Hebrew Congregation 31
Cass, Professor Bettina 115
Cass, Dr Moss 128
Cassab, Judy 116, 132
Castan, Ron 127
Chevra Kadisha (Holy Society) 14
Chifley, Ben 59

Child, Senator Joan 75
Church of England 13
Citizens' Electoral Councils 158
claims conferences 63, 70
Clarke, Sir Frank 52
Cohen, Barry 128
Cohen, David 38
Cohen, Edward 43
Cohen, Fanny 114
Cohen, Rabbi Francis Lyon 31, 46, 82
Cohen, George Judah 40
Cohen, Henry Emanuel 42
Cohen, Ida 107
Cohen, Israel 81
Cohen, John J. 42, 46
Cohen, Lysbeth 114
Cohen, Nerida 118
Cohen, Phillip Joseph 15
Cohen, Reike 109
Cohen, Sam 76
Cohen, Sir Samuel 40, 57, 83, 127
Cohen, Tirza 110
Cohen, Vera 109
Cohen family (Newcastle) 31, 40
Cold War 54, 72, 76
Coleman, Rabbi Shalom 38
colonies (ghettos) 53
Comay, Major Michael 84
commercial life 38, 121
communal life 106
Communism 54, 72, 76, 129
concentration camp survivors 60, 68, 74, 95, 143. *see also* Holocaust
Conference on Jewish Material Claims Against Germany 63, 70
Conservative Judaism 6, 7, 93
consumer affairs 127
conversions to Judaism 14, 142. *see also* intermarriage
Conversos (converted Jews) 3
convicts 11
Coonawarra Estate 41
Cooper, Daniel 13
Coppleson, Abram 41
Cornelius, Stella 115
Cornfield, Victor 35
Council of Jewish Women 107
country areas 25, 31, 37
Cowen, Sir Zelman 97, 126

Cox, Eva 118
Cromwell, Oliver 3
Cullen, Major-General Paul 40, 127
cultural life *see* social and cultural life
Curtin, John 58

Dadon, Rabbi 145
Danby, Michael 91, 128
Danglow, Rabbi Jacob 46, 82
Darling, Governor Ralph 15
David Cohen & Co 38
Davies, Lynn 112
Davis, Reverend Alexander Bernard 25, 82
Davis, Beverley 111
Davis, Margaret 115, 128
Davis, Phoebe 111
de Lissa, Lillian Daphne 115
de Medina, Solomon 3
de Rothschild, Lionel 42
de Vahl Davis, Gerald 67
Deakin, Alfred 44
Democratic Labor Party 76
Denominational Education Boards 28
Department of Immigration 73
diaspora (dispersion of Jews) 1, 69, 74, 89
Dintenfass, Dr Leopold 124
discriminatory policies 56
displaced persons 61, 72
Dobell, William 133
Docker, Dr John 161
doctors 53, 124
Don John of Austria (opera) 45
Dreyfus Affair (1894) 7, 80
Dreyfus, George 130
Dubossarsky, Vladimir 141
Dunera (ship) 58, 97
Dyte, Charles 43

Eastern Europe: European Jews *see* European Jews; fascists 72; Jews 29, 30, 82; Polish Jews, *see* Polish Jews
Eban, Aubrey (Abba) S. 87
ECAJ *see* Executive Council of Australian Jewry
economic depressions 49
economics and education 149
Eden, Anthony 57

education: Anglican Church 14; changes in 96; day school movement 96, 100, 105, 138, 145; Denominational Education Boards 28; economics and 149; kindergartens 99; part-time 101; women in 111, 114; Zionist 89
Egyptian 'escapees' 120
Einfeld, Marcus 75, 127
Einfeld, Sydney David 9, 64, 65, 70, 74, 127
Ellis, Dr Constance 115
Emunah 110
Encel, Professor Sol 124
'enemy aliens' 58
Ernst, Rudi 130
ethnic broadcasting stations 102, 145
Ettinger, Mark 81
Euro-Asian Jewish Congress 74
European Jews: Central 153; experience in Europe 5; German Jews 6, 22, 57; immigrants before 1930s 9; post-war immigrants 9. *see also* Eastern Europe
Evatt, Dr Herbert Vere 86
Evergood, Miles 46
Executive Council of Australian Jewry (ECAJ) 66, 70, 73, 74, 111
Ezra 110

Falk, Rabbi 83
Falstein, Max 128
family businesses 122
Family Planning Association 117
fashion industry 122
federation 43, 66
Feiglin, Moshe and Bere 32
Fein, Yvonne 116
feminism 117
Fiftieth Gate (Baker) 131
Fink, Leo 58, 63, 109
Fink, Mina 109
Fink, Theodore 45
First Fleet 11, 114
Fischl, Eva 110
Fitton, Doris 132
Fitzroy, Sir Charles 19
food and restaurants 133
Fortress (band) 158
Founding of New Societies (Hartz) 8

France: French Revolution (1789) 5; Monash on Western Front 49
franchise 69
Frankel, Rabbi Zacharias 6
Fraser, Malcolm 75, 91, 128
Freedman, Rabbi David 33, 38, 46, 80
Freeman, Sir Bernard 132
Freilich, Rabbi David 38
Freilich, Max 85, 88
'friendly aliens' 59
Friends of Refugees of Eastern Europe (FREE) 142
Fuhrman, Major-General O. C. W. 61

Gallipoli campaign 49
Geelong (Vic) 28
Geiger, Abraham 6
Gentilli, Joseph 93
George V, King 49
German democratic revolutions (1848) 22
German Jews 6, 22, 57
Gipps, Sir George 19
Glassgold, Charles 61
gold-rush era 22, 27, 33, 37
Goldhar, Pinchas 131
Goldlust, Dr John 95
Goldner, Richard 130
Goldreich, Reverend Israel M. 28
Goldstein, Dr Alexander 81
Goldstein, Vida 117
Goodman, Isadore 130
Goodman, Nerida 115
Goot, Robert 69, 75
Gordon, Hayes 129
Gorelik, Rabbi Eliozer 142
Goulston, John 41
Goulston, Dr Stanley 127
Grassby, Al 102
Greenwood, Bob, QC 73
Gregorian, Slavor 131
Grosz, Elizabeth 118
Gulf War (first) 154, 158
Gullett, Henry Baynton 54
Gutnick, Rabbi Joseph 157

Habad movement 94
Haddad, Michael 159
Hage, Associate Professor Ghassan 161

Hallenstein, Isaac 40
Hammerman, Bernhard 132
Hand, Gerry 160
Hansky, Dr Jack 124
Harbin (Manchuria) 33
Haredi Judaism 94
Harris, Alfred 62, 83
Harris, Ian 137
Harris, John 12
Hart, Hannah 117
Hart, Henri J. 23
hate emailing 157
hate music 158
Hawke, Robert J. 73, 75, 91, 128
Hebrew Immigrant Aid Society 63
Hebrew Standard 62, 83
Heilbrun, Rabbi Philip 138
Helfgott, Samuel 130
Herman, Rabbi Samuel 28
Herman, Sali 132
Herron, Justice Leslie James 84
Herz, Chief Rabbi Dr 34
Herzl, Theodore 7, 80, 105
Hess, Moses 80
Hess, Dr Walter 76
Heyes, Tasman H. E. 60
El-Hilaly, Sheikh Taj Eldine 159
Hill, Alfred 115
Hill, Mirrie 115
Hirsch, Baron de 30
Hirsch, Max 43
Hirsch, Rabbi Samson Rachael 6
history of Jewish people 1
Holocaust 57, 63, 120, 121, 152. *see also* concentration camp survivors
Holocaust museums 103
Holt, Harold 62, 76
Holzman, Ruth 110
Hort, Greta 118
housing 53, 150
Howard, John 91
Hughes, Billy 46
human rights 74, 161
Hungarian Jews 120, 122
Hungarian revolution (1956) 51
Hunter, Governor John 14
Hurford, Chris 159

immigration: ALP policies 54, 60; discriminatory policies 56; Eastern European 29, 85; from Israel 144; German non-Jewish 76; Iron Curtain embargo 61; Jewish immigration policy 59; post-war 59, 85; pre-1930s 22; quota restrictions 112; reception 112; to capital cities 23; white alien 59; 'White Australia' policy 52; women and 111
Independent Theatre (Sydney) 132
indigenous Australians 46, 127
interfaith activities 113
intermarriage 105, 151, 161. *see also* conversions to Judaism
International Refugee Organisation 61, 72
internees 52, 58
Intifada (1987) 144
Iraq war 157
Irish Catholics 13, 47
Isaacs, Sir Isaac Alfred 43, 83
Isaacson, Caroline 113
Isaacson, Peter Stuart 127
Islamic Youth Movement 161
Israel, Land of 1
Israel, State of: advocacy 91; ALP support for 129; Australia–Israel relations 90; claims conferences 70; ECAJ 68; Evatt 86; immigration from 144; Iraq war 157; Leibler 74; Soviet Jewry 140, 143
Israeli Synagogue (Melbourne) 145

Jacobs, Joseph 46
Jacobson, Reverend Dr Dattner 24
Jacobson, Nathan 78
Jetset Travel 74
Jewish Advisory Boards 66, 69, 75. *see also* Jewish Boards of Deputies
Jewish Agency 136, 139
Jewish Boards of Deputies 68, 70, 77. *see also* Jewish Advisory Boards
Jewish Care 104, 110, 136. *see also* Jewish Welfare
Jewish Communal Appeal (JCA) 69, 110, 154
Jewish Community Council of Victoria 69, 143

INDEX

Jewish Congregational Society (Melbourne) 20
Jewish Council to Combat Fascism and Anti-Semitism (JCCF&A) 72, 75
Jewish Employment Bureau 49
Jewish Freeland League 57
Jewish Herald 23
Jewish Learning Centre (Sydney) 138
Jewish Male Choir (Melbourne) 139
Jewish Museum of Australia 111
Jewish National Fund (JNF) 85, 87, 146
Jewish Secular Humanistic School 101
Jewish Sports Carnivals 34. *see also* Maccabi
Jewish Student Network 102
Jewish Unity Committee 75
Jewish Welfare 62, 63, 104, 141. *see also* Jewish Care
Jewish Welfare Guardian Scheme 63
Joel, Sir Asher 128
Johan de Witt (ship) 63
Johnston, Lieutenant George 12
Jona, Dr Leon 67
Jona, Walter 128
Jones, Jeremy 155
Joseph, Dr Max 71
Joseph, Moses 13, 18

Kadimah (Carlton) 32
Kahan, Louis 132
Kahn, Esther 115
Kalejs, Konrad 73
Kaplan, Yehuda 145
Kashrut 96
Kaye, Brett 139
Keating government 73, 91
Keesing, Nancy 116
Kerr, Sir John 126
Kessler, Hannah 110
Keysor, Leonard 46
Khoen, Menachem 145
Kimmel, Dr Hans 69
King, Poppy 115
Kipen, Aviva 114
Kleine Wiener Theater (Sydney) 132
Kloot, Leah 115
Kogus, Aviva 146
Kohn, Dr Rachael 116
Krips, Henry 130

Kristallnacht pogroms 57, 155
Kronheimer, Joseph 40

la Rouche, Lyndon 158
labour 59
Lacey, Josie 113, 114
Lamidey, Noel W. 60
Lampert, Rabbi Richard 138
Landa, Abe 127
Landa, Paul 128
Landau, Reverend Joseph 82
Lang, Jack 54
Larra, James 12
Lebanon war (1982) 144
Leibler, Isi 74, 91
Leibler, Mark 88, 92
Leiblich, Amia 113
Levey, Barnett 13, 45
Levey, Solomon 13
Levi, Friedl 112
Levi, Rabbi John 43
Levi, Nathaniel 43
Levi, Philip 21
Levi, Walter Jacob 15
Levien, Jonas Felix 43
Levine, Judge Aaron 126
Levy, Rabbi Aaron 16
Levy, Abraham 14
Levy, Sir Daniel 42, 46
Levy, Rabbi Ephraim M. 82, 83
Levy, Gerry 154
Levy, Julia 107
Levy, Sandra 116
Liberal Party 129
Liberman, Serge 131
Liberov, Motty 145
Liebman, Charles J. 62
Light, Dr Helen 111
Lipsius, Mr (Balt Stormtrooper) 73
Lipski, Sam 91
Lipton, Betty 112
Lithuania 137
Lowenstein, Nitza 145
Lowy, Frank 123
Lowy, Shlomo 85
Luber-Smith, Edna 112
Lubofsky, Rabbi Ronald 139
Ludendorff, General Eric 49
Luks, Betty 158

INDEX

Lynch, P. J. 54
Lyons, Samuel 13

Maccabean Hall (Sydney) 34, 62, 103
Maccabi 117. *see also* Jewish Sports Carnivals
McEwen, John 57
Machon L'Madrichei Hutz L'Aretz 90
Machover, Dr Jona M. 57
Macquarie, Governor Lachlan 14
Magid, Isador 90, 91
Magnus, Walter 133
Mahlab, Eve 110, 115
Malan, Dr Daniel 135
Mandelbaum, Reverend Zallel 31
Manne, Professor Robert 124
Marcus, Joseph 15
Marks, Ernest S. 46
Marks, Gladys (1883–1970) 114
Marks, Herbie 130
Marks, Percy Joseph 81
Marks, Rosetta 19
Marsden, Reverend Samuel 12, 14
Martin, Clarrie 124
Martin, Sir David 12
Martin, David 131
Masada College (Sydney) 138
Masel, Alec 60, 67
Mayer, Professor Henry 124
medical practitioners 53, 124
Melbourne: differences with Sydney 153; schisms with Sydney 75; synagogues 20, 23, 137, 145, 163–4
Mercer, Zosia 111
Merchant of Venice (Shakespeare) 2
Metro-Goldwyn-Mayer 132
Michaelis, Sir Archie 128
Michaelis, Moritz 23, 40
Mirkus, Roman 143
Monash, Sir John 43, 47
Mond, Haya 88
Montefiore, Claude G. 83
Montefiore, Dora 117
Montefiore, Jacob 21
Montefiore, Jacob Levi 28, 46
Montefiore, Joseph Barrow 16
Montefiore, Sir Moses 79, 104
Montefiore Homes for the Aged 104, 107
Morawetz, Paul 60

Moriah College (Sydney) 100
Morris, Ethel 109
Moses, Mordecai 17
Mother and Son (ABC TV) 132
Mount Scopus College (Melbourne) 97, 138
multiculturalism 100, 102, 129
Musica Viva 130
Muslims in Australia 158
Myer, Sidney Baevski 40
Myers, Jonas M. 25

Nagley, Harold 100
Nathan, Isaac 45
National Alliance 158
National Council of Jewish Women (NCJW): creation 109; feminism 118; Golden Age Clubs 143; role 106; South African Jews 139; Tarbuth 145
Nazi war criminals 72
Nazism 56, 72, 85
Negev 87
New South Wales Legislative Assembly 42
Newman, Horace B. 85
Ninio, Jackie 114
North Shore Temple (Sydney) 154
Norton, John 50

Office of Special Investigations 73
Oistralier Leben (Australian life) 34
Oliver Twist (Dickens) 19
Orthodox Judaism 6, 114, 142
Oslo Accords 155

Pacific war 59
Palestine: anti-refugee hysteria 53, 54; British mandate 82; immigrants from 38; Palestine Committees 85; Palestine Restoration Fund 81; World War II 58; Zionism 79, 84
Palestine Liberation Organization 91
Passfield White Paper 83
Passover 96
Patkin, Dr Aaron L. 83, 85
Patkin, Benzion 97
Pauline Hanson's One Nation party 158
Pearlman, Justice Mahla 115
Pellach, Peta Jones 113
Penny, Professor Ron 124

Perlman, Elliot 131
Perth Jewry: care and convalescence 104; education 101, 105; Fremantle 33; gold-rush era 37; immigration from Israel 144; post-war immigrants 65; South African Jews 136, 138; Swan River settlement 13; synagogues 166; women 110
Pevsner, Bella 107
philanthropic endeavours 106
philanthropic institutions 104
Phillips, Ada 113
Phillips Fox, Emanuel 46
Phillips, Nat 132
Phillips, Solomon 17
Pilcher, Bishop Charles Venn 85
Pinsker, Leo 80
Polack, Abraham 15
Polish Jews 51, 57, 60, 63, 122, 131, 153
politics: Jewish involvement in 42, 127; Jewish parliamentarians 28, 42, 115, 117, 127; political tensions 53; right-wing movements 50, 158; women in 115
Polyukhovich, Ivan 73
population distribution 148
Porat, Professor Dina 157
Port Phillip Bay Association 20
Porush, Bertha 107
Post, Shannon Mark 157
Power Without Glory (ABC TV) 130
Prague Trials 76
Pratt, Richard 92, 122
press: Arabic 159; Jewish 23, 34, 46, 62, 113; non-Jewish 30, 50, 56, 84
Preston-Stanley, Millicent 117
Price, Dr Charles 37
professions 38, 115, 123
Progressive Judaism 93, 113, 138
Public Instruction Acts (1872 and 1880) 29
public life 36
public relations 113
Pugno, Raoul 117

Queensland Jewry 25, 28, 33, 144

Rabinovitch, Abraham 97, 100
rag trade 122

Rapke, Julia 115
Rappaport, Yehoshua 131
Reading, Dr Fanny 84, 107, 112
Red Cross 107
referenda: on conscription 46; on scripture lessons 45
Reform Judaism 6, 7, 24, 93, 114, 138
Refugee Economic Corporation 62, 63
refugees: anti-refugee hysteria 51; children of 121; embrace Australia 120; post-war immigrants 59, 61, 63; pre-war 59; Zionist 85
Rene, Roy 132
reparations 70
representative structure 66
restaurants and food 133
Returned Services League (RSL) 51, 52, 54
Reuben, Abraham 19
Rich-Schalit, Ruby (1888–1988) 109, 117
Riesenberg, Yitzhak 137
Rintel, Reverend Moses 21, 23
Robinson, Dr Nehemiah 72
Roche, Jack 157
Rodriguez, Judith 116
Roosevelt, President Franklin Delano 57
Roozendaal, Eric 129
Rose, Reverend Michael 17
Rosenberg, Louise 111
Rothfield, Evelyn 113
Rubenstein, Dr Colin 91
Rubin, Hilton 139
Rubin-Zacks, Rabbi Louis 38
Rubinstein, Helena 115
Rubinstein, Professor W. D. 56
rural towns 25, 31, 37
Rush (ABC TV) 130
Ruskin, Dr Hans 97
Russia: Soviet Jewry 74, 140, 152; Tsarist pogroms 5, 8, 14, 15, 29, 38, 80
Russian Jewish Community Centre (Melbourne) 142

Sackville, John 29, 41
Sackville, Justice Ronald 41, 126
Salcman, Sam 75
Salomons, Sir Julian 42, 43, 45
Salzman, Theo 130

Same, Saul 90
Samson, Lionel 42
Samuel, Saul 42
Samuels, Gordon 126
Sanger, Rabbi Dr Herman 94
Saphir, Rabbi Jacob 34, 79
Saunders, John 123
Save the Children 63
Scarf, Reuben F. 91
Schechter, Solomon 8
Schenk, Rabbi Max 94
Schnabel, Arthur 117
Schneersohn, Chaim Zvi 79
Schneersohn, Rabbi Menachem Mendel 94, 142
Schneeweiss, Dr Joachim 77
Schwartz, Monique 116
Scullin, James 43
Scully, Olga 156
Seidler, Harry 124
Selby, Cecile 130
Sephardic Jews 2, 94
September 11 (2001) 158
settlement patterns 36
Shabbat 96
Shaheen, Taleb 159
Shalom Association 143
Shalom Institute 102
Shanghai 61
Shapiro, Baruch 142
Sharpeville massacre 135
Shein, Dr Bension 85
Shteinman, Diane 75, 111
Simmons, Joseph 16
Simons, Janet 110
Singer, Professor Peter 124
Sitsky, Larry 130
Six Day War (1967) 87, 154
Slutzkin, Rose 110
Smith's Weekly 56, 84
Snider, Barnett 40
Snider, Baron David 128
social and cultural life: the arts 129; Hebrew language 102, 145; institutions 102; theatre and art 45; women in 111; Yiddish language 31, 32
socio-economic class 37
Solomon, Emanuel and Vaiben 21

Solomon, Dr Geulah 114
Solomon, Isabel 107
Solomon, Judah and Joseph 19, 20
Solomon, Miriam 111
Solomon, Vaiben Louis 43
Solvey, Joseph 85
Soria, Karen 114
South African Jews 135, 152
South Australian Jewry 21, 37, 104
Soviet Union *see* Russia
Soweto riots 135
Special Investigation Unit 73
Spielvogel, Nathan F. 27
Spielvogel, Newman Friede 28
Spigelman, Jim 126
sport 116
Stalin, Josef 76
state aid 28
Steigrad, Brigadier Joseph 127
Steinberg, Dr Isaac N. 57
Steinman, Roy 139
Stone, Deborah 113
Stone, Professor Julius 83, 126
Street, Jessie 117
Sverdlin, Rimma 143
Swan River settlement 13. *see also* Perth Jewry
Sydney: differences with Melbourne 153; schisms with Melbourne 75; synagogues 15, 25, 31, 95, 107, 165
Sydney Board of Jewish Education 29
Sydney Hebrew School 28
Symon, Eve 113
Symonds, Saul 63, 64
Szeps, Henri 132

Tadros, Morris 159
Talmud Torahs 101, 123
Tasmanian Jewry 19, 20, 37
Tedeschi, Simon 131
Temple Emanuel (Sydney) 94
textile industry 122
theatre 45
Three Dollars (Perlman) 131
Toben, Dr Fredrick 157
Tofler, Dr Oswald 105
Torah 101, 123
Trotsky, Leon 47
Troy, Abe 105

Truth 50
Tsivlin, Vladimir 143
Turk, Hani-El 159
Tycho, Tommy 131

Ulman, Rabbi Yoram 142
United Ancient Order of Druids 41
United Emergency Committee for European Jewry 67
United Israel Appeal 87, 110, 154, 161
United Jewish Education Board 29
United Jewish Emergency Committee 57
United Jewish Overseas Relief Fund (UJORF) 57, 63
United Nations: human rights 74; Special Committee on Palestine 86; UNRRA 67
United Restitution Office 72
United States: American Joint Distribution Committee 61, 63; Eastern European immigrants 30; ECAJ 77; helps finance refugee integration 63; Iraq war 157; Jewish settlement in 7; Palestine 86; United States Reform 7; US Space Centre 124
Universal Service League 46

Valler, Rachel 131
Van Diemen's Land 19. *see also* Tasmanian Jewry
van Tongeren, Jack 157
Victorian Ladies' Zionist League 107
Victorian Legislative Council 52

Walford, Bernard 19
Waller, Professor Louis 126
Waten, Judah 76, 131
Waxman, Aaron 40
Wedgewood, Camilla 118
Weiser, Dr Ron 88, 89
Weissberg, Samuel 32
welfare institutions 104
Wenkart, Fred 130
Werder, Felix 130
Wertheim, Hugo 40
Wertheim, Solomon 85
West German government 70

Westfield Holdings 123
White, Thomas W. 57
Whitlam, Gough 90, 102, 126, 128
Wiener, Bono 76
Windeyer, Sir William 42
Wise, Rabbi Israel 7
Wistrich, Professor Robert 158
Wolinski, Reverend A. D. 30
Wolinski, Joseph 46
Wolinski, Naomi 117
women 106; and religious life 113; communal life 106; concerns 162; feminism 117
Women Power 119
Women's Electoral Lobby 118
Women's Interfaith Network 113
Women's International Zionist Organisation (WIZO) 88, 106, 109; Amit 145
work force 59
World Jewish Congress 69, 73, 74
World War I 46, 52
World War II 57, 127
World Zionist Organisation 81, 88
Wran government 128
Wynn, Ida 118
Wynn, Samuel 41, 85, 109
Wynvale Wines 41

Yedid, Mordechai 146
Yom Kippur 96
Yom Kippur war (1973) 87
Young, Mick 160
youth 89, 161
Youth Aliyah 112

Zable, Arnold 131
Zablud, Ann 88, 111
Zablud, Robert 91
Zionism, political 6, 7, 32, 54; anti-Zionism 79, 82, 161; beginnings of 79; identification with 87; South African Jews 139; support increases 85
Zionist Councils 88
Zionist Federation of Australia 81, 86, 88, 111
Zionist Leagues 81
Zox, Ephraim 43, 45

For EU product safety concerns, contact us at Calle de José Abascal, 56–1°, 28003 Madrid, Spain or eugpsr@cambridge.org.

www.ingramcontent.com/pod-product-compliance
Lightning Source LLC
LaVergne TN
LVHW040737250326
834688LV00031B/340